Y0-BDY-853

The Redaction of the Books of Esther

THE SOCIETY OF BIBLICAL LITERATURE
MONOGRAPH SERIES

Adela Yarbro Collins, Editor
E.F. Campbell, Associate Editor

Number 40
THE REDACTION OF THE BOOKS OF ESTHER
On Reading Composite Texts

by
Michael V. Fox

Michael V. Fox

THE REDACTION OF THE BOOKS OF ESTHER
OF ESTHER
On Reading Composite Texts

Scholars Press
Atlanta, Georgia

BS
1375.5
.F69
1991

THE REDACTION OF THE BOOKS OF ESTHER

by
Michael V. Fox

©1991
The Society of Biblical Literature

Library of Congress Cataloging in Publication Data

Fox, Michael V., 1940-
    The redaction of the books of Esther : on reading composite texts
    / by Michael Fox.
    p. cm. — (Monograph series / the Society of Biblical
    Literature ; no. 40)
    Includes bibliographical references and indexes.
    ISBN 1-55540-443-X (acid-free paper). — ISBN 1-55540-444-8 (pbk.)
    1. Bible. O.T. Esther—Criticism, Redaction. 2. Bible. O.T.
Esther—Criticism, Textual. 3. Bible. O.T. Apocrypha. Esther—
Criticism, Redaction. 4. Bible. O.T. Apocrypha. Esther—
Criticism, Textual. I. Title. II. Series: Monograph series
(Society of Biblical Literature) ; no. 40.
BS1375.5.F69 1990
222'.9066—dc20
                                    90-39349
                                    CIP

Printed in the United States of America
on acid-free paper

CONTENTS

ACKNOWLEDGMENTS

I thank Mr. Peter Flint for his careful editorial assistance in the preparation of this book, Joseph Abrahamson for making the index, as well as the others who helped me in the manuscript preparation: Dr. Kelvin Friebel, Paul Manuel, Karl Kutz, and Michael Rowe.

I am indebted to the Wisconsin Society for Jewish Learning for grants that aided me in the research for this study and in the preparation of the manuscript, as well as for its ongoing moral and financial support for academic Jewish learning in Wisconsin.

I dedicate this book to my mother, Mrs. Mildred Ross, for the unfailing encouragement she has given my efforts over the years.

ABBREVIATIONS

Add(s)	The deutero-canonical Addition(s) (A-F)
AT	The Greek Alpha-Text
AT-end	The current (redactional) ending of the AT, not including Adds E and F; = viii 39-52
BDB	Brown, Driver, and Briggs, *Hebrew and English Lexicon of the OT*
BH	Biblical Hebrew
BHS	Biblia Hebraica Stuttgartensia (1st edn., 1967)
D+	AT vi 13-18 (see ch. I, 6.1)
GKC	Gesenius-Kautsch-Cowley, *Gesenius' Hebrew Grammar*, 2nd English ed. (1910, 1963)
Her.	Herodotus, *The Histories*
Jos	Josephus, *Antiquities of the Jews*, XI 184-296 (= chap. vi)
LXX	Septuagint (Hanhart's edition used, see Bibliography)
MT	Massoretic text
OG	Old Greek
OL	Old Latin
R-AT	The redactor who turned proto-AT into AT
R-MT	The redactor who created the Massoretic book of Esther
Syr	Syriac Peshitta
Vul	Vulgate

Bibliographic references are by author and date. Commentaries are referenced *ad loc.*, by author's name only.

INTRODUCTION

1. *Finding the Redactor*

Redactors inscribe their thoughts in others' words. The decision to do so cannot be taken for granted, for ancient scribes obviously were not always constrained to rewrite earlier texts. They could and did compose original works of their own, perhaps incorporating older themes, plots, and motifs, while telling the tale anew in fresh words. But redactors take a less obvious approach, at once humble and presumptuous: by rewriting an existing text, they submerge their creativity in another's work while masking the other's creation in their own.

Not only does the redactor's form of creativity have the advantage of providing most of the wording and structure ready-made, it also allows the new text to partake in the respect, and even the sacredness, possessed by its predecessor. At the same time, this approach places material constraints upon the redactor, for each attempt to draw upon the earlier work's status, information, and quality effectively subordinates the redactor's own voice to the substance of that work. Simultaneously, each change *violates* the text being adapted, whether "for its own good," as it were—thereby making the text "better than it was before" (in the words of the preamble to the Egyptian Shabaka Stele[1])—or for the sake of conveying a new ideology by an ancient vehicle. The redactor's work thus proceeds in a tension between two poles: a self-effacing subordination to another's work, and a bold, even presumptuous, expropriation thereof.

Redactors are not will-o'-the-wisps. Whereas the "original author" may be a heuristic fiction in a work that took shape through a lengthy and fluid process of oral and written transmission, a redactor is real and specific. A redactor was an individual, a scribe who made deliberate changes in the text or texts in the course of transcribing them.

The definition of "redactor" is problematic. R. Knierim (1985:150–53) finds that redaction critics use three definitions of the relation between author and redactor. These are (in my wording): (1) traditional: redaction is the reworking of what an author wrote; (2) global: redaction encompasses the entire history of written texts; (3) temporal: redaction is the final formation of materials created earlier; earlier layers are formed by "composition."

---

[1] An Old Kingdom text copied—with "improvements"—in the late 8th century BCE. Translation in Lichtheim 1973:51ff.

1

None of these definitions is quite adequate. Definition 3 assumes that the "final form" is created in a way fundamentally different from the earlier stages, whereas a variety of types of composition can pertain at all stages, and there is no reason to call an earlier scribe a "composer" or "author" and a later one a "redactor" if their activity is essentially the same. Definition 2 does away with an important distinction in types of creativity, one that will have to be reintroduced in another form (see Knierim, p. 152). Moreover, this definition rests on (and tries to promote) the assumption that Biblical literature attained its essential form in the oral stage. This may be true of some texts, but we surely must allow for the possibility of active written authorship as well.

Definition (1), implicit in nineteenth century literary criticism, still accords with the common usage, and I will follow it. But this definition clearly refers not to a dichotomy but to a continuum, which runs from radically creative authorship to mechanical redaction. An author uses only raw materials — motifs, themes, story-lines, stock phrases — and shapes them into an original story, while a redactor adopts most of the text from earlier sources and makes only modest changes in wording. The distinction refers primarily to the source of a text's wording, not to its ideas or literary features, and certainly not to the talent or significance of its composer. Someone who recasts an older tale mostly in new words is an author — though he may be a dull, uncreative hack — while someone who derives the material of the new work mostly from the words of older texts is a redactor — though he may thereby create a profoundly new work of literature, theology, or history.[2]

It is probably impossible, and certainly artificial, to draw a precise boundary between these two types of composition. As Knierim observes, both authors and redactors can use the *techniques* of collecting, composing, compiling, combining, and connecting (p. 151). Conversely, redactors may create some material of their own from scratch. There is, however, no practical need to mark a boundary. Some writers are more innovative, others adapt more than they create. When discussing the more innovative writers or even the innovative passages produced by adaptors, we naturally use terms and concepts pertaining to authorship. When treating writers who primarily borrow and rework earlier material, while remaining dependent on its

---

[2] The foremost case of the latter is the Deuteronomistic redactor: "Here the compiler is unmistakably the historian who provides the text's narrative framework. . . . He is not an editor, or not solely an editor, but a historian" (Halpern 1988:29–30). (I would not oppose "editor" to "historian" but regard the Deuteronomist as an historian who composed primarily by redaction.) Halpern's book takes the redactor seriously as historian by giving full attention to compositional history rather than by submerging the redactor in the "final form" of the work. Halpern shows that the Deuteronomist's achievement as historian can be comprehended only by attention to the way he uses and interacts with his sources.

wording, we speak in terms appropriate to redaction. Yet the basic opposition — authorship is the creation of new material, redaction is the reworking of another's creation — is valid. The opposition refers primarily to wording, not to ideas or literary features, and certainly not to evaluations of the quality of the work.[3]

In the Esther traditions, the composer of the present AT ("R-AT") is clearly a redactor by any definition. He[4] never composes more than a few isolated phrases on his own. The redactor of the MT ("R-MT") is far more innovative, and when discussing his innovations I will occasionally refer to him as an "author." But he too adopts more than he produces anew, and on the overall he belongs in the ranks of redactors, a transmitter more than an originator.

The extent of a redactor's activity can range from trivial word-substitution and grammatical changes to fundamental reorganization and recombination of two or more donor texts.[5] The more extensive the changes, the more the redactor's involvement intrudes in the creative process and approaches authorship. Concurrently — even with relatively minor changes — the redactor's work is a screen between the reader and the earlier text. The redactor's role must therefore be taken seriously, sometimes as seriously as that of the original author — and not only by a scholar attempting to reconstruct the inner history of a text, but by any critical reader addressing a text's meaning in its fullness. To do this we must ask: was this text redacted? and if so, what has the redactor done, and how, and why?

It is possible, and nowadays regrettably common, to brush aside these questions by collapsing historical depth into literary surface — giving exclusive attention to a "final form" of a text, thereby obscuring both composition and redaction in an undifferentiated collective authorship.[6]

The notion of "final form":
It is better to speak of "a" rather than "the" final form, because there can be several. Each religious community can have a form final for itself. The Samaritan Pentateuch is as final as the MT, just as LXX-Jeremiah is final within *its* textual tradition (one that is still "the final form" for the Orthodox church). For that matter, there are various "final forms" even within the Massoretic tradition. And does anyone insist that for literary study the latest edition of Biblia Hebraica Stuttgartensia should be privileged over

---

[3] For a brief but thoughtful attempt to define redaction and redactors see Willis 1979.

[4] All scribes in antiquity were, as far as I know, male.

[5] The terms "redactor" and "editor" have not generally been distinguished. Given the use of the term "redactor" in Bible studies, we might use the term "editor" for one who makes only minor adjustments in a text and introduces a minimum of new ideas, reserving "redactor" for one who makes changes (even when they are small-scale) that significantly influence the message and literary shape of the product. There is obviously a continuum between the two.

[6] See ch. V, §1.

earlier editions and manuscripts? Consider too that there are several "final forms" of Shakespeare's works, such as the versions preserved in the early and sometimes corrupt (or abridged) Quartos, the later but often better (but sometimes "improved") Folios, and the later but vastly worse redactions of Cibber and Tate, as well as the numerous editions of varying quality currently on the market. Does the notion of "the final form" of Shakespeare even make sense?

The concept of "the final form" is deceptive because it sounds as if it had an objective reference—the biblical texts "as they actually exist" (Alter and Kermode 1987:4)—whereas the concept in fact rests on dogmatic or hermeneutical presuppositions. It is preferable to speak of the "canonical form" of biblical texts,[7] for then it is clear and open that we are classifying a text by a sociological criterion—the status of a specific form of the text for a religious community—and not claiming to identify a quality inherent in the text.

One common way of bypassing a work's internal history without denying the existence of that history is to posit that the end-product of development *is* the latest redactor's work, and that whatever it says or does represents that redactor's, rather than the author's, intention.[8] Or, to the same end, one may reify the discourse and speak of what the *text* communicates, in effect (and sometimes deliberately) investing all meaning in the act of reading, which is to say, in the scholar's abstraction from innumerable and irreplicable acts of reading. Reading with sole attention to the canonical text is legitimate, of course, and the vast majority of readers do so. The canonical form has its own meaning because the intentions of the original authors as well as later redactors usually combine to form a meaningful whole, sometimes close to the author's creation, sometimes more the redactors' product.

Yet restricting our perspective to the latest extant text can diminish our awareness of the individual thought and artistry that went into its creation. After all, the redactor takes the wording of the base texts as they come and does not create their motifs, themes, or rhetoric. These might be quite distinct from the particular ideas and attitudes of the redactor. To gain an awareness and understanding of the particular contribution of the redactors

---

[7] If one may be excused for the ethnocentricity of assuming the perspective of Judaism and Western Christianity. But even within this grouping, we have to set aside the "deuterocanonical" books and passages which are quite canonical for a Catholic.

[8] This is the point of Franz Rosenzweig's famous dictum that the "R" of the Pentateuchal redactor should stand for "Rabbeinu"—i.e. *Moshe Rabbeinu,* Moses our Master—since the redactor is responsible for the final shape of the Torah and it does not matter a great deal who this individual was (1965:29, in a letter from 1927). The problem with this equation is that it deprives both Moses and the redactors of their historical contexts and eliminates the dialectic between Moses and his scribal successors. In any case, it is certainly an oversimplification to claim that this redactor, "wer er auch war und was ihm auch vorgelegen haben mag, er ist unser Lehrer, seine Theologie unsre Lehre" (ibid.).

to the finished work is the goal of redaction criticism. Instead of dissolving the original creation and the subsequent reshapings in the end-product, redaction criticism attempts to follow a work through its development, of which the end-product is only one stage, and not always the most successful.

Redaction criticism seeks to describe, understand, and (sometimes) evaluate the individual artistry, goals, and ideology of both authors and redactors. It works toward this understanding by isolating and examining the different levels of creativity and analyzing them in terms appropriate to each.[9]

Redaction criticism proceeds from source criticism by reversing its thrust. Source criticism moves backward from the finished work, segregating its stages of development with a view to retrieving the work of the participants in the creative process. Redaction criticism moves forward from the results of source criticism, reconstructing the process from the parts. Redaction criticism and source criticism are thus two phases of a single operation. Both are oriented to intention — of author and redactor — and both regard literature as a medium and reading as communication. They seek to restore communications now muted in a multiplicity of superimposed voices.

Source criticism and redaction criticism together constitute literary-historical criticism, and this provides the only hope for achieving a literary history of ancient Israel. Without it there can be no history of Israelite culture or religion, and probably no history of Israel at all.

Still, literary-historical criticism is inherently a speculative enterprise. Indeed, it must be granted that many of its methods seem almost as anarchic, and many of its conclusions almost as solipsistic, as those of some current synchronic hermeneutics. For to use a later form of a text to reconstruct the process whereby it reached that form involves several postulations, each of which increases the uncertainty of the reconstruction.

The uncertainty is reduced, though never eliminated, when we have an external witness to the process, such as a prior version of the text, or at least a collateral version that developed from a common ancestor. For the book of Esther, such an external witness is available in the Greek Alpha-Text (AT). The AT is a variant version of the Esther story parallel to the LXX; it incorporates much of its wording but differs from it significantly. In the present monograph, a comparison of the AT with the LXX will provide a firm basis for the source and redaction analysis of the AT, which will identify the layers of that text and allow us to recover and interpret the achievement of its redactor. This in turn will afford an external standpoint for tracing the redaction history of the MT.

---

[9] There has been little inquiry into the methodology of redaction criticism of the Hebrew Bible. (It has flourished in New Testament studies, on which see Perrin 1969). For introductory methodological considerations see Richter 1971:165–73 and Barton 1984:45–60. See also Koch 1969:57–67. There have, however, been many applications of redaction criticism to biblical literature, though not always under that rubric.

My goal is to advance our understanding of the redactional process in general by studying the development of two particular representatives of the Esther tradition, the AT and the MT—the two "books" of Esther mentioned in the title of this monograph. For both I begin with source criticism to identify the material the redactors worked with, but since this study aims not at reconstructing sources but at describing the redactors' work, I subsume both steps of literary-historical analysis under redaction criticism.

This book proceeds from a minute examination of two particular redactions to a broad consideration of some fundamental questions about redaction criticism and the reader:

I. The first chapter examines the redaction that produced the present form of the AT, seeking to determine its scope, methods, attitudes, and purposes. This examination will show us—with some certainty, I believe—what one redactor did, and so provide an "empirical model" by which other biblical texts might be tested.[10]

    A scrutiny of the changes made by the AT's redactor (R—AT) in the Septuagintal material he was transferring will show how a redactor can express his own ideology through a series of seemingly unrelated changes, some of them minute.

II. MT-Esther's redaction history is the subject of the second study. Here the conclusions cannot claim an equally "empirical" status, but they do have a more secure basis than most biblical redaction studies, insofar as the conclusions of the first chapter provide an idea of the scope and shape of the material that the MT redactor (R—MT) drew upon. He too fashioned quite a different book with new ideas and goals.

III. This chapter describes and compares the texts that resulted from these redactions, the latest forms they attained within their respective traditions.

IV. Next I inquire into the practical implications of the above studies, considering the ways in which they provide a model for redactional studies.

V. In conclusion, I offer some thoughts about a literary approach to redaction.

Appendices: Appendix A shows the correspondences among the three versions of Esther and Appendix B is the AT text. The purpose of the last appendix is to allow the reader convenient reference to the AT, not to present the best edition of that version. For copyright reasons I have used the 1940 Cambridge edition, which copies Lagarde's 1883 text. This is not the edition I quote in the body of the book and count for statistical purposes (i.e. Hanhart's); the differences, however, are minor. (I thank the Cambridge University Press for permission to reproduce this text.)

---

[10] The value of external witnesses in redaction studies has been richly demonstrated by the essays in J. Tigay's anthology, *Empirical Models for Biblical Criticism* (1985). S. Kaufman (1982) undertook a similar study of the Qumran Temple Scroll.

2. Reference system

The AT has its own numbering system, which I use throughout. (The correct numeration can be found in the Brooke-McLean edition.) There is, however, severe confusion in the way scholars and editors number the chapters and verses of the AT. The LXX numeration follows the MT's except in the Additions ("Adds") and 9:31.[11] The AT's own system diverges from the LXX-MT system at many points, though some editions attempt to impose the MT system on the AT. Even the proper AT numeration has been partly assimilated to the LXX-MT, with the result that the AT system has gaps and violations of sequence.[12] Note that Hanhart's critical edition applies the LXX-MT numeration to the *chapters* in AT, and these numbers are mostly one behind the AT numeration (e.g., AT ch. iv = LXX ch. 3). In Hanhart's edition, the AT verse numbers are those not in parentheses.[13] Appendix A presents a concordance of the AT and MT numbering systems.

I distinguish AT references by using lower case roman numerals for the chapters (e.g., viii 17), whereas MT/LXX chapters are cited in arabic numerals (e.g., 7:17). In discussing synoptic material (in the Adds), I usually give both the AT and the LXX numeration, separated by a parallel-sign (//). When quoting other authors I convert whatever system they use into this one.

There has also been considerable confusion in the abbreviations used for the Greek Esther texts. The Alpha Text (AT) is often designated "L" or "Luc" because it was once thought to be Lucianic. Hanhart still uses this misleading abbreviation. What is worse, in older works the AT is sometimes designated the "B text" and the LXX the "A text" (thus Fritzsche), the reverse of the current practice. Note that the "A" in AT has nothing to do with the Codex Alexandrinus (LXX-A), which, like the Codex Vaticanus (LXX-B) is a manuscript of the LXX.

3. Special abbreviations

Add(s)   Addition(s) (A-F) in the Septuagint and the AT

AT   The Greek Alpha-Text, in accordance with Hanhart's
         (Göttingen) edition

---

[11] LXX 9:31 // MT 9:32; the LXX does not represent MT 9:30–31aα and handles the rest of MT 31 differently.

[12] The numeration at the end of AT ch. ii proceeds . . . 14 16 18 20 21; ch. iii proceeds 1 2 4 5 7 8 9 14 17 18; the middle of chap. iv proceeds . . . 6 8 9 11 10 7 13 . . . . In the Additions, the AT continues the sequential numeration of the chapters they are in, whereas the LXX numbers them separately (e.g., D 1, 2 . . . ; F 1, 2 . . .).

[13] In the AT, all the verses paralleling LXX chapters 7, 8 (including Add E), 9, and 10, as well as Add F, are counted as a single chapter, designated chap. 7 in Hanhart's numeration and chap. viii in the proper AT system.

AT-end The current (redactional) ending of the AT, not including Adds E and F. (This ending, I will argue, is to be limited to viii 39-52.)

D + AT vi 13–18 — material following Add D which is also to be ascribed to the redactor

R-AT The redactor who turned the proto-AT into the AT mainly by inserting the Septuagintal Adds and AT-end (R-AT should not be confused with the author of the original AT, who is sometimes called an "editor" or "redactor" because of the mistaken assumption that the AT originated as a recension of the LXX.)

R-MT The redactor who (I will argue) created the Massoretic book of Esther on the basis of an earlier Esther story ("proto-Esther")

4. *Sigla*

  // parallel or equivalent

  = virtually identical (apart from minor differences in grammar, use of articles, pronouns, sg./pl, and the like; also ignoring synonym variants in one-to-one correspondence and prefix-variants in verbs when their meaning is essentially the same)

  ≈ substantially similar (same content phrased differently; different numbers or names considered "pragmatic synonyms"). Used in cases of clear dependency.

  ≠ substantially different

  / . . . / substitution of synonymous material

  > missing in

  ≥ equal to or greater than

  ≤ equal to or less than

  ____ Underlining (unless otherwise designated) highlights significant differences between parallel texts.

  § section number. Unless otherwise noted, the sections referred to in cross references are within the same chapter.

  ---- Dashes (in comparisons among the versions) mark minuses common to the AT and the MT but not the LXX (unless otherwise indicated).

The following diagram represents my understanding of the development of the Esther texts.

Diagram 1: *The History of the Esther Texts*

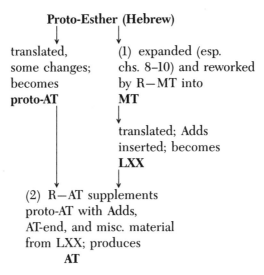

Proto-Esther (Hebrew)

translated,   (1) expanded (esp.
some changes;   chs. 8–10) and reworked
becomes   by R−MT into
proto-AT   **MT**

                     translated; Adds
                     inserted; becomes
                     LXX

(2) R−AT supplements
proto-AT with Adds,
AT-end, and misc. material
from LXX; produces
                AT

The stages marked (1) and (2) are the subjects of the present investigation, beginning with the latter.

I

THE ALPHA TEXT AND ITS REDACTION

1. *A profile of the AT*

The book of Esther is preserved in multiple versions:[1] the MT, the LXX (which, outside of the six Additions, is based on a text close to the MT), the Old Latin (which reworks and expands a Septuagintal-type text while maintaining some independent variants), and the AT (to be described below). The present study focuses on the history of the MT and the AT. Only in the case of these two editions do we find variations deriving from different — quite different — *Hebrew* texts.

The AT of Esther is preserved only in MSS 19, 93, 108, 319, and 392 (the last a mixed text), all from the 10th–13th centuries (see Hanhart 1983:15–16).[2] Ms 93 was printed by James Usher in 1665 alongside the LXX. In 1848 Fritzsche published both the LXX and AT versions of Esther. Lagarde produced a critical edition of the AT in 1871 and 1883, which was incorporated in the Brooke-McLean Cambridge Septuagint, where it follows LXX-Esther and is labeled "ΕΣΘΗΡ Α." Hanhart published a critical edition, with minor divergences from Lagarde's, in the Göttingen Septuagint (1966, 1983), which sets the AT at the bottom of the page and gives it the siglum *L*. For a handy synoptic printing of the AT (Lagarde's edition) alongside the MT (in German translation), Josephus (*Antiquities*), and the LXX, see the appendix to Scholz's commentary (1892). Clines (1984) includes an original English translation of the AT in its entirety alongside the Greek text from Brooke-McLean.

1.1. *The AT and the LXX*

The relation between the AT and the LXX is a puzzle. The AT resembles the LXX, often word for word, but also differs from it significantly, sometimes

---

[1] For a survey of the issue of double literary editions of biblical narratives, in particular those preserved in the Greek witnesses, see Ulrich 1988. Among the vast number of studies of variant editions within the Septuagint, the following may be noted as particularly relevant to redaction-critical problems of Hebrew texts: Tov 1985a and Barthélemy *et al.* 1986 on 1 Sam 17–18; Tov 1985b on Jeremiah.

[2] Manuscript groupings: 19' = 19–108; 93' = 93–319.

by lacking long passages found in the other version, sometimes by adding material or telling events in its own way. Most of the differences are in wording, word-order, and short pluses and minuses. Overall, in terms of a word-count, the AT is about 29% shorter than the LXX (see Table II), but since there is also material in the AT that is absent in the LXX, the portion of the LXX unparalleled in the AT is higher than 29%. For the quantitative relation between the two texts see Table II (in §7, below).

The most frequent type of difference between the AT and the LXX is in wording. Here are three examples in literal translation,[3] two from the canonical sections, one from the deuterocanonical:

(a) LXX 6:6

(6) The king said to Haman, "What shall I do for the man whom I wish (θέλω) to honor?" And Haman said to himself, "Whom does the king wish to honor if not me?"

AT vii 9–10

(9) When he [Haman] entered, the king said to him, "What shall we do to the man who reveres the king, whom the king wants (βούλεται) to honor?" (10) And Haman thought, "Whom does the king want to honor if not me?"

(b) LXX 6:11

(11) Haman took the cloak and the horse, and he cloaked Mordecai, and put him up on the horse, and led (him) through the squares of the city and cried out, saying, "Thus shall it be to every man whom the king wishes to honor."

AT vii 13–19

(13) When Haman realized that not he, but rather Mordecai, was the one to be honored, his heart was greatly crushed, and his spirit fell into faintness. (14) And Haman took the cloak and the horse, showing respect to Mordecai, whereas he had decided to impale him on that very day! (15) And he said to Mordecai, "Remove the sackcloth." (16) And Mordecai was very agitated, like one dying, and he removed the sackcloth in distress and put on the garments of honor. (17) And Mordecai thought to see a sign, and his heart was toward the Lord, and he was astonished in speechlessness.

---

[3] All English translations are my own.

(18) And Haman hurried to put him up on the horse. (19) And Haman led the horse out and brought him out, crying, "Thus shall be done to the man who reveres the king, whom the king wants to honor."

(c) LXX C 5–7

(5) You know everything. You know, O Lord, that I did this neither in arrogance nor in haughtiness nor in love of honor—not bowing to the haughty Haman—(6) for I would have been pleased to kiss the soles of his feet for the salvation of Israel—(7) but I did this so that I might not set the honor of man over the honor of God. And I will not bow down to anyone except you, my Lord, and I will not do thus [αὐτά] in haughtiness.

AT v 14–15

(14) For you know everything, and you know the race of Israel, (15) and (you know) that I acted neither in arrogance nor in love of honor—not bowing to the uncircumcised Haman—since I would have been pleased to kiss the soles of his feet for the sake of Israel—but I acted so as not to set anyone before you O Master! And I will bow down to no one except you, the True One, and I will not do this [αὐτό] (even) in trial.

In example (a) the versions are basically in agreement, but with several differences in word choice and one difference significant to the meaning. Example (b) shows radical variation in content and wording. Example (c) shows very close agreement, with only slight variations in wording and word order. Differences of these kinds occur throughout the book. The closest agreements are in the deuterocanonical sections, the greatest disparities elsewhere.

The plot of the AT—i.e., the current AT, not the pre-redactional version—is close to that of the LXX for most of the book. There are, however, a few notable differences:

(1) The AT lacks the motif of the inalterable Persian law (1:19; 8:8).

(2) The description of the treatment of harem entrants (2:10–15) is far less elaborate in the AT.

(3) Mordecai's discovery of the eunuchs' plot is absent from the section parallel to LXX 2:19–23. (It does appear as part of Add A [i 9b–17], as in the LXX. The LXX has the episode twice, in 2:19–23 and A 13–17).

(4) In the AT, Haman casts the lots *after* receiving permission to destroy the Jews[4] (iv 7 [follows vv. 11–10]).

---

[4] Thus showing definitely that the purpose of the lot-casting is to determine the day of

(5) The lengthy exchange of messages between Mordecai and Esther in 4:4–12 is considerably abbreviated in v 3–8.

(6) When Haman goes to carry out the honors the king has commanded for Mordecai, Mordecai's thoughts are described in detail: he is first greatly afraid, then amazed, believing he has seen a portent (vii 16–17; quoted above, example (b)).

(7) The reason for the king's anger against Haman is revealed after the denouement. This is that Haman had sought to kill the king's benefactor, for he did not know that Mordecai was a relative of Esther (viii 14).

(8) The AT refers to God (or heathen gods) at several points, not restricting this to the Adds, as does the LXX (AT v 4b–5, 7, 9, 11; vi 23; vii 1, 17, 22b; viii 2, 34). (Such reference is absent in the MT.)

Major differences between the LXX and the AT are most frequent in the last part of the book, viii 15–52 // 8:1–10:3. (For a translation of viii 18–21 and 33–38, see §5.) The AT concludes as follows: After Haman is hanged, the king summons Mordecai and gives *him* (not Esther) Haman's property (viii 15). Then Mordecai asks the king to annul Haman's decree, and the king entrusts Mordecai with the affairs of the kingdom (16–17). Esther requests permission to execute her enemies; she is granted that right and consequently many men are slaughtered (18–21). Then comes Add E, the king's public epistle countering Haman's plot. After this, Mordecai writes a public letter telling the Jews to celebrate their deliverance and explaining the background of his order (33–38). He then goes forth dressed in glory, the inhabitants of Susa rejoice, and the Jews celebrate (39–40). Many of the *Jews* circumcise themselves, meeting with no opposition (41); indeed, the authorities aid them out of fear of Mordecai (42). Haman and the opponents are named in Susa (43).[5] The Jews kill 700 men *and* the sons of Haman, and plunder their property (44). The king exclaims on the extent of the slaughter (45), and Esther asks that the Jews be allowed to annihilate and plunder at will (45). The king agrees, and they kill 70,100 men (46). Mordecai records all these matters in a book, instructs the Jews to celebrate the 14th and 15th of Adar, and sends portions to the poor (47–48). For this reason the holiday is called Phouraia (49). The king imposes taxes and writes of his wealth and glory, and Mordecai praises him and inscribes it all in the books of Persia and Media (50–51). Finally, Mordecai *succeeds* Xerxes, leads the Jews, and bestows honor on his people (52). The book concludes with Add F, the interpretation of Mordecai's dream.

---

destruction, not the day auspicious for Haman to approach the king. The MT is ambiguous on this point.

[5] On the meaning of this verse see §8.2.

1.2. *Views of the nature of the AT*

The AT has generally been considered a recension of the LXX. Fritzsche described the AT as "eine tiefeingreifende Umarbeitung" of the LXX (1851:71). According to Fritzsche, the redactor (whom Fritzsche called the "Verfasser"), while generally maintaining the narrative line, supposedly made changes where he did not understand the base text[6] or where it did not please him. He also, Fritzsche believed, condensed the LXX where it was too expansive, eliminated contradictions,[7] and made various additions. In his commentary, Fritzsche noted AT variants but did not usually offer a rationale for individual differences. Langen (1860), on the other hand, argued (rather obscurely) that the AT was an independent translation of Esther which was subsequently changed and glossed in various ways.[8]

At the end of the last century, it became the standard view that the AT is the Lucianic recension of LXX-Esther. Lagarde (1883:lxxxiv) had identified MSS 19, 93, and 108 as Lucianic in some other OT books, and B. Jacob (1890:258–62) took this to mean that the text of Esther in those MSS was likewise Lucianic—a view subsequently adopted by most scholars (see Hanhart, p. 25). Jacob considered this presumed recension to be based on a very poor text which often led Lucian astray. Bickerman (1951:103–108), who rejected the attribution of the AT to Lucian, still argued that it descended from the same translation as the LXX.[9] Almost all commentators who used the AT have treated it as a source for inner-Septuagintal variants, most of which they rejected, usually implicitly. Paton's text-critical apparatus (1908) is the most thoroughgoing application of this approach.

E. Tov (1982:10) has proposed a fresh solution to the problem. He contends that the AT is a recension of the LXX that underwent revision towards a Hebrew or Aramaic version different from the MT. Several considerations weigh against Tov's hypothesis: (a) The evidence for the AT's dependence on the LXX is restricted to the Adds and the ending, but these are later supplements to the original AT (Clines, p. 90). (b) The statistics brought below in §2.7 show that the correspondence between the AT and the LXX is not consistent throughout the book: it is very high in certain passages—not all of them deuterocanonical—and very low in most others. A single recension of a unified AT would have produced a text with a more consistent relation to the LXX. (c) Many sentences in the canonical sections of the AT are the same as the LXX in content but are worded quite differently; examples are given in §2.1. A recensor adjusting the LXX toward a variant Hebrew text

---

[6] LXX-Esther is actually quite comprehensible throughout, except in Adds B, E, and parts of F, but that is where the *fewest* changes are made.

[7] On the contrary, AT contains several contradictions *lacking* in the LXX (§11.2).

[8] According to Ryssel 1900:198, this was also the view of Archbishop Usher.

[9] Almost all of Bickerman's arguments for the common origin of the two versions are based on the Additions, which are indeed taken from the LXX (§3).

would not have changed the Greek wording so radically if the Hebrew text said essentially the same thing as the LXX. (d) It is hard to see what would have been the motive for adjusting the LXX to the variant Hebrew manuscript. The recension Tov hypothesizes added nothing in the way of moral or religious values.[10] Nevertheless, the view I will advocate resembles Tov's insofar as it recognizes the contribution of a non-Massoretic Hebrew text to the present AT.

J.-C. Haelewyck (1985) proposes an intricate, five-stage history of the development of the Esther texts: (1) The original Hebrew, which he identifies with the MT. (2) "G III"—the Greek vorlage of the OL—whose editor thoroughly remodelled the Hebrew text and composed Additions A, part 1 (A 1–11 // i 1–10), B, H 1–5, C, D, E, and F. (3) "L^0," the original AT. Its redactor (or author) used G III as base text, but reshaped it under the influence of the MT. From G III he borrowed Adds A, part 1, D, and F. He reduced and reworded his Greek vorlage considerably, but also added a few items, notably Add A, part 2 (i 11–18) and Mordecai's epistle in viii 33b–38. The differences between L^0 and the MT are to be explained by the liberties taken by the Greek translator. (4) The LXX. Its redactor aligned G III with the Hebrew. He also took elements from L^0, including Add A, part 2, and borrowed the other supplements from G III, while transferring elements of the prayer in Add H 1–5, in a radically modified form, to Add C. (5) The AT. Another redactor transferred Adds B and E and the prayer in C to L^0, giving the AT its current form.

Rather than arguing with this reconstruction in detail, I will offer my own as an alternative.[11] The intricacy of Haelewyck's theory and the multiplicity of its postulations weigh against its plausibility from the start. It is especially implausible that various Additions (and parts thereof) were transferred in different directions at different times. And, as I will show, the author of the AT was *not* working with the MT. Haelewyck's argumentation consists almost exclusively of a "critique littéraire," which is governed by a feel (often unconvincing) for literary coherence, a quality that Haelewyck is too quick to take as a mark of an earlier stage in literary development. (Yet when he

---

[10] It is, on the other hand, clear what would be achieved in this regard by a recension that moved deuterocanonical material from the LXX to a Greek variant version, namely a heightening of the religious aspect of the tale.

[11] As for the place of the OL in the developmental schema, it is almost certainly a translation of a Greek manuscript in the Septuagintal tradition, but one maintaining some older readings (Moore, 1965:117–21). Some of these are found in the AT as well. But the OL (which itself exists in notably diverse forms) is not simply a rendering of the first Greek translation, and Haelewyck does not prove it to be so. There are many aggadic expansions in the OL (Moore 1965:121–26), some of which may be earlier than the Latin translation, but which certainly do not belong to the first stage of the Greek tradition.

finds greater coherence in a supposedly later stage he considers it "harmonization."[12])

I agree with Haelewyck that Adds B, C, and E were copied from the LXX to the AT, but not that Adds A, D and F were borrowed in the other direction. The latter are no better ensconced in the AT than in the LXX. (In neither version are Adds A and F quite in harmony with the rest of the book).[13] My own reconstruction is simpler: *There was an original AT to which a redactor added material from the LXX.*

In 1944, C. C. Torrey argued that AT ii 1–viii 21 (corresponding generally to MT 1:1–8:8)—including the Septuagintal Adds—is independent of the LXX; it is a translation of a different Semitic original.[14] His arguments, however, were somewhat impressionistic and had no immediate impact. It was C. A. Moore (1965:133–39; 1967:352–53) who showed (quite decisively, in the view of most recent scholars) that the AT is not a Lucianic recension of the LXX and that, indeed, there was never any good reason to think it was. Moreover, he suggested, the AT may be an independent translation of a Hebrew (or possibly Aramaic) original quite different from the LXX's vorlage.[15] Clines (pp. 85–92) bolstered the argument, observing, most significantly, that the Septuagintal Additions A-F and the current ending of

---

[12] See, for example, his appeal to the LXX redactor's *harmonistic* treatment of the two assassination plots on p. 22.

[13] The LXX, but not the AT, has Mordecai serving in the court (αὐλή) from the beginning of the book (A 1), thus rendering superfluous the court appointment he receives in A 16. If an LXX redactor had taken Add A from the AT, we would have to suppose that he created that contradiction by unnecessarily adding the phrase "who served in the court of the king" to A 1. The linking of part 1 of Add A to part 2 by the phrase ἕως τῆς ἡμέρας in AT i 11 is no evidence that the two parts were combined first in the AT, for if the LXX were later it would hardly have removed the link.

In one regard Add A is indeed better adjusted to the AT than to the LXX, namely in reporting the eunuchs' plot only once (in i 11–15). But this greater smoothness could just as well be due to redactional omission of 2:21–23 in the AT (thus Tov, 1982:11–12) or to the original absence of a eunuchs' plot in proto-AT (thus Clines 1984:104–105; vii 3 does not require the scheme to have been reported earlier). Even so, the AT does not avoid the major contradiction between i 16, which has Mordecai rewarded early on, and vii 4, which asserts that he had not yet been rewarded.

AT vi 22, which refers to Mordecai serving in the court, does not (contrary to Haelewyck p. 32) prove that Add A (which has Mordecai appointed to the court in i 16) was integral to the original AT. Without Add A, proto-AT proceeds on the assumption that Mordecai had a position in the court, but sees this simply as Mordecai's office, not as a reward for special service.

Moreover, several variants in Adds A, D, and F are better explained on the hypothesis that they were made by the redactor of the AT rather than by a redactor of the LXX; see §§8.4.1–2; 8.6; 8.7. Strong evidence that material was taken from the LXX to the AT and not the other way around is provided by the "cut-and-splice" variant in i 17–18; see §8.6 (quoted in §9.3).

[14] Though on p. 7 Torrey speaks of ii 1–viii 21 as deriving from a separate Aramaic text, on p. 16 he says that viii 18–21 is a "transitional patch" leading into an ending taken from the LXX.

[15] Paton (p. 38), while assuming that the AT is Lucianic, suggested that it was influenced by an independent Hebrew original.

the AT (starting, in his view, with viii 17) do not belong to the original AT ("the proto-AT"[16]). Hence all arguments for the nature of the original AT must be based on non-Septuagintal passages alone.[17]

2. Evidence for the independence of the proto-AT version

I will now present arguments for two intertwined hypotheses: (1) The AT is composed of two levels—the proto-AT and a redactional level, the latter comprising mostly supplementary material taken from the LXX. (2) The proto-AT is a translation from a Hebrew vorlage independent of the MT. (The proto-AT's vorlage and the MT are nevertheless similar or the same in many passages.) Arguments on behalf of the second hypothesis support the first as well; in fact they exclude the alternative.

Moore and Clines adduce several arguments for the independence of the proto-AT from the LXX; these arguments are discussed (and expanded) in §§2.1–2.6. In §§2.7–2.9 I offer some new evidence for the theory.

2.1. *Passages translated differently in the AT and the LXX* that seem to presuppose the same or a very similar vorlage (Moore 1967:353–54; Clines 1984:87–89). These are more likely to result from two translations of the same Hebrew than from inner-Greek modifications.

vii 10 // 6:6b:

MT   *wayyōʾmer hāmān bĕlibbô lĕmî yaḥpōṣ hammelek laʿăśôt yĕqār yōtēr mimmennî?*

LXX   εἶπεν δὲ ἐν ἑαυτῷ ὁ Αμαν Τίνα θέλει ὁ βασιλεὺς δοξάσαι εἰ μὴ ἐμέ;

AT   καὶ ἐλογίσατο ὁ Αμαν λέγων ὅτι Τίνα βούλεται ὁ βασιλεὺς δοξάσαι εἰ μὴ ἐμέ;

Moore (1967:354) observes that the AT's ἐλογίσατο and the LXX's εἶπεν δὲ ἐν ἑαυτῷ clearly presuppose the same Hebrew in their respective vorlagen, as do the AT's βούλεται and the LXX's θέλει. It must be granted, however, that synonym substitution in a recension could account for this and similar examples (see §8.1). The example of iii 4 // 2:4 (Moore, ibid.) is also weakened by this objection. A better example is the following.

---

[16] "Proto-AT" is Clines' term (1984:84). I will be using it, although I differ with regard to the scope of proto-AT and its place in the development of the Esther tradition.

[17] See also Cook 1969. Clines (pp. 85–92) also refutes Tov's case for AT dependence on the LXX, as well as the position of Hanhart (pp. 81–84), who describes the AT as a reworking ("Neugestaltung") of the Greek Esther tradition with heavy dependence on the LXX.

ii 10 // 1:10. These verses are structured differently in the two versions. It is also significant that the LXX lacks AT's ἐγένετο, because this translates *wayĕhî*. It is more likely that the translator of the AT had *wayĕhî* in his vorlage than that it was removed by a recensor of the LXX—contrary to the MT.

iv 1 // 3:1. Not only are there three synonym variants here, but the AT seems more closely bound to the Hebrew: the AT's μετὰ τοὺς λόγους τούτους is a more precise translation of *'aḥar haddĕbārim hā'ēlleh* than is the LXX's μετὰ δὲ ταῦτα. Likewise ἔθηκε τὸν θρόνον αὐτοῦ ὑπεράνω (AT) is closer to *wayyāśem 'et kis'ô* than ἐπρωτοβάθρει (LXX) (Moore, ibid.). To be sure, a reading like the AT's *might* result from recensional adjustment toward the MT, but the AT differs from the MT too radically to allow us to explain the AT in that way.

An interesting case of variant translations of the same (consonantal) vorlage is vii 5 (Clines, p. 106). Clines observes that AT's "what shall we do [for Mordecai]" is awkward and is probably a mistaken reading of *n'śh* as imperfect rather than perfect (the LXX, like the MT, has the perfect).[18]

Moore (1967:354) and Clines (1984:87–89) mention several other cases, not all of them entirely convincing[19]: ii 9 // 1:9; ii 14 // 1:14; ii 21 // 1:21; iii 2 // 2:2; iii 5 // 2:5; iv 2 // 3:2; iv 8 // 3:8; iv 11 // 3:10; v 1–2a // 4:1; v 2b // 4:2; vi 21 // 5:10; vii 9–10 // 6:6; vii 11 // 6:7; vii 14 = 19 // 6:11; viii 12b–13a // 7:9. Some of these verses will be discussed in §2.9.

2.2. *Hebraisms in the AT lacking in the LXX parallels.* For example ii 2 // 1:2b:

MT   *kĕšebet hammelek 'āḥašwērôš 'al kissē' malkûtô*

AT   ἐν τῷ καθῆσθαι ὁ βασιλεὺς[20] Ασσυῆρον ἐπὶ τοῦ θρόνου τῆς βασιλείας αὐτοῦ

LXX   ὅτε ἐθρονίσθη ὁ βασιλεὺς Ἀρταξέρξης

Also ii 14 (// 1:14 [see below]); ii 21 (// 1:21); iv 1 (// 3:1) (Moore, 1967:355). Also see below, §2.9. Such Hebraisms support the hypothesis that the LXX was not intermediate between the original AT and its Hebrew vorlage.

2.3. *AT pluses lacking parallels in other versions.* These include all or parts of iv 1b, 3, 6, 7; vii 14b; viii 2, 4b, 5b–7, 9, 12, 13, 14, 36.

---

[18] On the other hand, Clines' explanation of most of vii 4–6 as a tangled addition by the AT translator is itself too tortuous to be convincing. It is possible, however, that the difficulties in AT vii 5 are in part translational in nature.

[19] In fact, iv 2, 11; vi 21aβ most likely are derived from the LXX; see §6.2.

[20] Hanhart omits ὁ βασιλεύς.

2.4. *AT minuses*—"repetitious elements," personal names, numbers and dates (all or parts of 1:3, 10, 14, 22; 2:16; 3:5; 5:3, 9, 11; 9:18–19, 23–25; Moore 1967:356–57).

2.5. *AT variants* that are "slightly reminiscent of Hebraic style" and *may* reflect a different Hebrew vorlage; e.g., καὶ ἀγαθὸς ὁ λόγος ἐν καρδίᾳ τοῦ βασιλέως (ii 21; MT *wayyîṭab haddābār bĕʿênê hammelek*, 1:21; 3:13) (Moore 1967:357).

2.6. A *near-absence of Septuagintalisms* outside the Additions and the ending (Clines, pp. 85–92). This argument will be developed in §2.7. There are, to be sure, several Septuagintal incursions that neither Moore nor Clines recognized—see §6.2—but once these are accounted for the argument is valid.

The third argument (§2.3) and especially the fourth (§2.4) are rather weak, since a redactor might both supplement his base text and remove passages from it. The redactor of the AT did just that—supplementing the proto-AT with passages from the LXX while omitting much of the material from ch. 9. The other arguments, however, establish at least a *prima facie* case for the theory that the proto-AT originated independently of the LXX, for they show that the AT stands at a considerable distance from the LXX without approaching the MT. I develop a stronger form of the first argument (§2.1) in §2.9 and of the second argument (§2.2) in §2.10. As formulated, the fifth argument (§2.5) is not a strong one, but once the independence of the proto-AT from the LXX is established, the LXX-AT differences—which exist in almost every verse and often concern matters of plot as well as wording—may be presumed to represent differences in the proto-AT's vorlage, since they certainly do not derive from the MT. The additional arguments I adduce in the following sections combine to isolate the redactional supplements from the *proto-AT,* show the independence of the proto-AT from the LXX, and establish a distance between the MT and the proto-AT's vorlage.

2.7. *The different frequency-ranges of vocabulary correspondences* ("matches"). It is necessary first to show that there are two distinct compositional levels in the present AT, one of them Septuagintal, the other not.

In some sections of the AT (class 1 passages), there are many LXX-AT correspondences (II B in Table II). In other sections (class 2 passages) there are very few (II A in Table II). Table II (§7) shows that there are two independent types of material in the AT: passages with a strong vocabulary overlap with the LXX (class 1) and passages with a vague, incidental overlap (class 2). Class 2 passages comprise the original AT; class 1 passages are redactional supplements.

"*Matches*": To compare the texts I counted the vocabulary correspondences between them.[21] Since exact correspondence is not necessary
to show dependence, I allowed a variety of equivalences. Both the exact and
the near equivalences are called "matches." The following are considered
matches: (1) occurrences of the same lexical item, irrespective of grammatical form, (2) close cognates in different parts of speech, and (3) prefix-
variants of compound verbs and nouns from the same stem. These classes of
words are included in the definition of "matches" because they are manifestly
among the types of variations the redactor allowed himself in AT passages
indisputably dependent on the LXX. Matches need not appear in the same
position in the sentence in each version, but they must fill the same syntactical slot. A tighter definition of "matches" would reduce their numbers but
not affect the relative differences between the two types of passages. We
would simply find a lower frequency of matches in *both* groups; the
dichotomy would remain. The following examples show by underlining what
types of correspondences are counted as matches and how the statistics for
Table II are calculated:

AT	LXX
vi 5 καὶ ἄρας τὸ πρόσωπον αὐτοῦ πεπυρωμένον ἐν δόξῃ ἐνέβλεψεν αὐτῇ ὡς ταῦρος ἐν ἀκμῇ θυμοῦ αυτοῦ	D 7 καὶ ἄρας τὸ πρόσωπον αὐτοῦ πεπυρωμένον δόξῃ ἐν ἀκμῇ θυμοῦ ἔβλεψεν

(16 AT words; 11 matches; frequency of matches: 0.69; 11 LXX words; portion
of LXX words represented in the AT: 1.00.)

AT	LXX
vi 7–8a καὶ μετέβαλεν ὁ θεὸς τὸ πνεῦμα τοῦ βασιλέως καὶ μετέθηκε τὸν θυμὸν αὐτοῦ εἰς πραότητα, καὶ ἀγωνιάσας ὁ βασιλεὺς κατεπήδησεν ἀπὸ τοῦ θρόνου αὐτοῦ καὶ ἀνέλαβεν αὐτὴν ἐπὶ τὰς ἀγκάλας αὐτοῦ, καὶ παρεκάλεσεν αὐτὴν	D 8 καὶ μετέβαλεν ὁ θεὸς τὸ πνεῦμα τοῦ βασιλέως εἰς πραΰτητα, καὶ ἀγωνιάσας ἀνεπήδησεν ἀπὸ τοῦ θρόνου αὐτοῦ καὶ ἀνέλαβεν αὐτὴν ἐπὶ τὰς ἀγκάλας αὐτοῦ, μέχρις οὗ κατέστη, καὶ παρεκάλει αὐτὴν λόγοις εἰρηνικοῖς

(34 AT words; 27 matches; frequency of matches: 0.79; 32 LXX words;
fraction of LXX words represented in the AT: 0.84.)

---

[21] The count was manual, because the AT is not available for the computer.

iv 8

λέγων
Ἔστι λαὸς διεσπαρμένος
ἐν πάσαις ταῖς
βασιλείαις, λαὸς πολέμου
καὶ ἀπειθής, ἔξαλλα νόμιμα ἔχων,
τοῖς δὲ νομίμοις σου,
βασιλεῦ, οὐ προσέχουσι, γνωριζόμενοι ἐν πᾶσι τοῖς ἔθνεσι
πονηροὶ ὄντες καὶ τὰ
προστάγματά σου ἀθετοῦσι
πρὸς καθαίρεσιν τῆς δόξης σου.

3:8
καὶ ἐλάλησεν πρὸς τὸν
βασιλέα Ἀρταξέρξην λέγων
Ὑπάρχει ἔθνος διεσπαρμένον ἐν
τοῖς ἔθνεσιν ἐν πάσῃ τῇ
βασιλείᾳ σου, οἱ δὲ νόμοι
αὐτῶν ἔξαλλοι παρὰ πάντα τὰ
ἔθνη, τῶν δὲ νόμων τοῦ
βασιλέως παρακούουσιν, καὶ οὐ
συμφέρει τῷ βασιλεῖ ἐᾶσαι
αὐτούς.

(39 AT words; 11 matches; frequency of matches: 0.282; 40 LXX words; fraction of LXX words represented in the AT: 0.275.)

It must be emphasized that *individual* correspondences are not evidence for a common origin. Almost all passages have some matches, because both the LXX and the AT tell basically the same story. What is important is the overall patterns that give each passage its statistical profile.

Table II shows that there are two fundamentally different types of material in the AT. Within class (1), 75% of the AT's words have matches in the LXX, and 62% of the words in the corresponding LXX passages are represented in the AT. In contrast, within class (2), only 35% of the words in the AT have matches in the LXX, and a mere 21% of the words in the LXX parallels appear in the AT. There is thus a gap, not a continuum, between the two classes. Only a few verses in class (2) show a high percentage of matches.

Separating the two classes even further is the fact that several verses in class (2) were probably transferred from the LXX (see §6.2), and once they are taken into account, the distinction between the two classes is seen to be even greater.

Also significant to the distinction is the disparity between the *medians* of frequency of matches per verse for each section. In class (2), the range of the median verse for each section is between 0% and 35% matches, the average median for all sections being 22%. In class (1), the range is between 57% and 97%, the average median for all sections being 93%. Such a disjunction cannot be explained by positing a single recensor for the entire AT. Someone who went through the LXX making various changes along the way would have produced a text with a more homogeneous relationship to the LXX base-text.

In places where the AT is indisputably dependent on Septuagintal material, i.e. the Adds, we do *not* find passages with low frequencies of matches. We would expect a single recensor to introduce some low frequency (class 2) passages there too. After all, such a recensor would not know (or care) that the deuterocanonical sections had a different background from the rest of the text. Conversely, the high match-frequency passages (class 1) are not distributed more or less evenly throughout the book, as we would expect if the variations in match-frequency merely reflected fluctuations in a recensor's style. Rather, they are densely clustered in eight places (the Adds, D +, and AT-end).

Except for AT-end, D +, and a few isolated verses, the close AT-LXX resemblances are confined to passages that lack MT parallels altogether— namely, the Adds; here the derivation is directly from the LXX to the AT. The *loose* resemblances, on the other hand, are confined to passages where the MT *is* represented. This dichotomy indicates that we should posit a different type of relationship for the loose resemblances, namely an indirect, collateral relationship between the two Greek versions. The proto-AT did not derive from the LXX. The proto-AT and the MT are descendants of the same story ("proto-Esther"), with the MT intermediate between that story and the LXX. In class 1 passages the relationship is:

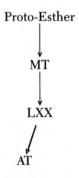

Proto-Esther

MT

LXX

AT

In class 2 passages the relationship is:

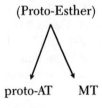

(Proto-Esther)

proto-AT   MT

2.8. *Density patterns of Septuagintal matches.* Statistical analysis of occurrence-patterns of matches clinches the argument that the AT is composed of two types of material with fundamentally different relationships to the LXX.

The segmentation of the book for the statistical profile in Table II was made in accordance with natural divisions, based on marking off the deutero-canonical additions from the material that comes between them. However, to avoid the possibility that the particular selection of "passages" has influenced the patterns revealed, we can examine the *density* of Septuagintal matches, as defined above. To what degree do matches tend to cluster with other matches, and non-matched words with other non-matches—irrespective of the delineation of the book's subdivisions?

The following chart describes the distribution of (1) *coordinate pairs,* in which either a Septuagintal match (M) is followed by another match (MM), or a non-match (N) is followed by another non-match (NN), and (2) *non-coordinate pairs,* i.e. either MN or NM. The numbers of occurrences of each type are:

coordinate pairs	MM 2102	1953	NN
non-coordinate pairs	NM 523	502	MN

The probabilities of occurrence of coordinate pairs and non-coordinate pairs are:

	first word	second word	frequency	number of observations
coordinate	M	M	80.72%	} 2604
non-coor-dinate	M	N	19.28%	
coordinate	N	N	78.88%	} 2476
non-coor-dinate	N	M	21.12%	

It is immediately evident that coordinate pairs are much more frequent than non-coordinate pairs. In other words, matches tend to co-occur and non-matches to do the same.

A statistical analysis of these figures, applying a chi-square test, argues strongly that the patterns are not random.[22]

In this test, the degree to which an M or an N occurring as the first word of a pair is associated with an M or an N occurring as the second word is tested against the null hypothesis of no association. Using the Yates' correction for 2-by-2 tables, the test generates a chi-square value of 1803. This is highly significant (p < .00001), indicating that the probability that the co-ordinate pairs in the AT are random is vanishingly small.

The above results are a strong indication that the AT was not produced by one person reworking the LXX, but rather by *two different acts of literary creativity* of two fundamentally different types. This conclusion rests on the assumption that a recension carried out by a single redactor will display on the overall the same relation to the donor text throughout. This assumption would be invalid if the redactor had reasons to treat different parts of the donor text differently, but no such reasons are at hand in the case of the LXX.

2.9. *MT-AT agreements against the LXX in proto-AT sections*, when these agreements are not hexaplaric. Sentences where the AT is closer to the MT than to the LXX, yet not identical to the MT, provide evidence that the AT is not a revision of the LXX. Since such AT-MT proximations are not derived from the LXX, and since the AT as a whole is too distant from the MT to be thought influenced by it, these proximations show that the MT and the AT had a common source. These agreements differ from the ones produced by the hexaplaric or pre-hexaplaric[23] recension. (In the following, underlining marks words that appear in the MT and the AT but not in the LXX, while dashes mark minuses in regard to which the MT and AT agree against the LXX.)

2.9.1. ii 2a // 1:2b: AT ἐν τῷ καθῆσθαι . . . ἐπὶ τοῦ θρόνου τῆς βασιλείας αὐτοῦ = MT "as King Xerxes was sitting on his royal throne" (*kĕšebet hammelek . . . ʿal kisseʾ malkûtô*). This clause, used above as an example of an AT Hebraism (§2.2), is also a case where the AT agrees with the MT against the LXX.

---

[22] I am grateful to Kurt Neuwirth of the Data and Computation Center of the University of Wisconsin for designing and calculating the statistical model. I report his results rather than attempting to argue for them. I also thank Zhao Xinshu for applying a logit model to these figures and arriving at the same conclusion.

[23] On which see Hanhart, pp. 67–68.

2.9.2. ii 3 // 1:3: AT τοῖς ἄρχουσι = MT "his princes"(*śārāyw*). LXX τοῖς φίλοις. Since the AT diverges from the MT in several ways in this verse, the agreement is unlikely to have resulted from a harmonization with the MT.

2.9.3. ii 13 // 1:13

MT	And the king spoke to the wise men who knew
AT	καὶ εἶπεν ὁ βασιλεὺς πᾶσι τοῖς σοφοῖς τοῖς εἰδόσι
LXX	καὶ εἶπεν τοῖς φίλοις αὐτοῦ

MT	the times, for thus was the word of the king before
AT	
LXX	Κατὰ ταῦτα ἐλάλησεν Αστιν, ποιήσατε οὖν περὶ τούτου

MT	all who knew law and justice:
AT	νόμον καὶ κρίσιν
LXX	νόμον καὶ κρίσιν

The AT shares with the MT three items that are lacking in the LXX: "the king," "the wise men," and "who knew."[24] The AT certainly did not pick these up from the LXX, which here, as often in Esther, is translating loosely. The MT plus, "the times . . . knew," may be a gloss by the MT author which was rephrased by the LXX translator or, alternatively, a later expansion absent in the LXX's vorlage.

2.9.4. ii 14 // 1:14

MT	And those who were near to him		were Karshena,
AT	καὶ	προσῆλθον πρὸς αὐτὸν	
LXX	καὶ	προσῆλθεν αὐτῷ	Αρχεσαῖος καὶ

MT	Shethar, Admatha, Tarshish, Meres, Marsena, Memuchan,	
AT		
LXX	Σαρσαθαῖος καὶ	Μαλησεαρ

---

[24] "The king" does appear in some hexaplaric MSS. Hexaplaric MSS also supply "knew," but as part of another phrase: "who knew the times."

MT   the seven princes of Persia and Media,

AT   οἱ   ἄρχοντες Περσῶν καὶ Μήδων

LXX   οἱ   ἄρχοντες Περσῶν καὶ Μήδων

MT   who saw   the face   of the king,

AT   καὶ οἱ   ὁρῶντες τὸ πρόσωπον τοῦ βασιλέως

LXX   οἱ ἐγγὺς   τοῦ βασιλέως,

MT   who sat first   in the kingdom.

AT   καὶ οἱ   καθήμενοι ἐν τοῖς βασιλείοις

LXX   οἱ πρῶτοι παρακαθήμενοι   τῷ βασιλεῖ

The underlined words are present in the MT but not represented in the free translation of the LXX; hence the AT could not have taken them from the LXX. On the other hand, the sequence of the passage in AT ii 13–14 differs from that of MT and LXX 1:13–15, with material corresponding to MT-LXX 1:15 appearing in AT ii 13. There are further AT divergences from the MT and LXX in this passage, and no reviser tried to change them.[25]

2.9.5. ii 16b // 1:17a.

MT   For the word of the queen will go forth to all the women, etc.

AT   καὶ εἰς πάντας τοὺς λαοὺς ἡ ἀδικία αὐτῆς ἐξῆλθεν κτλ.

LXX   καὶ γὰρ διηγήσατο αὐτοῖς τὰ ῥήματα τῆς βασιλίσσης καὶ ὡς ἀντεῖπεν κτλ.

The AT's ἐξῆλθεν renders consonantal yṣ' as an aorist; the MT correctly points it as an imperfect, yēṣē'. (Since Aramaic yinpaq would not occasion this ambiguity, we may conclude that the AT's vorlage was in Hebrew.) The phrase "to all" likewise was derived from a text common to the AT and the MT, not from the LXX.[26]

---

[25] The word "seven" seems to be a later addition in the MT. It is missing in the Syriac as well as in the LXX, AT, and OL. It is present in Josephus (Ant. XI, 192), who lacks the names themselves. He is probably simply counting the names rather than copying them, since he often omits irrelevant details.

[26] As for MT's "women," I would surmise that AT's "peoples" is the earlier reading, present in MT's predecessor, and that the MT changed it for greater specificity.

2.9.6. iii 7 // 2:7

(In this section the numbering in square brackets refers to clauses that appear in a different order in the LXX and have been rearranged here for purposes of alignment.)

MT	And he <u>was raising</u> (*'ōmēn*) Hadassah,	
AT	καὶ ἦν ἐκτρέφων πιστῶς	
LXX ([1]	καὶ ἦν τούτῳ παῖς θρεπτή,	

MT	that is Esther, the daughter	------------	of his uncle,	
AT	τὴν Εσθηρ θυγατέρα	----------	ἀδελφοῦ τοῦ πατρὸς αὐτοῦ	
LXX		θυγάτηρ	Αμιναδαβ ἀδελφοῦ	πατρὸς αὐτοῦ
LXX	καὶ ὄνομα αὐτῇ Εσθηρ.			

MT (7aβ) for she had no father or mother.

AT

LXX

MT (7bα)	And the girl was	lovely of form
AT	καὶ ἦν ἡ παῖς	καλὴ τῷ εἴδει σφόδρα
LXX [3]	καὶ ἦν τὸ κοράσιον	καλὸν τῷ εἴδει.

MT	<u>and comely of appearance.</u> (7bβ) And when her father and her
AT	<u>καὶ ὡραία τῇ ὄψει.</u>
LXX	27 [2] ἐν δὲ τῷ μεταλλάξαι αὐτῆς

MT	mother died, (7bγ) Mordecai took		her to him
AT			
LXX	τοὺς γονεῖς	ἐπαίδευσεν αὐτὴν ἑαυτῷ	

MT	as a daughter.
AT	
LXX	εἰς γυναῖκα.

---

27 The AT's final five words in iii 7 (// MT *ṭôbat mar'eh*), absent in the LXX, are supplied in hexaplaric MSS, but in a different order (καὶ ὡραῖον τῇ ὄψει σφόδρα), and with the singular ὡραῖον for the AT's plural.

The AT's ἐκτρέφων πιστῶς, "raised her faithfully," can only be an etymological rendering of 'ōmēn not derived from the LXX. This rendering shows, incidentally, that the AT's vorlage was in Hebrew rather than Aramaic, since Aramaic would use a form of *RBY*, not *'MN*, for "raising."

The AT is not dependent on the LXX here, as is shown by the fact that it was not influenced by the LXX's notion that Mordecai raised Esther to be his wife, or by its importation of the name of Esther's father from 9:29, or by its different ordering of the clauses (indicated by numbers in square brackets), or by the MT plus in v. 7aβ or the MT-LXX plus in 7bβ. Yet the AT is far from being in harmony with the MT.

2.9.7. iii 9b // 2:16aα

MT   And Esther <u>was taken</u>

AT   ὡς δὲ <u>εἰσήχθη</u>   Εσθηρ

LXX   καὶ   εἰσῆλθεν   Εσθηρ

The AT's "was taken" derives from Hebrew *wattillāqaḥ*, not from the LXX's "entered." (This does not result from a systematic attempt to adjust the AT to the MT at this point, since in iii 8 the AT renders *wattillāqaḥ* by the form ἐλήφθη.) But the AT diverges from the MT in omitting the king's name and everything following "the king." Furthermore, the AT goes its own way in the sequence of sentences in iii 6-9.

2.9.8. iii 17b // 2:17b

MT   and she received grace <u>and kindness before</u>   <u>him</u>

AT   καὶ   εὖρε   χάριν <u>καὶ ἔλεον</u>   κατὰ πρόσωπον αὐτοῦ

LXX   καὶ   εὖρεν   χάριν

MT   more than all the virgins,

AT

LXX   παρὰ πάσας τὰς παρθένους

MT   and   he put   ------ the <u>royal</u> crown

AT   καὶ   ἐπέθηκε   ------ τὸ διάδημα τῆς βασιλείας

LXX   και   ἐπέθηκεν αὐτῇ τὸ διάδημα τὸ γυναικεῖον.

MT   <u>on her head</u>   and made her queen in place of Vashti.

AT   ἐπὶ τὴν κεφαλὴν αὐτῆς.

LXX

The AT agrees with the MT in including "and kindness" (for *wāḥesed*), "before him," "on her head," and "royal." The AT's κατὰ πρόσωπον αὐτοῦ is surely a rendering of *lĕpānāyw* in a Hebrew vorlage. (The phrase "and kindness before him" is not an hexaplaric addition to the AT. Hexaplaric texts use καὶ ἔλεον ἐνώπιον αὐτοῦ here.) On the other hand, the AT agrees with the LXX against the MT in lacking the last clause in the verse. In the few cases of MT phrases that are unrepresented in the AT and the LXX of Esther, either the phrase in question is a later addition to the MT, or the original MT redactor added a clause that was later coincidentally omitted by the LXX.

2.9.9. iv 1 // 3:1

MT   After these things the king

AT   καὶ ἐγένετο   μετὰ τοὺς λόγους τούτους   <u>ἐμεγάλυνεν</u>   ὁ βασιλεὺς

LXX   μετὰ δὲ ταῦτα   ἐδόξασεν   ὁ βασιλεὺς

MT   Xerxes <u>exalted</u> Haman son of Hammedatha the Agagite and

AT   Ασσυῆρος   Αμαν   Αμαδάθου   Βουγαῖον   καὶ

LXX   Ἀρταξέρξης   Αμαν   Αμαδάθου   Βουγαῖον   καὶ

MT   lifted   him up and <u>placed his seat (*kis'ô*) above</u>

AT   ἐπῆρεν   αὐτὸν   καὶ <u>ἔθηκε τὸν θρόνον αὐτοῦ ὑπεράνω</u>

LXX   ὕψωσεν   αὐτὸν   καὶ ἐπρωτοβάθρει

MT   all   the princes who were with him.

AT   τῶν φίλων αὐτοῦ κτλ.

LXX   πάντων τῶν φίλων αὐτοῦ

The AT's ἐμεγάλυνεν renders *giddal* (as μεγαλύνειν normally does in the LXX; it is translated by δοξάζειν only here). In the first clause, the AT's καὶ ἐγένετο may represent a *wayĕhî* not found in the MT, but the AT's (μετὰ) τοὺς λόγους τούτους seems to derive directly from a vorlage reading *haddĕbārîm hā'ēlleh* (as in the MT) rather than being a rewriting of the LXX's (μετὰ δὲ) ταῦτα.

The AT's "placed his seat above" must render *wayyāśem 'et kis'ô mē'al*; it cannot derive from the LXX's "place (him) before" (though the LXX, for its part, does represent the MT). On the other hand, LXX equals AT in τῶν φίλων αὐτοῦ. Φίλος is one of the LXX's characteristic terms, used to render *śārîm* (1:3 [AT ἄρχουσι]; 2:18 [AT lacking]; 3:1 [AT φίλων]); *ḥăkāmîm* (1:13 [AT σοφοῖς]; 6:13b [AT σοφοί]); *'ōhăbîm* (5:10 [AT φίλους], 6:13a [lacking in AT]); and *rē'a* (9:22 [lacking in AT]). Since the AT shows no consistent attempt to follow the LXX in its treatment of these words, the presence of τῶν φίλων αὐτοῦ in iv 1 is probably an accidental agreement.

Βουγαῖον, on the other hand, does show LXX influence. Since it alone cannot testify to the dependency of the entire verse on the LXX, it can best be explained as a redactional incursion of the LXX, by either R—AT or a later copyist.

2.9.10. iv 5b // 3:6: AT's ἐζήτει represents *wayĕbaqqēš* more precisely than does LXX's ἐβουλεύσατο.[28]

2.9.11. iv 10 // 3:10a: AT's ἀπὸ τῆς χειρὸς αὐτοῦ is the equivalent of MT's *mē'al yādô*, absent in LXX. (The AT's phrase does not have its parallel in LXX's ἔδωκεν εἰς χεῖρα τῷ Αμαν, which describes a different action and translates the MT's "and gave it to Haman.") AT's καὶ ἔδωκε τῷ Αμαν is a literal translation of the same Hebrew as the MT, not a revision of LXX's "put it into the hands of Haman." AT iv 10 otherwise differs considerably from the MT in both its placement in the story and its wording.

2.10. The language of the proto-AT

Linguistic considerations show that the proto-AT is a translation from a Hebrew vorlage, not a revision of the LXX.

Raymond Martin's study of the syntax of Greek texts (1974, cf. 1975) provides a method for determining whether a text was originally composed in Greek or is a translation from a Semitic language (Hebrew or Aramaic). Examining various texts whose origin is known, Martin looked at the distribution of seventeen syntactical features and found a sharp difference in the patterns of their use in "original-Greek" and "translation-Greek" texts.

An example of a criterial feature is the use of καί to introduce main clauses. This syntagm can, of course, occur in texts originally composed in Greek. What is decisive is the *ratio* of occurrences between καί = main clause and the particle δέ. Martin found that in texts translated from Semitic the ratio is typically equal to or greater than 2.1 to 1. It is not the syntagm καί = main clause that constitutes the translation-Greek trait, but rather the appearance

---

[28] The LXX in MS 392 has καὶ ἐζήτει τὸν Μαρδοχαῖον ἀνελεῖν καί, but according to Hanhart (ad loc.), this is taken from the AT (there is much cross-contamination in this manuscript).

of the syntagm in the specified relative frequency range. The 17 syntagms tallied are listed in the first column of Table I below.

A translation-Greek *trait*[29] refers not to a specific realization of a syntactic feature (e.g., διά = genitive) in a text, but to a case where a syntactic feature occurs in the frequency-range characteristic of translated texts (as shown in Table I), and conversely for original-Greek traits.

Not every translation-Greek trait, of course, need occur in every translated text. It is the overall profile of the text that is significant: how many translation-Greek traits it has in proportion to its original-Greek traits. To arrive at this profile one looks at the *net* number of translation-Greek or original-Greek traits; this is calculated by subtracting the smaller number from the larger. I Kgs 17, for example, has ten translation-Greek traits and four original-Greek traits, yielding a net of six translation-Greek traits, and this accords with what we know of the origin of that text. (In some texts, certain syntagms occur too infrequently to contribute to the profile and are therefore left out of the count; I Kgs 17 has three such.)

Martin found that texts translated from Hebrew or Aramaic always had at least four more translation-Greek traits than original-Greek ones, whereas texts composed in Greek always had a net plus of at least 15 original-Greek traits. Moreover, no original-Greek texts had *any* traits characteristic of translation Greek (1974:40–42),[30] while translated texts had at least *nine* traits characteristic of translation Greek.

The results of Martin's methods are impressive, especially for selections longer than 50 lines, and they leave little doubt that texts originally composed in Greek show clear differences from translated texts. Application of his criteria to a selection of 57 lines from the proto-AT produces the results listed in Table I on page 32.

These statistics leave little doubt that the proto-AT is a translation from a Semitic language — in this case Hebrew[31] — and not a recension of the LXX. The proto-AT has 11 translation-Greek traits and only 5 original-Greek ones — a net difference of 6 translation-Greek traits. Martin's original-Greek texts had *no* translation-Greek traits, while the translated texts had between 9 and 14 translation-Greek traits (the average was 12.4).

Now there is no dispute that the proto-AT is a translation at *some* remove; somewhere behind its version of the Esther story obviously lies a Semitic text. The issue is whether the proto-AT is a translation or a *recension* of a translation, in particular, of the LXX. The above statistics provide strong evidence that the proto-AT as we have it is close to the original translation.

---

[29] I have chosen the term "trait" for what Martin, rather ambiguously, calls "frequencies."

[30] When the profile of an original-Greek text shows less than 17 original-Greek frequencies, this is only because one or two syntagms do not occur at all in that text and so cannot be taken into account.

[31] See above §§2.9.5–6.

TABLE I
CHARACTERISTICS OF TRANSLATION-GREEK
IN THE PROTO-AT
in comparison with LXX parallels
translation-Greek traits underlined

col. I				col. II proto-AT	col. III LXX
1.	διά	+ gen.	.06 – .01 as freq. as ἐν[32]	.14	1.16
2.	διά	+ all cases	.18 – .01 as freq. as ἐν	_.14_	1.16
3.	εἰς		.49 – .01 as freq. as ἐν	_.21_	.83
4.	κατά	+ acc.	.18 – .01 as freq. as ἐν	.28	.50
5.	κατά	+ all cases	.19 – .01 as freq. as ἐν	.35	.66
6.	περί	+ all cases	.27 – .01 as freq. as ἐν	_.21_	.33
7.	πρός	+ dat.	.024 – .01 as freq. as ἐν	.07	--
8.	ὑπό	+ gen.	.07 – .01 as freq. as ἐν[33]	--	.66
9.	καί in main clauses ≥ 2.1 times as frequent as all occurrences of δέ			_3.86_	1.7
10.	≤ .05 of articles separated from their substantive			_.006_	_.016_
11.	≥ 22 dependent genitives following the word they qualify for each such genitive preceding the word qualified			_65_	_23_
12.	≤ 9 lines of Gk. for each dependent gen. personal pronoun			_2.95_	_4.7_
13.	≤ 77 lines for each gen. personal pronoun dependent on anarthrous substantive			_29.5_	_0_
14.	≤ .35 attributive adjectives preceding the word they qualify for each attrib. adj. following the word it qualifies			.50	1

[32] In the samples studied, ἐν occurs five times in the AT, and six times in the LXX.

[33] According to Martin (1974:5, n. 3), the absence of a preposition cannot be used as a criterion for identifying the type of Greek in a particular text.

15. ≥ 10.1 text lines for each attrib. adj.   _19.6_   _16_

16. ≥ 6 lines for each adverbial participle   _10.72_   _6.6_

17. ≤ 2 datives *not* used as object of   2   5
     ἐν[34] for each occurrence of ἐν

	orig.-Gk texts	tran.-Gk texts	proto-AT	LXX
transl.-Grk traits	0	≥ 9	_11_	_6_
orig.-Grk traits	≥ 15	≤ 5	_5_	10
net transl.-Grk traits		≥ 4	_6_	
net orig.-Grk traits	≥ 15			4

It is doubtful that a recensor of a Greek text would or could vary the content of that text extensively while maintaining a strongly "Semitic" character. A recension that moved as far from its base text as the proto-AT is from the LXX would certainly have taken on a stronger *original-Greek* character. Josephus, who retells biblical stories with a fair degree of faithfulness to the content of his source (i.e, the Septuagint), produces a Greek style *all* of whose features are in the frequency ranges for original-Greek.[35] We may say, then, that the proto-AT is far less of a reworking of a Greek vorlage than is Josephus, at least with regard to style.

The LXX cannot be the intermediary between a Hebrew text and the proto-AT. First of all, most of the particular realizations of syntagms whose frequency-ratios produce the pronounced translation-Greek character of the proto-AT sample are *absent from the parallel passages in the LXX*.[36] Surely no recensor would or could have introduced these traits. Even one who wished to give his work a Hebraic "tone" would not have realized that these features, though all acceptable Greek on their own, become characteristics of

---

[34] Excluding the objects of λέγειν, εἰπεῖν, and διδόναι (Martin 1974:36).

[35] Martin's statistics are based on selections from *Contra Apionem* and *Antiquities*, not *Wars*, which was originally written in Aramaic (*Wars* I i 3).

[36] For example, in AT viii 2–3 the underlined words are elements in syntagms that appear with frequencies characteristic of translation Greek: (2) <u>καὶ</u> ἠγωνίασεν Εσθηρ <u>ἐν τῷ</u> ἀπαγγέλειν, ὅτι ὁ ἀντίδικος <u>ἐν</u> ὀφθαλμοῖς <u>αὐτῆς</u> καὶ ὁ θεὸς ἔδωκεν αὐτῇ θάρσος <u>ἐν τῷ</u> αὐτὴν ἐπικαλεῖσθαι αὐτόν. (3) <u>καὶ</u> εἶπεν Εσθηρ Εἰ δοκεῖ τῷ βασιλεῖ, καὶ ἀγαθὴ ἡ κρίσις <u>ἐν</u> καρδίᾳ <u>αὐτοῦ,</u> δοθήτω ὁ λαός <u>μου τῷ</u> αἰτήματί <u>μου</u> καὶ τὸ ἔθνος τῆς ψυχῆς <u>μου.</u> Vs. 2 has no parallel in the LXX. Vs. 3 in the LXX reads (with the same words underlined): <u>καὶ</u> ἀποκριθεῖσα εἶπεν Εἰ εὗρον χάριν ἐνώπιον τοῦ βασιλέως, δοθήτω ἡ ψυχή τῷ αἰτήματί <u>μου</u> καὶ ὁ λαός μου τῷ ἀξιώματί μου. Thus in these two verses, the LXX could provide 3 of the 13 words that will enter into the ratios that characterize the AT as translation Greek.

translation-Greek when they appear in certain ratios with other syntactical features.

The application of Martin's methodology to the Greek Esther texts shows the proto-AT to have a radically more pronounced translational character than LXX-Esther. This character can hardly have been produced by recension of the LXX. Looking at net translation-Greek traits, the simplest index of origin, we find a figure of 6 for the proto-AT. This is, to be sure, below the 12.4 average for the 10 translated texts Martin studied,[37] but it remains well within the range presented by those texts, namely between 4 and 14 net translation traits. LXX-Esther, on the other hand, has a net of 4 *original-Greek* traits! (This surprising finding does not undermine Martin's methodology, since the latter figure is well below the net count of 15–17 original-Greek traits that Martin found in the original-Greek texts he studied. Moreover, LXX-Esther does have six translation-Greek traits, whereas *none* of the original-Greek texts had *any* of the traits characteristic of translated texts. So LXX-Esther is still closer to Semitic style than original-Greek texts.)

In sum, it is hardly conceivable that a recension of the LXX produced the proto-AT. While a harmonizing recension (like the hexaplaric) would enhance a text's Semitic character, the proto-AT is *farther* from the MT than the LXX is. A recension creating a text like the proto-AT could hardly produce such a highly translational character. The proto-AT must be fairly close to its Hebrew vorlage, which was quite different from the MT.

3. *The development of the Alpha Text.*

The AT arose in two distinct stages: first the original composition of the proto-AT, unrelated to the LXX, and second a redaction that drew upon the LXX as its source or donor text, working some of its material into the proto-AT, the receptor text.

> *A remark on some terms:*
> The term *source* should, in my view, properly designate the text from which material was transferred into the redacted text, rather than denoting the borrowed material as it presently stands in that text. Thus the "source" of the Adds and some other material (to be delineated below) in the AT is the LXX. The material taken from the LXX forms a redactional *layer* in the AT where it is not itself a source. Kings is a source of Chronicles, but the synoptic material *in* Chronicles, in the form it has there, is not and should not be called a "source." In the Pentateuch the "E" material is not a source but (according to the usual theory) was taken *from* a source, which we can likewise call E. Of course, in some cases there is no practical way of distinguishing between the borrowings and the source it came from. In the

---

[37] Namely Gen 1–4; 6; 39; 1 Sam 3; 4; 22; 1 Kgs 17; 2 Kgs 13; Daniel LXX and Theodotion (both the Hebrew and Aramaic portions); Ezra (Hebrew and Aramaic portions).

case of the AT, the *source* of the redactional borrowings, LXX-Esther, is easily distinguishable and quite different from the Septuagintal *layer* in the AT.[38] Two other useful terms are "receptor text"—in this case the AT—and the "donor text"—in this case the LXX.

The two stages are distinct. I cannot agree with Tov (1982:11-13) that the canonical sections in the AT and the Additions are one "organic unit," by which he seems to mean that the canonical parts were translated by the same person who transferred the Adds. (Actually, the term "organic," if it is to be used properly, must signify that the entire unit developed as part of a single process, as the AT certainly did not.) It is true that the canonical sections in the AT contain several allusions linking them to the Adds (Tov pp. 11–12), but these links are redactional, not integral to the AT (i.e., the proto-AT). An example of such an allusion is ii 1a, "And it happened after these things," which is simply the redactor's transition from Add A to the beginning of the proto-AT. The echos of Add C in v 4b and Add D in vi 1 that Tov mentions are merely borrowings from the LXX and say nothing about the affiliations of the non-redactional parts of the AT.[39] There may well have been certain "excisions" from proto-AT sections to avoid redundancies with the Adds, as Tov thinks (pp. 12–13), but these excisions could just as well have been the work of the AT's redactor (especially in 3:12), for he frequently omitted redundancies in LXX material (see below, §8.5). Alternatively, the "omitted" material may have been absent from the proto-AT. This is probably the case in LXX (= MT) 2:6; 2:21–23; and 8:7–13.[40]

---

[38] Richter (1971) also prefers the term "layer" (*Schicht*), objecting to the term "source" (*Quelle*) on the grounds that it leads one to premature use of the material so designated for historical information (p. 66) and because the concept may be taken to imply originality (p. 167). The term "source," used as I have suggested, should not have those implications.

[39] On the other hand, Esther's injunction to Mordecai, "And pray to God" (v 11), need not allude specifically to Mordecai's prayer (Add C), but may stand alone. If this sentence was in the *MT*'s source, it may have been changed to a call to fasting in MT, if Clines is right that the absence of explicitly religious language in MT is secondary. Alternatively, it may be a translator's or glossator's way of introducing religious language into the AT.

[40] Bickerman adduces several minuses common to the AT and the LXX (as well as Jos and the OL) as evidence that the Greek versions are interdependent reworkings of a single translation. He thinks that these gaps must have existed in the translator's vorlage, inasmuch as it is "unbelievable" that a later redactor of the Hebrew would have inserted such difficult passages in the story (1951:108). But in almost all cases of minuses shared by the Greek versions, the AT is lacking much more than just the clause adduced, so the absence of a few words within the larger minus is hardly evidence of AT dependency on the LXX. These shared minuses are:

(a)   6:8bβ (crown on horse's head). But in any case 9 of the LXX's 18 words have no parallel in the AT.

(b)   1:22 ("and speak in the language of his people"). But all of 1:22 is absent in the AT.

(c)   2:19a (second gathering). But all of 2:19–23 is absent in the AT.

(d)   4:6. But 4:6 is absent in the AT and 4:4 and 7 are only loosely paralleled.

One might hypothesize that the AT arose from two separate redactions of the LXX, the first (which supposedly produced the proto-AT from the LXX) very free, the second (which introduced the Septuagintal material) closely bound to its source. But this supposition would undo the hypothesis that gave rise to it; for once we make this distinction, we can no longer use the second type of material in determining the origin of the first type, leaving little with which to connect that material with the LXX—scarcely more than miscellaneous words inevitably shared by two versions of the same basic story.

The passages shared by the LXX and the AT were copied from the former to the latter and not the other way around. Several considerations show this:

(a) The "cut-and-splice" technique (§8.6) can only be explained as a deliberate reduction of the LXX, not as an expansion of the AT.

(b) The AT's αὐτῶν ἅμα (v 27) must derive from LXX's Αμαν (C 28; see Hanhart, p. 88), and the AT's τὸν ἀδελφὸν αὐτοῦ (viii 44) must precede the LXX's καὶ Δελφων (9:7). (On these changes see §8.2.)

(c) Add E fits awkwardly in the AT version of the story, whereas it is well integrated into that of the LXX (see §11.2.2).

(d) Though scattered LXX verses appear in the AT, no proto-AT material shows up in the LXX. If a redactor were moving material from the AT (proto-AT + the Additions) to the LXX (in its pre-deuterocanonical form), we would expect some sentences to appear in those two versions (outside the deuterocanonical passages) that are not represented in the MT, but this does not happen.

4. The redaction of the proto-AT

The redaction that introduced the Septuagintal material into the AT has never been studied in its own right. Torrey and Clines looked at the redactor's additions only in order to prove that the ending he added is not an integral continuation of the preceding story. In large part the proof consisted in pointing out the artistic deficiencies of the ending. According to Clines (pp. 78–83), the narrative logic "falls apart" after viii 17, the logic of viii 18 is "strange," vs. 19 contains an "awkward juxtaposition," vs. 21 constitutes a "meaningless repetition," vs. 47 seems to be "a rather unintelligent abbreviation of a longer account of the institution of the festival" (p. 83), and so on. It is true that the AT's ending is deficient when considered as a continuation of the earlier narrative. But AT-end is part of a broader redaction with its own

(e)   8:10 (bassûsîm . . . hārammākîm) and
(f)   8:14aα (difficult words). But all of 8:8–14a is absent in the AT!
Bickerman (ibid.) concedes that other words omitted by the versions (AT, OL, LXX, Jos) may be later additions to MT. He considers 'eḥād in 3:8, "Ahashuerus" in 1:15 and the clause "who waited upon him" in 2:2 to be such MT additions. I consider "Hadassah" in 2:7 another likely gloss.

goals, methods, and logic, and these are obscured when the ending is judged only by how well it serves the dynamics of the preceding narrative. The ending the redactor provided cannot be understood outside the context of his entire activity.

The dating of this redaction is very uncertain. According to the colophon, LXX-Esther was brought to Egypt in the fourth year of the reign of Ptolemy and Cleopatra. This Ptolemy is probably Ptolemy XII Auletos, making the date 73 BCE (according to Bickerman's understanding of the colophon; 1944:347). An even later *terminus a quo* is indicated by the identification of Adar-Nisan with Dystros-Xandikos (i 1). A retardation of the Macedonian series in the Macedonian-Babylonian month correlation was introduced sometime between 15/16 CE and 46/47 CE. Prior to 15/16 CE, Adar corresponded to Xandikos and Nisan to Artemisios (Samuel 1972:142–43). The *terminus ad quem* could be much later. Macedonian month-names, which R-AT uses to gloss Hebrew month names in i 1 and iv 18, were in widespread use in the East well into the Byzantine period and thus provide little help in narrowing down the *ad quem* of the redaction.

The nature of the Septuagint text that R-AT used is of uncertain bearing on the issue. The AT frequently agrees with hexaplaric LXX manuscripts (hexaplaric, that is, in the canonical sections.) Strictly speaking, the agreements are not themselves hexaplaric, since they appear in deuterocanonical sections and cannot reflect adjustment toward the MT. The hexaplaric readings in the AT's redactional additions are probably later incursions. However, even if the agreements between the AT and hexaplaric manuscripts in these sections were in fact present in the LXX text that R-AT used, this might indicate only that these variants existed in the particular LXX tradition used by Origen, not that the redaction is post-hexaplaric.

Further evidence for the antiquity of the AT redaction is to be found in the appearance of apparent AT characteristics in the OL, both in redactional and proto-AT sections.[41] It is unlikely that these reflexes of the AT were originally Septuagintal readings first taken into the OL, and then lost from the Septuagintal tradition while somehow infiltrating the AT. The existence of AT-OL correspondences suggests that the AT in its entirety was influencing the Greek tradition by the end of the third or (at the latest) fourth century CE.[42]

---

[41] Of the AT-OL correspondences listed by Moore (1965:108–109, 110–17), only the following verses include distinctive AT-OL agreements against the LXX in redactional passages (numbered according to the AT): i 10 (Add A); v 20 (Add C); v 25 (Add C); vi 5 (Add D); vi 9 (Add D); viii 26 (Add E); viii 28 (Add E); viii 40 (AT-end); viii 54 (Add F).

[42] The listing in Moore (1965:110–17) includes 32 cases of OL-AT correspondences (against the LXX) in proto-AT sections. Some of the correspondences are quite distinctive, such as the major plus in vii 4. On the other hand, the supposed (proto-)AT correspondences Moore finds in Josephus (1965:169–70) are too vague to prove AT influence on Josephus' vorlage. Josephus rephrases the LXX in so many ways that his version inevitably coincides with the AT in various details.

One peculiarity of the redaction — the notion that Jews rather than gentiles "circumcised themselves" after Haman's fall (viii 41a // 9:17b) — seems to reflect the Hellenistic-Roman period, when many hellenizing Jews were uncircumcised, leading the redactor to envision Jewish self-circumcision as a concomitant of Jewish repentance. But because other explanations are possible, this is not a strong criterion for dating. (One might, for example, interpret the change as an attempt to avoid affirmation of proselytism and gentile circumcision, which were forbidden, under the most severe sanctions, by the Justinian Code and later Byzantine codes.) Nevertheless, viii 41a does seem to presume that many Jews are uncircumcised, a situation not reflective of Byzantine Jewry.

There are no other ideological features that require a certain historical setting. The ideas and interpretations of the redactor could, so far as I can tell, appear at any time.

A linguistic analysis of the redactor's Greek, which I cannot undertake, might help in determining the date of the redaction. A study of word-choice in synonym substitutions might be especially helpful in this regard.

The uncertainty of the dating and the vagueness of historical indices of the redaction of the AT, as well as of the MT, means that one of the tasks of redaction criticism — the interpretation of a book's development as a response to specific historical exigencies — cannot be undertaken in the present study.

5. *The original ending*

Where did the AT originally end? This is not merely a matter of assigning a few verses more or less to the author. Our understanding of the nature and purpose of the redactions of both the AT *and the MT* hinge upon how we define the scope of the AT's original ending.

Clines (pp. 74–84, following Torrey 1944:14–15) contends that the proto-AT did not include any material beyond viii 17, in which the king puts Mordecai in charge of the kingdom's affairs. Clines recognizes, however, that this verse is not itself a suitable conclusion to the original book (p. 189 n. 25). There must have been additional material in the original conclusion, but he does not find it in the present AT. I suggest that most if not all of the original conclusion is indeed extant in the AT, and that it includes two key passages, (A) viii 18–21 and (B) viii 33–38.

> (A) (viii 18) Next Esther said to the king, "Permit me [Δός μοι] to punish my enemies by death. (19) And Queen Esther also took counsel with the king against the sons of Haman, that they too might die with their father. And the king said, "So be it." (20) And she ["he"?] smote the enemies *en masse*. (21) In Susa the king came to an agreement with the queen that the men would be killed, and he said, "Behold, I permit you to hang (them)." And so it happened.

> [Add E intervenes, 22–32]

(B) (viii 33) And a decree concerning these matters was issued in Susa, and the king empowered Mordecai to write whatever he wished. (34) And Mordecai sent word via letters that he had sealed with the king's ring, to the effect that his people should remain each in his own place and hold celebration unto God. (35) And the epistle that Mordecai sent contained the following: (36) "Haman sent you letters saying thus: 'Make haste swiftly to send forth the disobedient Jewish people to destruction for me.' (37) But I Mordecai inform you that the one who did these things has been hanged before the gates of Susa and his household has been executed, (38) for he sought to kill us on the thirteenth day of the month, which is Adar.'"

As the following considerations show, these passages belong to the proto-AT and are not the work of the redactor. They are an appropriate continuation and conclusion to the proto-AT.

5.1. Of the material after viii 17, these verses alone are not based on the LXX. To be sure, later in the LXX (9:13) Esther does ask to hang Haman's sons, as she does in viii 19, but her request in viii 18–19 has no linguistic resemblance to that passage, nor does her petition in passage A include another day of slaughter, as it does in LXX 9:13. Likewise, although Mordecai's letter in passage B has thematic parallels in Mordecai's epistles in LXX-MT 8:11–13 (where he tells the Jews to prepare for self-defense) and 9:20–25 (where he institutes the celebration of Purim), the similarities in language and detail are slight. Elsewhere R-AT stays much closer to the LXX; in fact, there are fewer verbal matches in the above quoted passages than in most proto-AT passages.

5.2. These passages show no evidence of being later additions (post R-AT).[43] They certainly do not derive from the MT or the LXX, nor would there be any reason for a later scribe to invent them. They do not reinforce the religious dimension (except for the words "unto God" at the end of vs. 34), nor do they tone down the brutality, contribute to the etiology of Purim, or enhance the liturgical instructions. Passage A is not a "transitional patch" (*contra* Torrey 1944:16)—it does not smooth the way from the grant of authority to Mordecai (viii 17) to Add E any better than if Add E had been joined directly to viii 17.

5.3. There is no evidence for the secondary character of these passages. Clines (pp. 78–84) has vigorously argued the case for excluding them from the proto-AT. His basic contention is that "[t]he concluding verses, viii 17–21,

---

[43] Langen (1860:254–55) suggested that viii 34–38 is a secondary addition in the AT, supposedly added because of the apparent lack of a letter from Mordecai. But the author, no less than a later scribe, could have felt the need for such a letter.

33–52, are a poorly written narrative, almost unintelligible at places, that cannot be attributed to the same author or level of redaction as the principal part of the book, and can only be regarded as secondary to it" (p. 84).

Some of Clines' observations on the character of viii 18–52 are to the point, but the ones that pertain to the two passages in question — (A) viii 18–21 and (B) 33–38 — are not valid. Following are Clines's main assertions, each one followed by my rebuttal.

> (a) The use of τῇ ἑξῆς ("next," "moreover") as a connective (viii 18) is "a feeble and suspicious narrative link" (p. 79).

In fact, τῇ ἑξῆς may render a hypothetical *wattōsep* in the original — a natural connector here as at 8:3 — or it may have been supplied by the Greek translator of the proto-AT.[44]

> (b) There is an awkwardness in the juxtaposition in vs. 19 of Esther's request in indirect speech with the king's reply in direct speech (p. 80).

There is no awkwardness here. Esther's request is reported in indirect speech and the king's answer is *quoted* in the same indirect-speech frame.

> (c) Esther's intervention in Mordecai's audience with an "imperious" Δός μοι, "Give me!" (vs. 18) is "astonishing" (p. 79).

Δός is not too "imperious" a locution even for so pious a writer as the author of Add C, who has Esther address God in just that fashion (C 24 // v 25; sim. Bar 2:14). Daniel uses δός μοι in addressing Cyrus (Bel 25). In Hebrew the imperative *tēn* is addressed to God in Hos 9:14; Pss 25:4; 72:1; etc.

> (d) viii 20 is "strangely vague"; even the subject of the verb is ambiguous (p. 80).

This is true.

> (e) viii 21 appears to be a "meaningless repetition" of viii 18 = 20 (p. 80).

This is indeed a repetition, with vs. 21 summing up the preceding two verses. But would anyone contend that Hebrew narrative style was devoid of repetition?

> (f) Since Mordecai has already been appointed to run the affairs of the kingdom (viii 17), Esther's request in viii 18 to punish her enemies is pointless (p. 79).

---

[44] ἑξῆς appears three times in the Greek translation of Hebrew Scriptures (Exod 10:1; Deut 2:34; Judg 20:48), never rendering a Hebrew word for "next." In Deut 2:34 ἑξῆς renders *mĕtim* ("men") and in Judg 20:48 it corresponds to *mĕtōm*. This may represent an interpretation of the rare *mtm* as *mittōm*, "at the end," whence "afterwards" or "next." (It is not rendered in LXX Job 24:12).

Mordecai was not given a carte blanche in vs. 17. The vizierial authority was not thought to be absolute, as is shown by the fact that Haman, though at the height of his power, had to get special permission to carry out a massacre.

> (g) There is no reason for Esther to request the execution of Haman's sons in vs. 19, since in vs. 18 she already received permission to kill her enemies. And since Haman is already dead, how can his sons die "with their father"? (pp. 79–80).

Esther makes a separate request for the execution of Haman's sons because she wants them killed *immediately* —"with their father." The latter phrase does not contradict the earlier narrative, because although Haman's fate was "sealed" earlier (viii 13), he has not yet been executed.[45]

> (h) There is a contradiction between viii 34, which implies that Mordecai's letter was sent to the Jews, and vss. 36-38, which are addressed to the provincial governors (p. 81).

On the contrary: the letter, which is quoted only in vss. 36–38, is addressed to everyone in the empire (or to everyone via the governors), not specifically to the Jews. In viii 34b, before quoting the epistle, the narrator makes reference *to* the Jews in indirect speech. (It is unclear how this sentence is related to the decree proper; it is formulated as a purpose of the decree but is not quoted in the decree itself.) When Mordecai says "us" in viii 38, he is speaking as a Jew, but that does not mean he is addressing only Jews. It is quite reasonable for Mordecai to refer to the Jewish merrymaking in a letter addressed to everyone, so that all will realize that the Jewish activity has royal sanction. In any case, a contradiction such as Clines sees here is internal to passage B and would not prove it to be secondary.[46]

> (i) Mordecai fails to make one "pressing point"— that Haman's edict has been annulled (p. 81).

For the proto-AT, the plot has no life beyond the man who engendered it, and the annulment need not be stated. In any case, as Clines grants —"that information could no doubt be guessed at fairly easily" (p. 81).

> (j) According to viii 37, Haman was hanged at the gates of Susa, whereas viii 12–13 has the king agreeing to have him hanged in his own courtyard (p. 81).

Though it is possible that the author forgot this point, it is more likely that R-AT interfered in vs. 37. The redactional importation of the phrase ταῖς

---

[45] Even if the logic of the passage were flawed in this regard, it would not show that passage A is secondary, since both parts of the putative contradiction lie within the same block, not in passages arguably belonging to different historical layers.

[46] On the contrary, it would show that contradictions are not necessarily evidence of different literary strands.

Σούσων πύλαις from Add E (E 18 = AT viii 28b) was for the sake of harmonizing the place of hanging with the immediately preceding passage. To be sure, this produces disagreement with the more distant viii 12–13, but those verses had received less of the redactor's attention than Add E—which he had just copied from the LXX immediately before turning to viii 37.

Some of these features—(d) and (e), perhaps, and some others that Clines mentions—may indeed be stylistic or literary flaws (one must also reckon with the translator's imperfections), but such defects may come from authors as well as redactors. Even a single-author narrative may not maintain its excellence from beginning to end.

Passage A is of a piece with the preceding chapter and finds its natural continuation in passage B. Now that the danger is past, Mordecai wishes the Jews to hold festival unto God.[47] Since in the AT (both originally and in its current form) the crisis is over, this appeal makes good sense. Mordecai informs the empire that the author of the plot has been executed together with his family, his death bringing the scheme to an end. These facts are revealed in the king's epistle (Add E)—but that epistle is not part of the proto-AT. With Mordecai's letter summing up the events and calling upon the Jews to celebrate their deliverance, the book comes to its original and natural conclusion.

6. *Other Septuagintal transfers: D + and isolated short passages*

Clines speaks only of the deuterocanonical Additions as deriving from the LXX. (He also mentions a few Septuagintal "contaminations by a LXX-type text" [p. 92], which seems to imply that they were introduced by later copyists.) Torrey also sees the ending of the AT as borrowed (by memory) from the LXX (1944:15; he is apparently referring to everything after viii 21). It is, however, quite certain that the redactor copied a few additional sentences besides the Adds and AT-end from the LXX. We should not picture the redactor isolating the Adds and LXX ch. 9 as "additions" of a special sort, since these passages were embedded in the Septuagint as the redactor knew it. (There is nothing whatsoever to suggest that R—AT compared the LXX with the MT). We may surmise that the redactor proceeded sequentially, comparing the two versions and transferring Septuagintal material when he felt that something substantial was lacking. In so doing, he naturally transferred the Adds and AT-end—the major blocks lacking in the proto-AT—but he also picked up a few additional verses along the way.

6.1. One clearly Septuagintal passage is the section directly following Add D, namely vi 13–18, which I have designated D + . Sixty-nine percent of its words are Septuagintal matches, well within the frequency-range for the

---

[47] "To God" might be a later addition. Clines (pp. 107–112) argues that most of the religious language in the proto-AT is original, but the evidence is inconclusive.

Adds.[48] With regard to the percentage of LXX words it preserves (84%), it is well above the 62% average for the transferred passages. The proto-AT must have had something corresponding to these verses, which quote the king's query and Esther's invitation. The proto-AT could not have skipped from v 11 (where Esther resolves to go to the king) to vi 19 (where the king grants her wish). Some material must have been displaced by the introduction D +, either because the redactor felt that the AT was somehow inadequate when compared with the LXX, or, more likely, because he did not notice that he had continued beyond the gap. The likely explanation for the presence of D + in the AT is that the redactor copied Add D and simply kept on going for a few verses before noticing that the "gap" in the receptor text had ended. Instead of erasing the LXX verses he chose to forget about the material he had overwritten.

6.2. Isolated Septuagintal transfers include ii 1a; ii 5b–8; iv 2; iv 9b–11–10a; v 4b–5; v 9b–10; vi 21ab; vii 1.[49]

There are various additional sentences and short passages drawn from the LXX as well. The use of statistics in identifying short, isolated transfers raises the problem of how we should define the scope of the segments in which we count the frequency of matches. If we focus on the sentences with a high density of matches, the results of the count become self-verifying. If we choose a larger unit, we fail to show the density of matches in the borrowed segments. Although a more sophisticated statistical analysis than I could attempt might solve the problem, I will rely on more intuitive arguments, which are adequate to the case at hand. Once we recognize the low frequency of matches that usually pertains in the non-redactional sections, the clustering of the matches in a few verses makes their Septuagintal derivation

---

[48] Some of the pluses in D + (vis-à-vis the LXX parallel) may be hexaplaric, in particular αἴτησαι ἕως ἡμίσους τῆς βασιλείας μου in vi 17 (included in a larger hexaplaric addition in O-S^c; MT has "unto half the kingdom"), and καὶ εἰ ἐπὶ τὸν βασιλέα ἀγαθὸν δοῦναι τὸ αἴτημά μου καὶ ποιῆσαι τὸ ἀξίωμά μου in vi 18 (= MT; present in O-S^c, except for εἰ). Either these are to be removed from the AT as hexaplaric contaminations, or we are to posit their presence in R-AT's vorlage. Another AT plus in D +, δεῖπνον πολυτελές (vi 16), is attested in MS 93, where, however, it may be an incursion from the AT (MS 93 has both versions with much cross-contamination [Hanhart, p. 9]). Whichever explanation is correct, the proportion of LXX matches in the AT is higher than given here, but on principle I have kept to Hanhart's text throughout rather than making adjustments that favor my hypotheses.

Though AT-end too was presumably subject to hexaplaric incursions, this did not actually happen. AT-end agrees with the hexaplaric MSS only at viii 44 (// 9:7), where we cannot speak of an actual hexaplaric reading; see §8.2.

[49] The AT also shows a high degree of correspondence to the LXX in iii 5 (14 matches of 19 AT words) and might be influenced by it here too. On the other hand, correspondences in names and genealogies could arise simply because the same man is being identified rather than because of direct influence. In any case, it is clear from iii 7 that Mordecai was introduced at this point in proto-AT too.

fairly obvious—especially when this argument can be strengthened by additional considerations.

The appearance of a few identical words in two texts that relate essentially the same story does not, of course, prove dependence. If, as I believe to be the case, the MT is based on a predecessor of the proto-AT and the LXX is based on the MT, some verbal similarity between the proto-AT and the LXX is inevitable. We must also consider what *sort* of words are matched. Words that frequently and inevitably recur (such as "Esther," "the king," and "he said") are no indication of borrowing, though for statistical purposes they must be counted along with the other words.

The hypothesis that a certain passage is derived from the LXX is reinforced in cases where the AT agrees with the LXX against the MT. Where AT = MT = LXX, the agreement might have arisen because all three versions ultimately descend from the same Hebrew story. But in cases where AT = LXX ≠MT, the AT is probably directly dependent on the LXX, since it shows a peculiarity of that version.

6.2.1. AT ii 1a // LXX 1:1a

LXX   καὶ ἐγένετο μετὰ τοὺς λόγους τούτους ἐν ταῖς ἡμέραις

AT   καὶ ἐγένετο μετὰ τοὺς λόγους τούτους ἐν   ἡμέραις

LXX   ᾽Αρταξέρξου

AT   Ασσυήρου

While the proto-AT would have had some preface of this sort, the sentence as now formulated is a transitional link between Add A and the body of the narrative.

6.2.2. AT ii 6–8 // LXX 1:6–8

In ii 6–8, forty-two words, or 65% of the AT, are matches. Forty-eight percent of the words in the corresponding LXX passage are represented in the AT.

The AT derived κύκλῳ ῥόδα in ii 6b from the LXX. As B. Jacob observed (1890:270), κύκλῳ ῥόδα πεπασμένα represents *wrd* [MT *wdr*] *wsḥrt*, understanding *wrd* as "rose" (as in rabbinic Hebrew) and interpreting *wsḥrt* on the basis of Aramaic *sḥr*, "around." This double misinterpretation could hardly have arisen independently in both Greek versions.[50]

---

[50] The AT also has καὶ ὑακίνθινα, corresponding to MT's *tklt*, but the hexaplaric tradition and the OL share this plus and it does not prove that R−AT knew the Hebrew. Another AT plus,

The *omissions* that the LXX and the AT share against the MT are less significant, since both the LXX and R-AT often leave out material present in their sources (namely the MT and the LXX respectively) and it is also possible that words were added to the MT *after* the LXX was translated. The LXX as the redactor knew it may already have undergone some harmonization with MT; conversely, some of the AT-LXX differences may be due to later developments in the LXX.[51]

6.2.3. AT v 4b–5 // LXX 4:8b > MT:

LXX   μνησθεῖσα ἡμερῶν ταπεινώσεώς σου <u>ὡς</u> ἐτράφης ἐν   χειρί μου,

AT   μνησθεῖσα ἡμερῶν ταπεινώσεώς σου <u>ὧν</u> ἐτράφης ἐν τῇ χειρί μου,

LXX   διότι Αμαν ὁ δευτερεύων τῷ βασιλεῖ ἐλάλησεν   καθ' ἡμῶν

AT   ὅτι Αμαν ὁ δευτερεύων λελάληκε   τῷ βασιλεῖ καθ' ἡμῶν

LXX   εἰς θάνατον. ἐπικάλεσαι   τὸν <u>κύριον</u> καὶ λάλησον

AT   εἰς θάνατον. ἐπικαλεσαμένη οὖν τὸν θεὸν   λάλησον

LXX   τῷ βασιλεῖ περὶ ἡμῶν καὶ ῥῦσαι ἡμᾶς ἐκ θανάτου.

AT   περὶ ἡμῶν τῷ βασιλεῖ καὶ ῥῦσαι ἡμᾶς ἐκ θανάτου.

It is not clear which segment of the text should be used for comparison here. If we look at the entire verse starting from ἀλλ' εἶπεν, we find that 38 of 64 words are matches (= 59% of the AT) and that 46% of the words in the corresponding LXX passage are represented in the AT. But if we focus only on the LXX plus, as quoted above, 32 of 35 words are matches (= 91% of the AT words). The differences—synonym substitutions, transpositions, minor grammatical variations and plus/minus particles and articles—are of types well attested in the Septuagintal sections of the AT and do not argue against dependency.

It is unlikely for such agreement as we see in the above sentence to arise in two unrelated translations. Yet Clines uses this sentence as evidence for

καὶ κόκινα ἐμπεπλεγμένα ἐν ἄνθεσιν, need not derive from a Hebrew text *'ḥwz bhbṣlt, supposedly a mistaken doublet of 'ḥwz bhbly bwṣ (contrary to Moore 1965:120). Though ἄνθος does render ḥbṣlt in Cant 2:1, ἐμπλέκειν does not elsewhere translate 'ḥwz. Moreover, the presence of κόκινα in the plus shows that the AT is expanding the description with some freedom.

[51] In LXX 1:8, οὗτος is missing in 93-S c-A and οὐ is omitted in the original S (a MS that Hanhart thinks may have undergone some redaction in accordance with MT and the AT [p. 53]). οὗτος is missing also from the OL and Armenian a p. The οὐ looks like a moralizing addition in LXX, and its absence in the AT may represent the OG. LXX-A has (οὕτως) γάρ for δέ.

the *independence* of the AT from the LXX. He argues that the versions translate the same consonantal vorlage, namely *ky 'mr hmn hmšnh lmlk,* which the LXX takes to mean "because Haman, the second to the king, has spoken" and the AT understands as "because Haman the Second [i.e., the vizier[52]] has spoken to the king" (pp. 91–92).[53] In the LXX, the clause διότι Αμαν ὁ δευτερεύων τῷ βασιλεῖ ἐλάλησεν is indeed best translated "because Haman, the second to the king, has spoken . . ."—the point of emphasis is the danger presented by Haman's position of favor. Josephus understood the sentence in this way, rephrasing it "Haman, who possessed honor second to the king" (*Ant.* XI 225). But this clause *can* be understood to mean "because Haman the Second has spoken to the king," and this is how R-AT construed it, making that (mis)interpretation clearer by transposing the phrases. The sentence as a whole is a Septuagintal expansion in the AT and there is no reason to suppose that the AT translated it directly from a Hebrew text. The passage v 4b–6 makes good sense even without the sentence in question, reading: "But he said, Thus shall you say to her: 'Do not avoid going to the king and cajoling him on behalf of me and the people.' And he told her of the misery of Israel." This is how the passage originally stood in the proto-AT.

6.2.4. AT vii 1 // LXX 6:1a

LXX   Ὁ δὲ <u>κύριος</u>   ἀπέστησεν τὸν ὕπνον ἀπὸ τοῦ βασιλέως

AT   Ὁ δὲ <u>δυνατὸς</u> ἀπέστησε τὸν ὕπνον   τοῦ βασιλέως

LXX   τὴν νύκτα ἐκείνην

AT   τὴν νύκτα ἐκείνην καὶ ἦν ἀγρυπνῶν

This is clearly a theologizing addition (thus Clines, p. 111). Clines notes — and finds it surprising — that the rare divine epithet ὁ δυνατός occurs in i 9, where the LXX (A 11) has ὁ θεός. He suggests that the term comes from the "same redactional influence" that introduced the term in i 9. But instead of imagining a vague "influence" introducing isolated terms, we should explain the choice as a mark of the same redactor, namely R-AT. In v 29 the redactor rephrases ὁ θεὸς ὁ ἰσχύων (C 30) as δυνατὸς ὤν.[54] Other divine-name substitutions appear in i 6; v 13 (twice), 15 (twice), 16, and 28. In some

---

[52] Clines (p. 91) points out that *hammišneh* is used absolutely in 1 Chr 5:12; 16:5; 2 Chr 31:12; Neh 11:9, 17; cf. 1 Sam 23:17.

[53] Clines apparently forgets that on p. 111 he argues that AT v 4–5 is a Septuagintal contamination. Clines (p. 109) speaks of v 4–5 as a religious plus with "an unusually close correspondence" to the LXX. It is puzzling that he would extract one phrase from this plus as evidence of the AT translator's independence of LXX.

[54] Δυνατός renders *gibbôr* in Zeph 3:17 and appears in Luke 1:49.

cases the redactor is replacing "God" or "Lord" with a more descriptive, specific epithet—"Master," "True One," "who covenanted with Abraham"— and this is true in vii 1a as well.

The following passages too are likely Septuagintal borrowings, though the evidence for them is not as strong as for those given above.

6.2.5. iv 2 // 3:2. Nine words are matches = 77% of the verse. 45% of the LXX is represented.

6.2.6. iv 9b–11–10a [AT transposes verse order] // 3:9b–11. 29 words are matches = 70% of the AT in this passage. 64% of LXX words are used.

Note the unexpected διαγράφειν in both Greek versions for *šāqal* (only here in the LXX). The AT agrees with the LXX in lacking "to bring into the king's treasury" (iv 9b) and "the son of Hammedatha the Agagite, the persecutor of the Jews" (iv 10).

6.2.7. v 9bβ (σὺ κτλ.)–10 // 4:14b. The end of v 9 and all of v 10 are identical to the LXX (4:14b), although the first part of v 9 diverges sharply from the LXX and is closer to the MT.

6.2.8. vi 21ab // 5:10bβ, καὶ Ζωσάραν τὴν γυναῖκα αὐτοῦ. The name Ζωσάραν agrees with the LXX against MT's *zereš*. The agreement is significant because the AT (in both original and redactional passages) frequently differs from the LXX in its treatment of names.

The identification of these passages as redactional has little bearing on the statistics. But it does show something about the redactor's method: he is working with the entirety of the proto-AT and transferring smaller and larger units as he thinks fit.

7. R-AT's use of the LXX

The following table shows the degree of verbal dependence of the AT on the LXX in the redactional sections in comparison with the proto-AT sections. The procedure of comparison and the definition of "matches" are discussed in §2.7. Since, as argued earlier (§§2.6–10), the redactional sections and the proto-AT have different origins, the matches have different significance in each. In the former they are Septuagintal borrowings; in the latter they are usually coincidental—the natural appearance of the same wording in independent translations of different versions of the same tale. (Also, there may well be minor Septuagintal incursions in addition to those listed in §6.2.)

D + is included among the redactional sections because its dependence on the LXX seems undeniable. Table II A–B counts the isolated borrowings among the "proto" sections, showing that even without removing these borrowings there is a sharp disjunction between the proto-AT and the redactional passages. The disjunction is even more pronounced when we include the isolated redactional verses with the other redactional passages (Table II C).

TABLE II. R-AT's Use of the LXX

Column 1:   the units. "A→B" etc. = the verses between Additions A and B, etc. LXX 8:13–14 is taken to correspond to E→AT-end. 8:15–10:3 in the LXX corresponds to AT-end.

Column 2:   the number of matches found in each passage.

Column 3:   the number of words in the AT of that passage.

Column 4:   the frequency of matches in the AT (= col. 2 divided by col. 3).

Column 5:   the number of words in the LXX of that passage.

Column 6:   the percentage of LXX words represented in the AT (= col. 2 divided by col. 5). For AT passages that are derived from the LXX, this column shows how much LXX material the redactor chose to use.

Column 7:   the median verse. In other words, if we list the percentages of matches in each verse in the AT passage, which percentage is the *median* for that passage? This figure shows the "typical" degree of correspondence between the two versions in each passage. It thus counterbalances instances where a small segment of a passage varies radically from the LXX, which might yield a statistical profile that downplays the overall relation between the two versions in that passage.

1 passage	2 matches	3 # AT wds	4 freq AT matches	5 # LXX wds	6 % LXX wds used	7 median vs.

II A. *Proto-AT* (including miscellaneous LXX incursions)

1 passage	2 matches	3 # AT wds	4 freq AT matches	5 # LXX wds	6 % LXX wds used	7 median vs.
A→B	284	927	0.31	1381	0.21	.27
B→C	104	266	0.39	445	0.23	.35
D + →E	216	446	0.48	1058	0.20	.29
E→AT-end	1	98	0.01	43	0.02	.00
Totals	605	1,737	0.35	2,927	0.21	.22

II B. *Redactional Sections*

1 passage	2 matches	3 # AT wds	4 freq AT matches	5 # LXX wds	6 % LXX wds used	7 median vs.
A	189	308	0.61	298	0.63	.57
B	210	249	0.84	246	0.85	.81
C	447	577	0.77	597	0.75	.79
D	206	261	0.79	254	0.81	.85
D +	97	140	0.69	115	0.84	.74
E	338	429	0.79	472	0.72	.86
AT-end	196	281	0.70	718	0.27	.76
F	125	171	0.73	199	0.63	.97
Totals	1,808	2,416	0.75	2,899	0.62	.93

II C. *AT borrowings if ii 1a, 5bβ–8; iv 9b–11–10a; v 4b, 9b–10; vi 21aβ; vii 1 are included in the redactional material (see §6.2):*

# wd matches	# AT wds	freq. matches	# LXX wds	% of LXX used by AT
Non-redactional Sections:				
466	1,539	0.30	2,927	0.16
Redactional Sections				
1,959	2,614	0.75	2,899	.68

Diagram 2. *The extent and placement of Septuagintal transfers in the AT.*

xxx = verses (or half-verses) introduced by R-AT
--- = Proto-AT

i 1-18 (A)   ii 1a   6-8
x x x x x x x x x x x x x x x x x x x x | x - - - - - x x x - - - - - -

          iii   5   iv
- - - - - - - | - - - - x - - - - - - - - - - - - - | - - - - - -

  9b-11-10a   14-18 (B)   v   4b
- - - x x x - - x x x x x - | - - - - x - - - - - - - -

12b-29 (C)   vi 1-12 (D)

x x x x x x x x x x x x x x x x x x x x x | x x x x x x x x x x x x

13-18 (D +)   21a   vii 1a   7-10

x x x x x x - - x - - - - | x - - - - - - x x x x - - - - - - - -

               viii   22-32 (E)

- - - - - | - x x x x x x

                    39-52 (AT-end)   53-59 (F)

x x x x x - - - - - - x x x x x x x x x x x x x x x x x x x x x x x x

7.1 *A single redactor for the entire AT*

It cannot be proved that the above listed sections (Table II B–C) were all transferred by a single redactor, but we see similar types of changes in the various Adds and AT-end. (The steep rise in frequency of omissions in the last two sections, AT-end and F, suggests a copyist-redactor hurrying to the end of his work.) Moreover, a person who thought it necessary to supplement the proto-AT from the LXX for one major block would probably have thought it important to fill in the other major gaps as well. Also, Adds B and E are paired and would have been transferred together. Likewise, the dream in Add A calls for the interpretation in Add F and Add F is meaningless without Add A. To be sure, Add F in the AT handles some details differently from Add A (see §9.1), but these differences are not so contradictory as to indicate a second redactor, especially since the same tensions between these two Additions exist in the LXX as well. And whoever borrowed Adds A and F from the LXX almost certainly borrowed the other Additions. It is very unlikely that someone would have copied the Addition that begins the LXX, then copy the proto-AT, and then transfer the Add that ends the LXX—yet ignore the major pluses in the middle of his donor text.

7.2. *Editing within the redactional sections?*

Another issue that should be addressed, though it cannot be resolved, is whether the same redactor both copied the blocks from the LXX and made the changes within them. It is possible that a later copyist or copyists modified the wording (by synonym substitutions, transpositions, etc.) after the redactional blocks were already in the AT. In the absence of intermediate manuscripts, there is no evidence to prove or disprove this possibility, but certain considerations militate against large scale editing *after* the transfer by R-AT:

(a) The modifications in the Septuagintal transfers (to be described in §8) are far more extensive than what we see in manuscript transmission within the Septuagintal tradition (except for hexaplaric interventions, which are of quite a different sort). It is likely that the same redactor who took the bold step of adding major supplements to the proto-AT also made the local alterations.

(b) The specific modifications in the Septuagintal transfers are highly consistent within the AT manuscripts. This too weighs against the possibility of miscellaneous changes made by various later copyists.

(c) There is significant internal consistency in the modifications; many of them work together to express a coherent ideology. This consistency probably witnesses to the work of a single redactor. If, nevertheless, the modifications were made by later copyists, "R-AT" may be considered a collectivity, and most of my observations about the redactional process should still be valid.

8. *What the redactor did*

Although we can identify the sections of the AT that the redactor added to the proto-AT, we cannot know if he *subtracted* anything. One likely overwriting is at D + (see §6.1). Another possible omission is 2:21–23, Mordecai's discovery of the eunuchs' plot. The redactor may have recognized that this passage was otiose after i 11–16 (Add A), but it is also possible that 2:21–23 was absent from the proto-AT (thus Clines, pp. 110–111). The reference to the conspiracy in vii 3 does not require it to have been reported earlier.

Nevertheless, it is unlikely that there were any major subtractions or overwritings of proto-AT material. The proto-AT, in the form recoverable from the AT, still tells a complete story of Esther. All the main elements of the story known from the MT version (prior to ch. 9) are represented in the proto-AT. Moreover, the fact that the redactor chose to transmit the proto-AT by filling in its "gaps" from the LXX—rather than simply making do with the LXX— suggests a respect for the proto-AT's authority.

It is also very unlikely that the redactor made any significant redactional rearrangements. It is hard to find a motive for such changes, and in any case the temporal structure of the plot does not leave much room for changes of sequence. Still, the model of redaction the AT provides is strictly verifiable only in the sections that are manifestly redactional. The redactor may have done *more* than we know.

I will now describe the changes the redactor made in the donor text, the LXX, in the course of copying text from it to his receptor text, the proto-AT. This description is based on Hanhart's edition (which essentially follows LXX-B). However successfully this edition approaches the OG, it is not necessarily the very text used by R-AT. There are many inner-Septuagintal variants agreeing with the AT, particularly in D + , and if these were present in R-AT's donor text, the frequency of R-AT's changes would be lower. On the other hand, it would obviously be a circular operation to reconstruct R-AT's donor text by choosing the variants that agree with the AT. But whatever Septuagintal text we posit as R-AT's donor text, the relative frequencies of these types would, as far as I can tell, remain almost the same. Even if R-AT may have been quantitatively less innovative than a comparison with Hanhart's LXX indicates, all *types* of variants are well testified regardless of the LXX text used for comparison.

The redactional techniques to be described appear most clearly in AT-end, where R-AT is most active, but are in evidence throughout the Septuagintal portions.

8.1. *Synonym substitution*

The redactor often replaces a word by a synonym. Usually it is hard to discern the reason for the change: e.g., ἐσθῆτα for LXX στολήν (viii 39 // 8:15), ἀναστάς/διεγερθείς (i 9 // A 11), πένησιν for πτωχοῖς (viii 48; taken from the end of 9:22).

Prefix variation in compound verbs is another type of substitution that usually has little effect on meaning; e.g. περιπόρφυρον (viii 39) for πορφυροῦν (8:15), ἐπανέστη (viii 41) for ἀντέστη (9:2), ἀπέστειλε (viii 48) for ἐξαποστέλλοντας (9:22). A more detailed examination might discover the motives for some prefix variants, but for the most part they seem to have little lexical significance.

Prepositions, particles, etc. are sometimes replaced by virtual synonyms: e.g., ἐναντίον for ἐνώπιον (v 21 // C 17, vi 18 // 5:8, etc. (but three times ἐνώπιον is left unchanged [v 25 // C 24; vi 4 // D 6; viii 59 // F 10]), once it is changed to κατὰ πρόσωπον [i 17 // A 17]), and once it is omitted [viii 56 // F 8]). Such inconsistency is typical of the redactor's treatment of prepositions and particles); καὶ X for X δὲ (often); εἰ μή for πλήν (v 28 // C 29), but also πλήν for εἰ μή (v 19 // C 14). These rarely have a discernible effect on meaning and (for that very reason) may have significance for the redactor's style and possibly the dating. However, I do not see any patterns of selection.

An *entire clause* may arise by synonym-substitution; e.g., καὶ ὑπέγραψε τὴν ὑποτεταγμένην ἐπιστολήν for τῆς δὲ ἐπιστολῆς ἐστιν τὸ ἀντίγραφον τόδε (iv 14a // B 1). Since the AT has not yet said that something was written, the redactor needs a clause stating that the decree was inscribed. The reformulated introduction to Add B serves to summarize 3:12–13, according to which the scribes were summoned and the decree was written and sent. A similar change is introduced at the seam of Add E (viii 22a // 8:13a).

Personal names are often changed, never for any noticeable reason: Φαρνα (viii 44) for Φασγα (9:7), Μαρμασαιμα for Μαρμασιμ, Ιζαθουθ for Ζαβουθαῖον (Haman's sons, viii 44 // 9:7–9). Name-switching may occur in proto-AT passages too, since some of the names in the proto-AT sections resemble the

LXX's forms more than the MT's: Βουγαῖος (ii 16)≈Μουχαῖος (1:16) ≠MT *mĕmukān;* Ζωσάρα (vi 21, 23) = Ζωσάρα (5:10, 14; 6:13) ≠MT *zereš;* Αγαθας (viii 12)≈Βουγαθαν (7:9) ≠MT *ḥarbônā'.* The resemblance between the AT forms of the names Μουχαῖος and Βουγαθαν is slight, as in the case of some of the names in viii 44 // 9:7–9.

Nearby phrases may supply synonym-variants. The Jews' celebration is called πότος κώθων in the AT (viii 40b) in place of the LXX's εὐφροσύνη (8:16). The AT's variant is taken from the next sentence in the LXX (8:17a), which is otherwise unrepresented in the AT and which adds nothing new. In this way, R-AT combines two sentences while removing a redundancy.

In some cases the substituted synonym seems *more vivid or specific:* ἐπέπεσεν ἐπ' (viii 42) for ἐνέκειτο (9:3), πότος κώθων (viii 40) for εὐφροσύνη (8:16; κώθων is transferred from the next verse). In other cases, the substitution is consequent upon another change in the verse; e.g., having changed "the humble" to "the rivers," the redactor appropriately replaces "devoured" (κατέφαγον) by "drank down" (κατέπιον) (i 8 // A 10).

Sometimes a substitution gives a different nuance while remaining essentially synonymous, as in μοναρχία (iv 17b) for the somewhat surprising συναρχίαν, which implies joint rule and may suggest a display of modesty on the king's part (B 4b; cf. Fritzsche ad loc.).

Some further examples: κύριον (i 6) for θεόν (A 9); κραυγῆς (i 6) for βοῆς (A 9); κεκρυμμένον ἦν ἐν τῇ καρδίᾳ αὐτοῦ (i 10) for εἶχεν αὐτὸ ἐν τῇ καρδίᾳ (A 11); σατράπαις (iv 14) for τοπάρχαις (B 1); ἀντιδικοῦντα (iv 16b) for ἀντίθετον (B 4); ἀφανίσαι (v 16) for ἀπολέσαι (C 8); χαρείησαν ἐπί (v 23) for καταγελασάτωσαν ἐν (C 22); κακοποιΐας (viii 23c) for κακοηθείας (E 6); ὠμότητι (viii 24) for λοιμότητι (E 7) (note the play on sound); διεξάγοντες (viii 24) for διαχρίνοντες (E 9); νόμοις (viii 29) for νομίμοις (E 19).

Among synonyms I include *pragmatic synonyms,* words that *in the context of that particular sentence* function in essentially the same way. For example, εὐφροσύνην (v 17) for εὐωχίαν (C 10); ἀληθινοῦ (v 15) for κυρίου μου (of God) (C 7); κατέπιον (i 8) for κατέφαγον (A 10); ἀντιτάξεται (v 13) for ἀντιδοξῶν (C 2; of rivaling God); βασιλέως (v 25a) for λέοντος (C 24; both referring to the king). For the present purposes I reckon as synonyms cases such as "you" for "he," where the pronouns actually refer to the same person (e.g., vi 14 // 5:4), or "their" for "our" where both refer to Israel (v 20 // C 16). Synonyms and non-synonyms are not discrete categories, and someone else might distribute some of the items differently. But the exact distribution of changes among the various categories is not crucial to the typology.

8.2. *Non-synonym substitution*

Non-synonym substitution is the replacement of one item (a word or a short phrase) by another of different meaning while maintaining the word's function in the sentence. When this happens, I have counted the change as a non-synonym substitution (*one* occurrence, regardless of the number of words); e.g., πατρικῆς μου βίβλου (v 20) for ἐκ γενετῆς μου ἐν φυλῇ πατριᾶς μου (C 16). When a sentence in the LXX is replaced by a substantially different one, so that the addition does not correspond to a particular omission (e.g., viii 30 // E 21), the change is considered to be compounded of an omission from the LXX and an addition to the AT, since the redactor is not "manipulating" the LXX's wording.

Sometimes the new word expresses a different concept of narrative, character, or ideology. Examples include: ("I heard," Esther says,) πατρικῆς μου βίβλου (v 20) for ἐκ γενετῆς μου ἐν φυλῇ πατριᾶς μου (C 16; giving credit to the Torah rather than just vague tribal traditions as the source of historical information); ἐχθρῶν (v 22) for ἐθνῶν (C 21; the redactor is less inclined than some of the Adds and the LXX translator to assume that the nations are essentially inimical to Israel, and so chooses a narrower term to designate the hostile idolaters); ἐφοβήθη (vi 6) for ἔπεσεν (D 7; the AT makes Esther somewhat less servile and weak; likewise, whereas Esther falls in a faint a second time in the LXX [D 15], she merely perspires in AT [vi 12]); ἐπιφάνηθι ἡμῖν (v 24) for μνήσθητι (C 23; the AT makes Esther's request more dramatic); "sole and true God" (τοῦ μόνου θεοῦ καὶ ἀληθινοῦ; viii 27) for "highest and greatest living God" (τοῦ ὑψίστου μεγίστου ζῶντος θεοῦ) (E 16; this makes the king a monotheist); ποταμοί (i 8) for ταπεινοί (A 10; see discussion in §9.1.4); "Jews" for "nations" as the subject of "circumcised themselves" (viii 41a // 8:17; the act becomes one of Jewish repentance rather than superficial conversion of gentiles).

Variation of numbers is a type of non-synonym substitution, as in 700 (viii 44a) for 500 (9:6) and 70,100 (viii 46b) for 15,000 (9:16). These changes increase the casualty figures.[55]

Clarification or regularization of an obscure or unusual (or subtle) concept is often the motivation of a non-synonym substitution. Mordecai says he will not bow to anyone but God in πειρασμῷ (v 15) rather than in ὑπερηφανίᾳ (C 7). It seems no special virtue not to bow "in arrogance"; more heroic is not bowing *even* "under trial." The king declares that henceforth he will not heed διαβολαῖς (viii 24), rather than saying that he will pay attention to μεταβολαῖς (E 9)—"slanders" rather than "vicissitudes" were the cause of the crisis this book recounts.

Often, however, the non-synonym substitution makes no significant difference to the story, the tone, or the ideology. For example, Mordecai was trying to understand his dream ἐν παντὶ καιρῷ (i 10) for ἐν παντὶ λόγῳ (A 11). The Jews are accused of being hostile to "our decrees [προστάγμασιν]" (iv 17) rather than "our affairs [πράγμασιν]" (B 5). Esther prays, μὴ θραύσῃς ἡμᾶς "do

---

[55] Since the numbers do not resemble each other either as words or as abbreviations, the changes are probably not due to scribal error. The fact that the changes always increase the figures also argues that they are deliberate.

not shatter us" (v 24) for ἐμὲ θάρσυνον, "give me courage" (C 23). A peculiar substitution is αὔριον "tomorrow" (vi 14) for σήμερον "today" (5:4, twice)—the redactor shifts Esther's first banquet to the *next* day, for unclear reasons).

Occasionally prefix-variants are not synonymous: e.g., διαβολαῖς "slanders" (viii 24) for μεταβολαῖς "changes, vicissitudes" (E 9). A significant case is ἐπισχύειν "prevail" (viii 29) for συνεπισχύειν "give aid" (E 20), on which see §9.8.

Sometimes the word is not changed but its context is altered in such a way as to give the word a new sense; this may be counted as a clever form of non-synonym substitution. In viii 43, the AT uses ὀνομασθῆναι pejoratively: Haman and the other enemies are "named" as a byword for disgrace. The LXX (9:4) uses the word in praise of Mordecai: he is "named" in the sense of being celebrated and made famous; see §9:6. In B 7, the LXX reads καὶ ἀτάραχα παρέχωσιν ἡμῖν διὰ τέλους τὰ πράγματα, "and make our concerns forever untroubled"; the AT (iv 18b) has καὶ μὴ διὰ τέλους παρέχωσιν ἡμῖν πράγματα, "and not cause us trouble forever" (παρέχω πράγματα τινί = "cause someone trouble"; see Liddell & Scott, p. 1457b). In Add E, the LXX has the king vowing χρώμενοι ταῖς μεταβολαῖς, "[to] *deal with* [those] vicissitudes" which come before his eyes, that is, to be alert to them (E 9), whereas the AT adds the negative and reads οὐ χρώμενοι ταῖς διαβολαῖς, "not *paying heed* to slanders" (viii 24b), thereby making it clear that such things as Haman's lies should be ignored.[56]

Some apparent non-synonym substitutions may actually be mechanical errors due to graphic similarity, but it is often difficult to distinguish these from changes in which graphic similarity combines with other factors. The AT reads καὶ τὸν ἀδελφὸν αὐτοῦ (viii 44) for καὶ Δελφων (9:7). τὸν ἀδελφόν is present in some LXX MSS as well (of the O tradition). The latter variant may have been occasioned by simple graphic error in the AT plus subsequent adjustment (Tov 1982:5). But it is also possible that R-AT found this variant in his Septuagintal donor text. In the *LXX* transmission someone may have deliberately eliminated one of the eleven names in LXX's list in order to produce ten names, the number given in 9:10 (Moore 1965:47).[57] In favor of this explanation is the fact that the change has a clear motive in the LXX but not in the AT.

Deliberate play on orthography may motivate some substitutions, especially when they maintain graphic resemblance in uncials. The AT's ΔΙΑ ΤΩΝ ΝΟΜΩΝ (iv 17) resembles the LXX's ΔΙΑΓΩΓΗΝ ΝΟΜΩΝ (B 5). This change is probably not accidental, because the redactor seems not to have

---

[56] The textual evidence is complicated by the fact that the negative particle is prefixed in certain LXX MSS (mostly hexaplaric), the OL, Vul, and the Coptic. Two LXX MSS (93, 108) read διαβολαῖς for μεταβολαῖς as does Jos, though in a differently structured sentence.

[57] In LXX-B, Φαρσαννεσταιν is split into Φαρσαν καὶ νεσταιν; some other MSS render this as two names without καί.

overlooked the ἄγω stem in the LXX phrase, but rather to have "transposed" it by replacing παραλλάσσον with παραγωγήν two words later. Another change sometimes considered a copyist's error is αὐτῶν ἅμα for Αμαν in v 27, where the AT has "Your maidservant has not eaten at their table *together* with them" for the LXX's "Your maidservant has not eaten upon the table of *Haman*" (C 28; thus Hanhart, p. 88). But the change may be deliberate, for the AT's variant enhances the virtue (if not the syntax) of Esther's declaration. In the AT, Esther not only avoids *Haman's* table but *all* non-kosher meals. (Compare the change augmenting Mordecai's virtue in v 15, discussed in §9.3.) Another case is Esther's prayer that God not give his scepter (i.e., his rule over Israel) to τοῖς μισοῦσί σε ἐχθροῖς, "the enemies who hate you" (v 23), replacing the LXX's μὴ οὖσιν "those who do not exist" (C 22). Since the reading μισοῦσί σε appears in several LXX MSS (ἐχθροῖς is witnessed by MS 93), it may have been present in R-AT's vorlage. But whatever its origin, the AT's variant makes sense: It avoids suggesting that the non-existent, i.e. heathen, gods *could* receive God's "scepter." In all these cases, the hypothesis of graphical error requires an additional assumption, namely that a later scribe added words to make sense of the AT. The AT variants may be more simply explained as non-synonym substitutions influenced by the form or sound of the original. The redactor frequently maintains an orthographic or phonic resemblance in substitutions even when changing the meaning; e.g., μὴ θραύσῃς ἡμᾶς (v 24) for ἐμὲ θάρσυνον (C 23); ἐχθρῶν (v 22) for ἐθνῶν (C 21); διαρτησάμενος (viii 26) for αἰτησάμενος (E 13); ὠμότητι (viii 24) for the hapax λοιμότητι (E 7); προστάγμασιν (iv 17) for πράγμασιν (B 5); κυριεύσεως (viii 56; see §9.1.2) for κρίσεως (F 8). The latter change involves using a hapax legomenon, perhaps in order to maintain an echo of the earlier word.

TABLE III. SUBSTITUTIONS

III A. Substitutions *by number of occurrences*, each of which may comprise more than one word. The synonym and non-synonym counts include the prefix-variants as appropriate.

	words in AT	syn subs	freq	pfx vars	freq	non-syns	freq
A	308	23	0.075	2	0.006	4	0.013
B	249	9	0.036	2	0.008	2	0.008
C	577	33	0.057	1	0.002	17	0.029
D	261	7	0.027	4	0.015	1	0.004
D+	140	7	0.050	0	0.000	2	0.014
E	429	32	0.075	9	0.021	12	0.028

AT-end	281	19[58]	0.068	4	0.014	9	0.032
F	171	2	0.012	2	0.012	3	0.018
total	2,416	132	0.055	24	0.010	50	0.021

III B. Sections in order of *frequency of substitutions*

Synonym-subs.		Non-synonym subs.	
A	0.075	AT-end	0.032
E	0.075	E	0.029
AT-end	0.068	C	0.028
C	0.057	F	0.018
D +	0.050	D +	0.014
B	0.036	A	0.013
D	0.027	B	0.008
F	0.012	D	0.004

8.3. *Transpositions*

Sometimes the redactor changes the order of words or (far more rarely) phrases that he transfers. Transposition rarely has a discernible effect on meaning; nor, as far as I can tell, is it relevant to the style of the Greek.

In the following, "word-transposition" refers to relocations in which a single word is moved (the item with which it has changed places may contain more than one word), excluding articles and frequent particles (δέ, καί, μέν, etc.). "Phrase-transposition" refers to relocation of longer units, including clauses. The number of (AT) words moved is noted to indicate the extent of the redactor's activity. Individual items may be moved to an adjacent slot or to a more distant position. As an additional index of redactional intervention, I note the average distance of each move, counting the number of words *over which* the first word in the item has moved. (The diagonal marks the point of transposition; καί is moved as necessary.)[59]

---

[58] Counting five of the names of Haman's sons (viii 44b // 9:7–9) as the "same" words (being graphic variants of the names that appear in the LXX), four as omissions, and one ([τὸν] ἀδελφὸν [αὐτοῦ]) as a non-synonym substitution (for Δελφων).

[59] If a word or phrase maintains its lexical context relative to words other than those that have moved, it is considered as not having moved. For example, if each letter in the following represents one word, then:

LXX	AT		counts as:
ab cd ef gh	cd a b	ef gh	1 phrase transposition
ab cd ef gh	cd b a	ef gh	1 phrase transposition and 1 word transposition
ab cd ef gh	ef c d	ab gh	2 phrase transpositions
ab cd ef gh	gh c d	ef ab	2 phrase transpositions (ab and gh are considered as moving).

Nested variations, such as a word-transposition within a phrase-transposition, or a synonym

Examples of minor transpositions (grammatical and other inconsequential changes not noted): οἱ τύραννοι καὶ / οἱ σατράπαι (viii 42 // 9:3); τοῖς μακράν/ καὶ τοῖς ἐγγύς (viii 47 // 9:20); ἀπέκτεινον (-αν) / ἐν Σούσοις (viii 44 // 9:6); φιλούμενος / ὑπὸ πάντων τῶν ᾽Ιουδαίων (viii 52 // 10:3).[60] Longer moves may change the contextual function of the phrase; nevertheless they too seem to have little ideological significance. There is a double switch in iv 16–17 // B 3–5, where the phrase πρὸς τὸ μὴ κατατίθεσθαι τὴν ὑφ᾽ ἡμῶν κατευθυνομένην συναρχίαν is moved down (from B 4 to iv 17; with συναρχίαν changed to μοναρχίᾳ and ἀμέμπτως dropped), while the phrase πρὸς τὸ μὴ τὴν βασιλείαν εὐσταθείας τυγχάνειν is moved up (from B 5 to iv 16). This long-distance switch has little effect on the meaning of the passage. A transposition combined with condensation is exemplified by the move of οὐ φορῶ αὐτό ("I do not wear it") to the preceding sentence in the same verse (v 26 // C 27). The result is that while in the LXX, Esther declares that she does not wear the crown when off-duty (ἐν ἡμέραις ἡσυχίας μου), in the AT she says that she only wears it when making public appearances. The redactor then drops the last phrase of D 2—for unclear reasons but with no loss to the overall meaning.

Nested transpositions are the transposition of words within a transposed phrase; e.g., σὺν γυναιξὶν καὶ τέκνοις ἀπολέσαι ὁλοριζεί (B 6) becomes ὁλορί-ζους ἀπολέσαι σὺν γυναιξὶ καὶ τέκνοις (iv 18). These are counted as two separate transpositions.[61]

TABLE IV. TRANSPOSITIONS

IV A. *Word Transpositions*

section	AT wds	word trns	freq	avg dist (in wds)
A	308	1	0.003	1.0
B	249	5	0.020	3.0
C	577	6	0.010	1.3
D	261	5	0.019	4.3

substitution within a phrase-transposition, are counted as multiple variations, since the purpose of the count is to quantify the extent of the redactor's activity. For the same reason, when a word is transposed and "then" exchanged for a synonym, both changes are counted. This requires us to assume that the synonym somehow *is* the word that was moved, but this assumption is inherent in the identification of a word as a synonym-substitute. A justification for this assumption is the freedom the redactor allowed himself in retelling the same events in different words.

[60] The last move is in conjunction with the other adjustments in viii 52 (// 10:3), see below, §9.3.

[61] I.e., ἀπολέσαι ὁλοριζεί is transposed with σὺν γυναιξὶ καὶ τέκνοις, and ἀπολέσαι with ὁλοριζεί.

D +	140	2	0.014	1.0
E	429	19	0.044	2.8
AT-end	281	5	0.018	2.8
F	171	0	0.000	0.0
total	2,416	43.00	0.018	2.0

IV B. *Phrase Transpositions*

section	AT wds	phrase trns	freq	avg # wds in trns	fraction of AT wds moved	avg dist
A	308	2	0.006	2.5	0.008	11.0
B	249	4	0.016	5.5	0.022	14.5
C	577	2	0.003	5.0	0.009	5.0
D	261	0	0.000	0.0	0.000	0.0
D =	140	0	0.000	0.0	0.000	0.0
E	429	2	0.005	4.0	0.009	13.5
AT-end	281	0	0.000	0.0	0.000	0.0
F	171	0	0.000	0.0	0.000	0.0
total	2,416	10	0.004	2.1	0.007	5.5

IV C. *Sections in order of frequency of transpositions*

Word transposition		Phrase transposition	
E	0.044	B	0.016
B	0.020	A	0.006
D	0.019	E	0.005
AT-end	0.018	C	0.003
D +	0.014	AT-end	0.000
C	0.010	D +	0.000
A	0.003	D	0.000
F	0.000	F	0.000

8.4. *Additions*

The redactor has made numerous additions in the course of copying. Some pluses are trivial or (perhaps) stylistic — conjunctions, prepositions, articles, etc. Most of the additions clarify, emphasize, or elaborate details, but some introduce new concepts.

8.4.1. *Emphasis and vividness*. Additions commonly reinforce an idea already present in the donor text; for example: κραυγή "cry" is added to θορύβου "noise" (i 3 // A 4) to emphasize the general clamor as the dragons clash. The additions εὖ δὲ φρονήσας ὁ Μαρδοχαῖος "Mordecai, being well-disposed" (i 13 // A 13) and καὶ εὖρε τοὺς λόγους Μαρδοχαίου "and he found the words of Mordecai (to be true)" (i 14 // A 14) emphasize Mordecai's loyalty. The clause ἐπίκρισις αὐτοῦ διασαφηθήσεται αὐτῷ "its verification would become clear to him" (i 11 // A 11) seems to bring out Mordecai's eagerness to understand the dream; it also modifies the sequence of events (see §9.2). (Esther removed the garments of her glory) καὶ πᾶν σημεῖον ἐπιφανείας αὐτῆς "and every sign of magnificence (v 18 // C 13) — this reinforces her humility. (The king looked) αὐτῇ ὡς ταῦρος "at her like a bull" (vi 5 // D 7) — this makes Esther's situation even more dramatic). (The king tells Esther) ἰδοὺ τὸ σκῆπτρον ἐν τῇ χειρί σου "Behold the scepter is in your hand" (vi 9 // D 11) — this augments her status and emphasizes the king's favor.

8.4.2. *Exegetical clarification* (glosses): The addition of τοῦ μνημονεύειν "to remember" in i 15 (// A 15) explains the purpose of Mordecai's being written in the chronicles. To clarify in what sense Esther περιεβάλετο τὴν δόξαν αὐτῆς "put on her glory" (LXX D 1) — a phrase open to misunderstanding — the redactor adds τὰ ἱμάτια, reading: "she put on the garments of her glory" (vi 1). In i 18 (//A 17) the redactor adds the italicized clauses to explain why Haman sought to harm Mordecai and his people: "*Mordecai had spoken to the king* about the eunuchs, *for which reason they were destroyed.*" The latter expansion accords with the absence of an AT parallel to MT-LXX 2:21–23, in which the scheming eunuchs are hanged.[62]

Additions in *dates*: In the dating of Mordecai's dream, "Adar" is prefixed to "Nisan" in i 1 (// A 1). The redactor was probably influenced by the importance of Adar in the Purim story. A similar case of attraction occurred in the LXX with the shift of Esther's marriage from "Tebeth" in the MT to "Adar" (2:16). In both case, the transfer of an item to Adar makes incidental dating portentous of the month of crisis. Rather than substituting Adar for Nisan,

---

[62] There is no unequivocal statement in LXX Add A to the effect that the eunuchs were executed. Haelewyck (1985:22) explains this absence as harmonistic, since it allows the eunuchs — if these are indeed supposed to be the same ones — to remain alive until 2:23, when their execution is explicitly reported. But this explanation is shaky because the harmonization, if that is what it is, is so inadequate. It requires the reader to assume that after the first attempt the eunuchs were merely "led away" (ἀπήχθησαν; A 14), then at a later date (2:21–23) *again* grew angry at the king, *again* tried to assassinate him, and *again* were discovered by Mordecai, this time to be executed. It is more likely that the reader is to understand that the "leading away," i.e., arrest, of the eunuchs in A 14 was their demise (Fritzsche, p. 81) and that it was a new plot that Mordecai uncovered in 2:21–23. The doublet is still clumsy, but its purpose is clear: to augment Mordecai's value to the king.

R-AT combines the two, in imitation of the proto-AT's Adar Nisan in iv 7 (where the MT has Adar).[63] The meaning and function of the double month-specification are unclear. While one might imagine the dream extending from the last night of Adar into the morning of first day of Nisan, this explanation cannot be applied to iv 7, where the day indicated by Haman's lots is the thirteenth of "the month" Adar-Nisan — the day designated 13 *Adar* in viii 38. Fritzsche suggests that the compound name refers to the intercalary month of Adar. This explanation fits the context, but the intercalary month is elsewhere called "Adar Sheni." Whatever the significance of the compound, the redactor then glosses both with a double Macedonian month name, Dystros Xanthikos. There could be an intercalated month only in a lunar calendar, which the Macedonian was not. But the doubling in Greek may simply imitate a doubling in the original, since the Macedonian month-names were sometimes used as exact equivalents of the Jewish ones. (This is Josephus' usual practice; see Schürer 1973: I, 596). In Add B (iv 18), R-AT again adds a gloss identifying Adar as Dystros.

8.4.3. *Harmonistic details:* In iv 18 (// B 6) the redactor repeats "to murder all the Jews and rob their young" from iv 7b, thereby coordinating the decree of Add B with the proto-AT, according to which the Jews are to be despoiled *of their children* (in contrast, LXX 3:13 says that the Jews' *property* is to be seized). The phrase joining Add A to the start of the proto-AT is also harmonistic; see §6.2.1.

8.4.4. *New concepts or nuances:* Mordecai was appointed to "guard every door visibly" (i 16), emphasizing the king's trust in Mordecai even at this early stage. The LXX says that before praying, Esther "covered every place of glad adornment on her with her braided hair (στρεπτῶν τριχῶν)" (v 18 // C 13). The redactor might have wondered how, if Esther's hair is lovely, exposing it would *diminish* her attractiveness, as appropriate to one praying in mourning attire.[64] R-AT brought out the meaning of Esther's act — as he understood it — by replacing στρεπτῶν by an unambiguous τερπνῶν[65] and adding a clarification, producing: "And every sign of her adornment and gladness on her *delightful* hair [τερπνῶν τριχῶν] she covered with humiliation [ταπεινώσεως]" (v 18 // C 13). In Add D, the redactor removes some of Esther's thick flattery of the king and replaces the second fainting spell by a statement that perspiration appeared on her face (vi 11–12 // D 13–15).

---

[63] It is, of course, possible that the redactor created the compound in iv 7 too, perhaps by adding Adar to an original Nisan.

[64] In the LXX, στρεπτός might mean twisted in the sense of dishevelled (thus Moore 1977:208). But used of hair it commonly means plaited, and so could easily be understood as a means of increasing attractiveness.

[65] Ms 93, which is often influenced by the LXX, has στρεπτῶν.

Perhaps the redactor feels that there has been enough flattery and fainting already.

The additions in AT-end, though rather short, have special interpretive or ideological significance, which will be discussed below, §§9.3, 5–11: πάντα τὰ αὐτῶν (viii 44b // 9:11); τοὺς πεσόντας εἰς (viii 49b //9:26a, 27b); τὰ τέλη (viii 50 // 10:1; may have been present in R-AT's vorlage); καὶ ἐδόξασε Μαρδο-χαῖος (viii 51 // 10:2); καὶ δόξαν and περιετίθει (viii 52 // 10:3). The last mentioned change, like several additions elsewhere, occurs in conjunction with other restructuring, notably the omission of δεδοξασμένος (viii 52 // 10:3). The AT reads: (And Mordecai was) "beloved by all the Jews. And he led them and bestowed honor on all his nation." By the shifting of the word signifying honor, the redactor indicates that Mordecai was a source as well as a recipient of honor. The addition of καὶ ἐδόξασε Μαρδοχαῖος in viii 51a (// 10:2) makes the same point.

Only four additions are longer than ten words. These are a prayer of thanksgiving (viii 58 // after F 9; 22 words), an interpretation of the light in Mordecai's dream (viii 54b // after F 5; 13 words), a repetition of Esther's formula of polite request (vi 18 // 5:8; 15 words), and an elaboration on the king's expressions of favor toward Esther (vi 9 // D 11; 13 words). The redactor largely avoids using his own words to introduce his ideas into the text.

8.5 Omissions

Omissions range from scattered single words, most of them inconsequential, to the major blocks excised in AT-end.

Harmonization can motivate an omission, as in the deletion of the clause "who served in the court of the king" from i 1b (// A 2). Similarly, by removing mention of Mordecai's position in i 1b (// A 2), R-AT eliminates the LXX's contradiction between A 2—which says that Mordecai served in the court even before his dream—and A 16, which has him appointed to serve in the court after uncovering the plot.

The motive for minor omissions is often difficult to discern. Though the redactor often adds words for explanation or greater specificity (see above, §§8.4.1–2)—a clear enough motive—he also removes words that serve that very function in the LXX, as in the following sentences (the italicized words are absent in the AT): ". . . and her face was *glad*, as one dearly loved, but her heart was constricted *from fear*" (D 5 // vi 3); ". . . and [the king] took her in his arms *until she regained her composure*. And he comforted her *with peaceful words*" (D 8 // vi 8).

Only a few long omissions occur in the Adds, most notably in C and F. The whole of C 11, which states that all Israel called out to God, is lacking in the AT (after v 17). It is hard to imagine any ideological or narratival reason for the omission. Moore (1977:204) suggests that it was lost by haplography, though the beginnings of this verse and the next have only a καί in common.

The AT also leaves out "O king of the gods and ruler of all governments" in C 23b (∥ v 24), again for no apparent reason. The AT also omits τῇ μόνῃ καὶ μὴ ἐχούσῃ εἰ μὴ σέ, κύριε ("[help me], who am alone and have no one but you, O Lord") (v 25b ∥ C 25b). This phrase is a virtual repetition of one in C 14, where R-AT maintained the phrase but substituted ταπεινῇ "lowly" for μόνῃ "alone" (v 19). Perhaps the redactor is playing down Esther's loneliness because she does have the support of God and Mordecai. Most of F 6 (up to τῶν κακῶν τούτων) is omitted (viii 55); here Mordecai identifies his people as "Israel, who cried out to God and were saved" (but the omission is compensated for later in the text; see below). The redactor removes E 22, in which the king commands the Jews to celebrate the holiday, apparently feeling it inappropriate to give a foreigner such a role in the Jewish liturgical calendar (see §10.2).

Sometimes the redactor compensates for an omission by employing the lost wording elsewhere. For example, when the sentence καὶ οὐκ ἔστιν ὅς ἀντιτάξεταί σοι τῷ κυρίῳ ("and there is none who can stand up to you, Lord") is omitted from the end of C 4b (perhaps because it repeats καὶ οὐκ ἔστιν ὁ ἀντιδοξῶν σοι ["there is none who can oppose you"] that appears in C 2b). Then the redactor uses ἀντιτάξεται in v 13a as a synonym-substitute for ἀντιδοξῶν of C 2b. The omission of the prayer for help in F 6 is balanced by the addition of a prayer of thanksgiving in viii 58 (∥ F 9). The omission of 20 words of dream interpretation (F 3) is balanced by the new interpretation of the light in viii 54b. (This might be viewed as extensive non-synonym substitution; however the passages are formulated quite differently and do not deal with exactly the same topics).

In the extent and significance of their omissions, AT-end and, to a lesser degree, Add F differ notably from the other redactional sections, which preserve almost all of the parallel LXX material.[66] Since the redactor is most active here, I will survey these omissions and their apparent motives. Most serve to eliminate redundancies.

LXX 9:1 is omitted. R-AT dissociates the Jews' slaughter of their enemies from 13 Adar (see §9.8), and the removal of this verse contributes to this purpose. The redactor excises 9:11, in which the number of the dead is reported to the king, and 9:12b, in which the king promises to do whatever else Esther wants (they would appear after viii 44 and 45 respectively). This was done because these phrases do not advance the story, for the body count has already been mentioned (viii 44a), and the king's assurance of generosity is no longer necessary.

The repetitiveness of MT 9:13–32 has been recognized by many commentators, who often take this quality as a sign that the passage is secondary. R-AT

---

[66] The LXX already lacked MT 9:2a, 5, and 30. There is considerable inner-Greek divergence in 29–31 (∥ MT 29–32), and it is unclear just what R-AT's LXX would have had. All my counts follow Hanhart's edition.

reduces that repetitiveness (and thus runs counter to what redactors are commonly supposed to do). He removes most of LXX 9:13–31,[67] leaving only an abridged version of Mordecai's letter establishing Purim and a new etiology for the holiday's name. LXX 9:13–31 includes various items: the two letters sent to establish the holiday, the people's confirmation of the holiday, its acceptance by subsequent generations, the careful distinction between Susan Purim and provincial Purim, and the historical retrospective giving the rationale for the holiday. These issues are treated in Mordecai's first letter (viii 33–38), which was already present in the proto-AT, and in the few sentences preserved from the LXX (viii 47, 49 // 9:20, 21, 26a). Redundancy in such matters would make sense at a time when the legitimacy of the holiday was still an issue and when the dates of celebration were still a matter of some uncertainty. This seems to be the case in the MT. But these issues do not seem to have engaged R-AT (who was at work no earlier than the latter part of the first century CE). It is reasonable to imagine R-AT, nearing the end of his task and wearied by transferring repetitive material of dubious relevance, deciding to abridge his donor text drastically.

By now it should be clear that the minuses in AT-end (like those elsewhere in the AT) are no evidence whatsoever for the extent of the original MT. The redactor is working off the LXX at every step.

TABLE V. ADDITIONS AND OMISSIONS

Table V tallies the additions and omissions of words in the redactional sections. The frequency of additions is given as a percentage of the AT words. The number of AT omissions refers to the *Septuaginal* words not transfered, and the frequency of omissions is calculated as a percentage of the number of words in the corresponding LXX passage.

V A. *Additions and omissions in the redactional sections*

	# AT wds	# wds added	addns as % of AT wds	# LXX wds	# LXX wds omitted	omissions as % of LXX wds
A	308	60	0.195	298	45	0.151
B	249	20	0.080	246	11	0.045
C	577	47	0.081	597	71	0.119
D	261	43	0.165	254	35	0.138
D + [68]	140	24	0.171	115	18	0.157

[67] Note that LXX 30, 31 correspond to MT 29, 32.

[68] The 15-word plus in AT vi 18 ("and if it seems good to the king to grant my wish and to carry out my request") is present in MSS of the hexaplaric group O S^c. Therefore in the AT

E	429	43	0.100	472	84	0.178
AT-end	281	33	0.117	718	523	0.728
F	171	41	0.240	199	71	0.357
total	2,416	311	0.129	2,899	858	0.296

V B. *Sections in order of frequency of additions and omissions*

additions		omissions	
F	0.240	AT-end	0.728
A	0.195	F	0.357
D +	0.171	E	0.178
D	0.165	D +	0.157
AT-end	0.117	A	0.151
E	0.100	D	0.138
C	0.081	C	0.119
B	0.080	B	0.045

8.6 *Condensation. "Cutting-and-splicing"*

As well as merely omitting blocks of words, the redactor sometimes condenses them, conveying their gist in fewer words. Some of the condensation in AT-end conveys the redactor's new conception of the holiday's meaning (e.g., viii 30–31 // E 21b, 23), but some may just be a way of reducing wordiness (e.g. viii 24 // E 7–9; viii 32b // E 24b). Condensation may take the form of summarization, as in viii 46a, where καὶ συνεχώρησεν, "and he agreed," replaces 17 words (of 9:13–16a), which state that Esther's request was carried out. The redactor condenses C 27 by restructuring the sentence. The LXX has: "(I despise the sign of my superiority [i.e., the crown]) which is on my head on the days of my public appearance . . . I do not wear it in the days of my leisure." The AT (v 26) reads: ". . . which is on my head, and I do not wear it *except on* the day of my public appearance. . ."

A clever redactional device is the "*cut-and-splice*" technique, which condenses by omitting words to create new sentences from those that remain, often with a significantly different import. In this way the redactor compresses the donor text while still affording some representation to omitted material. Cutting-and-splicing may be combined with other changes, as in the following examples.

In viii 40b, the AT repeats part of LXX 8:16 to the effect that "the Jews

---

too the words may be a hexaplaric intrusion. In that case, the frequency of additions in D + is 0.064.

had light," then adds πότος "drinking" and then skips 21 words to pick up κώθων "banqueting" from the middle of 8:17b. The resulting sentence is "And the Jews had light, drinking, and banquetting'; this corresponds to 29 words in the LXX.[69]

The best example of cutting-and-splicing is viii 49 // 9:26–27 (underlining in the following LXX quotations marks material *not* transferred; in the AT quotations it indicates non-LXX material. Virgules (/ . . . /) mark substitutions):

LXX	AT
(26) διὰ τοῦτο /ἐπε/κλήθησαν αἱ ἡμέραι αὗται Φρουραι διὰ τοὺς κλήρους, ὅτι τῇ διαλέκτῳ αὐτῶν καλοῦνται Φρουραι, διὰ τοὺς λόγους τῆς ἐπι- στολῆς ταύτης καὶ ὅσα πεπόνθασιν διὰ ταῦτα καὶ ὅσα αὐτοῖς ἐγένετο. (27) καὶ ἔστησεν καὶ προσ- εδέχοντο οἱ Ἰουδαῖοι ἐφ' ἑαυτοῖς καὶ ἐπὶ τῷ σπέρματι αὐτῶν καὶ ἐπὶ τοῖς προσ- τεθειμένοις ἐπ' αὐτῶν, οὐδὲ μὴν ἄλλως χρήσονται.	(49) διὰ τοῦτο ἐκλήθησαν αἱ ἡμέραι αὗται Φουραια διὰ τοὺς κλήρους
(27b) αἱ δὲ ἡμέραι αὗται μνημόσυνον ἐπιτελούμενον . . .	τοὺς πεσόντας εἰς τὰς ἡμέρας ταύτας εἰς μνημόσυνον. [rest of 27b-31 omitted]
(26) Because of this, these days were designated "Phrourai," because of the lots—for in their language they are called "Phrourai"— (and) because of the words of this epistle and the things they had undergone, because of these matters and those things which happened to them.	(49) Because of this, these days were named "Phouraia," because of the lots

---

[69] Homoioteleuton (from εὐφροσύνη in 8:16 to εὐφροσύνη in 8:17) is a less likely explanation, since AT does not record this word even once.

(27a) And he established (it),
and the Jews accepted (it) for
themselves and their seed and
those who are joined to them,
and that they would not behave
otherwise.

(27b) And these days are
celebrated as a memorial . . .

that fell upon
these days
as a memorial.

By this revision, the name of Purim is made to memorialize the lots that selected the days of festival rather than the lots that Haman cast.

In i 5b–6, a combination of inventive cutting-and-splicing, addition of material, and transposition of words produces notable changes in Mordecai's dream (its significance is discussed in §9.1).

LXX A 5b–9a

(5b) καὶ ἐγένετο αὐτῶν φωνὴ μεγάλη, (6) καὶ τῇ φωνῇ αὐτῶν ἡτοιμάσθη πᾶν ἔθνος εἰς πόλεμον ὥστε πολεμῆσαι δικαίων ἔθνος. (7) καὶ ἰδοὺ ἡμέρα σκότους καὶ γνόφου, θλῖψις καὶ στενοχωρία, κάκωσις καὶ τάραχος μέγας ἐπὶ τῆς γῆς. (8) καὶ ἐταράχθη δίκαιον πᾶν ἔθνος φοβούμενοι τὰ ἑαυτῶν κακά, καὶ ἡτοιμάσθησαν / ἀπολέσθαι /, (9a) καὶ ἐβόησαν πρὸς / τὸν θεόν/.

(5b) And their sound grew great. (6) And at their sound every nation prepared for war, so as to fight against the nation of the righteous. (7) And behold, a day of darkness and gloom, affliction and distress, harm and great disturbance upon the earth. (8) And the entire righteous nation was disturbed, fearing their own harm, and they prepared / to die /, (9a) and they cried / to God /.

AT i 5–6

(5) καὶ ἐγένετο αὐτῶν φωνή, καὶ ἐταράσσετο πάντα ἀπὸ τῆς φωνῆς τῆς κραυγῆς ταύτης. (6) μαρτυρομένη πᾶσι τοῖς λαοῖς ἡμέρα σκότους καὶ γνόφου καὶ ταραχὴ πολέμου, καὶ ἡτοιμάσατο πᾶν ἔθνος / πολεμῆσαι /, καὶ / ἀν/εβόησα/μεν/ πρὸς /κύριον/.

(5) And there came their sound, and all were disturbed because of the sound of this cry, (6) witnessing to all peoples a day of darkness and gloom and the disturbance of war, and every nation prepared /to fight/; and /we/ cried out to /the Lord/.

Only about a quarter of the words of LXX F 2–3 are extracted and maintained in viii 54; the result is a different interpretation of Mordecai's dream.

The words ἡ μικρὰ πηγή and Εσθηρ ἐστίν, separated by 11 words in the LXX (F 3), are preserved and joined into a unit in the AT (viii 54). Cutting-and-splicing is also used in ii 6–8 (probably redactional; see §6.2.2), where the alteration tightens up the description of the banquet-room. Another example is i 17–18 // A 16b–17 (quoted in §9.3).

Cutting-and-splicing, we may note, proves that the Adds were transferred from the LXX to the AT and not the other way around, since the technique constitutes a deliberate reduction of the LXX. It would be extremely difficult to start with the AT sentences, interlace words in them, and produce sentences of such different structure and import as the LXX has in the above-mentioned verses. Similarly, the cutting-and-splicing in AT-end confirms the priority of the LXX to the AT of those verses. We can hardly imagine a redactor of the LXX interlacing words in sentences taken from the AT so as to produce a text much closer to the MT—yet remaining at some distance from it.

8.7. *Minor alterations: grammatical changes, particles, prepositions, etc.*

R-AT makes numerous minor changes: adding and subtracting articles, conjunctions, and prepositions; changing singulars to plural and plurals to singular; changing cases without significantly altering the sense (e.g., [εἰσάκουσον] φωνῆς for φωνήν [v 29 // C 30]); changing tense or person (e.g., 2nd sg. for 3rd sg., with reference to the king, in vi 18 // 5:7). Sometimes the redactor changes the tense of verbs—present to aorist, or aorist to present—without much effect on the meaning.

As far as I can tell, no pattern emerges from these changes. Also, since many grammatical alterations—particularly case and mode—are entailed by other changes, such alterations shed less light on the redactor's techniques and motives than do ones over which he has full control, such as synonym and non-synonym substitutions. I have not pursued such changes further because they do not seem to offer much insight into the redactor's attitudes, interpretations, or ideology.

Occasionally, however, grammatical changes do affect the meaning. For example, according to the LXX, Mordecai *writes* a favorable account of his own deed at the beginning of the book (A 15), while at the end it says that the king's glories *were written* (10:2). The AT reverses the voice of both verbs, informing us in i 15 that "Mordecai *was written* in the royal book for a remembrance" and in viii 51 that Mordecai *wrote* the king's glories. These changes make Mordecai more modest and emphasize his value to the king. Furthermore, in A 15 (// i 15) it is premature for Mordecai to record his revelation of the scheme; what is important is that his *deed* be recorded in the royal records, and R-AT's grammatical change makes this adjustment. Another case where a small change makes a big difference is viii 44c, where an added καί in the phrase, "*and* the ten sons of Haman," means that the men named in 44b are *not* Haman's sons. A switch from singular to plural that seems significant occurs in viii 56 (// F 8) —"days" of God's rule instead of the "day" of his judgment. Another noticeable change in person is in viii 54 (//F 2), where the first-person of two verbs, spoken by Mordecai (ἐμνήσθην and εἶδον) is changed to the third-person, so that the narrator now says that Mordecai remembered the dream that *he* saw. After this change it became necessary to prefix "And he said" to Mordecai's explanation of the dream (viii 54b), since the quotation of Mordecai's words now starts there.

There are various differences between E 23 and viii 31, but the most significant of these are grammatical: the change of an adjective to a verb (with a similar appearance) and the change of the case of a noun. In the LXX, the king tells the Jews to celebrate the day of salvation as a special commemorative festival, and continues:

ὅπως καὶ νῦν καὶ μετὰ ταῦτα σωτήρια ᾖ ἡμῖν καὶ τοῖς εὐνοοῦσιν Πέρσαις,
τοῖς δὲ ἡμῖν ἐπιβουλεύουσιν μνημόσυνον τῆς ἀπωλείας.

. . . so that now and henceforth it shall be a festival of deliverance[70] for you[71] and the well-intentioned Persians, but for those scheming against us, a reminder of destruction.

In the AT parallel, the king announces that the Jews have decided to celebrate 14–15 Adar as a festival, adding that the Almighty made salvation and joy for them (30a). The AT omits E 22 (in which the king declared the day a festival) and continues (31):

καὶ νῦν μετὰ ταῦτα σωτήριαν μὲν εὖ ποιοῦσι τοῖς Πέρσαις, τῶν δὲ
ἐπιβουλευσάντων μνημόσυνον τῆς ἀπωλείας.

This difficult sentence is probably to be rendered:

And now, they shall properly make (them) henceforth into a Festival of Deliverance for the Persians, but a reminder of destruction for schemers.[72]

---

[70] Following Fritzsche's accentuation σωτήρια (sc. ἱερά), "festival of deliverance," instead of σωτηρία (Hanhart, Brooke-McLean), "deliverance." The text makes better sense if it is understood to say that the day shall be a *festival* of deliverance rather than that the day—which commemorates a past deliverance—"shall be a deliverance." Furthermore, "festival of deliverance" is a more direct antonym of "reminder of destruction."

[71] Reading ὑμῖν (LXX-S and some other MSS) with most commentators, instead of ἡμῖν, "us."

[72] Or, ". . . a reminder of the destruction of schemers." The subject of ποιοῦσι is apparently "Jews," to be supplied from the preceding verse. The sentence is a double accusative construction, with the first object not expressed. The ellipsis ("them" = the two days, or "it" = the festival) can be supplied from the preceding context. Clines (1984:243) translates: "And now they do well [to regard it] hereafter as salvation for the Persians . . ."

The new version has the Jews initiate the *Persian* celebration. This is in line with R-AT's undoubtedly deliberate changes in the preceding verses. These emphasize Jewish independence by having the king announce the *Jewish* decision to inaugurate a festival rather than decreeing it himself.

8.8 *The scope of R-AT's changes*

Changes of the sorts described above, particularly synonym-substitutions, transpositions, additions, and minor alterations, appear to some extent in all manuscript transmission, whether as accidental alterations or as deliberate stylistic and exegetical modifications. This is not surprising, since for the most part R-AT is in fact simply copying text from one manuscript to another.

Of course the extent of changes that texts undergo in copying varies considerably. But we can get a sense of how much change would occur in normal — non-redactional — copying by looking at manuscript differences *within* each Greek tradition. The following table brings the results of two comparisons. Within the LXX tradition, it compares the Codex Alexandrinus (LXX-A) with the Codex Vaticanus (LXX-B); and within the AT tradition, it compares MS 93 with Hanhart's AT text (based on MSS 19' and 93'). The passages studied in this exercise are the redactional sections in the AT (Adds A–F, D + , AT-end) and their LXX parallels. I describe the variants in LXX-A as if it derived in a straight line of descent from LXX-B, and those in MS 93 as if derived from the Hanhart's AT text. Since the point is to describe relative *extent* of change, the angle from which the variations are approached should not affect the essential results.

TABLE VI. FREQUENCY OF CHANGES
IN NON-REDACTIONAL COPYING

Table VI compares the frequency of redactional alterations made by R-AT in LXX material (line 1) with copyist changes in two manuscript traditions, the LXX and the AT. In the LXX (line 2), LXX-A is compared with LXX-B; in the AT (line 3), MS 93 is compared with Hanhart's AT ("*L*") text (19', 93').

VI A. *Substitutions*

	total wds	syn subs	freq	pfx vars	freq	non-syns	freq
(1) R-AT	2,416	132	0.055	24	0.010	51	0.021
(2) LXX	2,899	38	0.013	13	0.004	17	0.006
(3) AT	2,416	15	0.006	2	0.001	13	0.005

VI B. *Transpositions*

	# AT wds	word-trsps	freq	avg distance
(1) R-AT	2,416	43	0.018	2.6
(2) LXX	2,899	22	0.008	1.68
(3) AT	2,416	3	0.001	1.00

	phrase trsps	freq	avg distance	freq wds	avg dist
(1) R-AT	7	0.003	11.8	0.005	6.28
(2) LXX	0	0.000	0.0	0.000	
(3) AT	0	0.000	0.0	0.000	

VI C. *Additions and omissions*

	# wds	# wds added	freq of addns	# LXX wds	# wds omitted	freq omissions
(1) R-AT	2,416	294	0.122	2,899	849	0.29
(2) LXX	2,899	63	0.022	2,899	107	0.04
(3) AT	2,416	13	0.005	2,899	23	0.01

The frequency of the changes made in the course of transferring Septuagintal material into the AT is far greater than the frequency of changes within either the LXX or the AT manuscripts studied—even allowing for subsequent modifications in the AT's own transmission. The differences are even greater than the statistics suggest. Almost all the "synonym substitutions" in LXX-A are trivial—e.g., δέ for καί and deictic pronouns for articles. Moreover, in the two LXX manuscripts compared, 39 words were lost through obvious cases of homoioteleuton, mainly in C 26 and F 6–7. Without these omissions, we find only 68 words omitted in LXX-A vis-à-vis LXX-B, yielding a frequency of .024. In the redactional sections of the AT, on the other hand, the only minus that may be due to homoioteleuton is C 11 (13 words).

9. *Reinterpretation*

Some changes, particularly in combination with modifications elsewhere, express an understanding of the holiday and its history that differs from that of the Septuagint.

9.1. *Mordecai's dream and its interpretation*

The AT differs from the LXX both in the narration of the dream (Add A) and its interpretation (Add F). Analysis of these passages is hindered by obscurities and internal tensions within both versions of these passages, but certain differences stand out and have thematic significance.

Synopsis of the dream and its interpretations

Add A: LXX	Add A: AT	Add F: LXX	Add F: AT
(a) Noise;	Noise;		
(b) 2 dragons approach to fight.	2 dragons approach to fight.	= Mordecai and Haman	= Mordecai and Haman
(c) A great sound, and the nations prepare for war against the righteous nation.	A great sound, and all are shaken up.	the nations = those who arose to destroy the name of the Jews Cf. (i)	
(d) Darkness & disturbance.	Darkness & disturbance.		
(e) The righteous nation is terrified and prepares to *die*	*Every* nation prepares to *fight*.		
(f) and cries out to God.	And *we* cried out to God.	Israel cried out for help and was saved.	
(g) A small spring becomes	A small spring becomes		
(h) a river.	a river.	= Esther	Cf. (i)
(i)			The river = the peoples who gathered to destroy the Jews.

(j) Sun rises.	Sun rises.	And there was light of sun and much water (not symbolic).	Sun and light are God's manifestation.
(k) *The humble* arise and devour the powerful.	The *rivers* arise and swallow the powerful.		
(l)		God made miracles and two lots	God made miracles and two lots
(m)		that came to the hour and time of *judgment.*	that came to the hours and days of God's *rule.*
(n)			Israel cried out in thanks.

The AT and the LXX differ in their treatment of several elements in the dream and its interpretation:

9.1.1. *Israel and the nations.* The sequence of events in the two versions conveys a difference in attitude toward the gentiles. According to the LXX (A 5–9a), (1) at the dragons' noise, (2) every nation (πᾶν ἔθνος) prepared to fight against Israel; (3) *then* (καὶ ἰδού introducing a new event) there were darkness and distress, etc., and (4) a great disturbance (τάραχος) on the earth; (5) whereupon the *entire righteous nation* (δίκαιον πᾶν ἔθνος = Israel) was disturbed and prepared to *die;* and (6) Israel cried out to God. In other words, the gentiles seem to be waiting for the opportunity to destroy Israel, and they seize upon the dragons' battle as the destined moment. Their preparations to attack Israel are accompanied by disturbance both cosmic and human (darkness and affliction). Only Israel sees itself as threatened—so much so that it prepares to die.

In the AT (i 4-6), events proceed differently: (1′) At the dragons' noise, (4′) *everything* (πάντα) was disturbed (ἐταράσσετο); (3′) there was darkness, etc., and the disturbance of war; then (2′, 5′) *every nation* prepared to *fight;* and (6′) *we* cried out to the Lord. The AT shows the gentiles in quite a different role. "Every nation" reacts fearfully to the noise and darkness—with the darkness causing their reaction rather than following upon their stirrings.

Every nation sees itself in peril and prepares for war, but not specifically against Israel.[73]

As general disaster loomed, *we* called upon God. The first-person plural seems to retroject an historical event into the dream itself rather than just aligning event with symbol afterwards in the interpretation. The use of "we" also highlights the contrast between Israel's wise behavior and the martial preparations of the others. We are probably to understand that "every nation" preparing for war does not include Israel, for there is an implicit contrast between Israel ("we"), who called upon God, and the others, who did not.

Thus in the AT the world does not unite against Israel. The hostile force is circumscribed; it is one of the dragons (= Haman) and his allies (who are not mentioned in AT Add A, unless they are among "the powerful").

9.1.2. *The gentiles' fate.* Whereas the LXX (F 8) regards God's lots as desig-nating the day of their *judgment* (κρίσις), in the AT (viii 56) they indicate the day of God's *rule* (κυριεύσις) among the nations. This change softens the hostility toward the gentiles.

9.1.3. *The little spring.* In F 3 (= viii 54) the LXX identifies "the little spring" as Esther:

> The little spring, which became a river, and there was light and sun and much water[74]: the river is Esther, whom the king married and made queen.

The AT too identifies the spring as Esther but removes the descriptive clauses (viii 54a). Later (54b) the AT identifies the *river* as the hostile nations. This cannot be the same river that (according to both versions of Add A [A 9 // i 7] as well as the LXX's version of Add F) grew out of the small spring.

There is a contradiction, or at least a disharmony, within the AT's treat-ment of the water symbols. In its version of Add A, the small spring grows

---

[73] The version of Add A found in the midrash (Est. Rab. VIII 5), taken from the Yossipon, mixes the two: All the nations are terrified at the dragons' clamor and flee. Then (in a non sequitur) they rise against one small nation (Israel) to destroy it. The small nation cries out to God and everyone is saved.

[74] The first clause in F 3, which is a sort of caption, might mean "the little spring, which became (ἐγένετο) a river and was (ἦν) light and sun and much water" (Fritzsche) — implying that both the light and the sun were somehow an outgrowth of the spring. But this rendering does not straighten things out, since it has a spring becoming a river which was (composed of) light, sun and water. Jerome tries to make sense of the progression in this way: et in lucem solemque conversus est, et in aquas plurimas redundavit, ". . . spreading out into sun and sunlight, and so went rolling on in full tide" (Knox transl). But this is not justified by the Greek. The addition of ἦν, where the ἐγένετο would have sufficed, suggests that ἦν is to be taken not as a copula but existentially ("there is") (thus Moore [1977:245 note], among others).

into a river, whereas in Add F (AT) there are two bodies of water: the small spring and the river that endangers the Jews. In neither the LXX nor the AT of Add A is there a river *hostile* to the Jews. In fact, the AT (unlike the LXX [A 6]) does not even mention nations gathering to destroy the Jews.

9.1.4. *The punitive rivers.* According to the LXX, the *humble* (ταπεινοί) were exalted (ὑψώθησαν) and devoured the eminent (A 10), whereas in the AT the *rivers* (ποταμοί) rose up (ὑψώθησαν) and swallowed the eminent (i 8). These "rivers" (plural) have not been mentioned earlier, so their appearance is unexpected. They seem to be a re-application of the river-image, which in the preceding verse represents Esther. The spring grows to a mighty river, which spreads into many rivers (Fritzsche), and these execute justice on the arrogant. The rivers are not identified, but they are most naturally interpreted as a symbol for the Jews, who punish their enemies after the failure of Haman's plot.

9.1.5. *Light and sun.*[75] The image of the "light and the sun" is scarcely integrated into the LXX's interpretation of the dream (F 3; quoted above). The AT provides a separate (and awkward) explanation for the light-image: "Sun and light is a manifestation of God which came to the Jews. This[76] is the judgment" (viii 54). The AT's ἥλιος καὶ φῶς in Add F (viii 54) seems to be derived from the LXX's φῶς καὶ ἥλιος in F 3 rather than from R-AT's own φῶς, ἥλιος in Add A (i 8). But the inversion of the words as well as the new interpretation of the symbols shows that he is not mechanically copying the LXX.

9.1.6. *Israel's outcries.* The AT (viii 54–55) omits F 6a, in which Mordecai (rather unnecessarily) identifies his people as "Israel, who cried out to God and were saved." An "outcry" does occur later on, in viii 58, which says that all the people cried out in *thanksgiving* to God.

9.1.7. *The relation between dream and interpretation.* Some confusion in the interpretations of the dreams is probably due to errors in transmission. In part, however, the interpretation offered by Add F in the LXX may simply be mistaken. Moore (1977:249) points out various incongruities between the dream and the story and persuasively argues that the dream was originally

---

[75] The phrase φῶς καὶ ὁ ἥλιος + sg. verb (A 10) may mean "(There was) light, and the sun arose" or, as a hendiadys: "The light of the sun arose." In F 3, φῶς καὶ ἥλιος is probably a hendiadys, as apparently is ἥλιος καὶ φῶς in the AT (viii 54). In any case, the two nouns are interpreted as one symbol. The AT's φῶς, ἥλιος + sg. verb in i 8 seems to be an apposition identifying the two, to the same effect.

[76] The demonstrative τοῦτο has no neuter antecedent and must refer to the events generally.

a separate entity secondarily adapted to the Esther story. Indeed, read by itself Add A has little to do with the story. In particular, no distinction is drawn between the two dragons; both seem to be an indiscriminate source of danger. Also, Mordecai's role in salvation has no symbol in the dream. Esther would be appropriately represented by the little stream who turned into a mighty river, but the role of the river in salvation is indefinite. Add F, on the other hand, was written primarily with attention to the body of the Esther story, not to Add A, as is evident from the fact that (as Bardtke 1963:54 observes) the interpretation is structured according to the development of the narrative rather than according to the sequence of the dream. In other words, the author of this Add is less concerned with explaining the enigmas of the dream than with showing how the story fulfilled its portents.

Whether or not the dream text ever existed independently of the Esther story, the incongruities suggest that Add F was composed not by the author of the dream but by a later writer who was trying to apply the mysterious symbols to the Esther story but could do so only imperfectly. The interpreter in the version of Add F that got into the LXX does not know quite what to make of φῶς καὶ ὁ ἥλιος (A 10), so he merely associates the terms uneasily with the great waters. He ignores the statement about the "humble" arising and devouring the powerful. R-AT had to work with this material as presented in his donor text and did not achieve much greater congruity. His one "improvement" is in finding a symbolic application for the sunlight.

9.2. *The eunuchs' plot* (Add A). The sequence of events is restructured. The LXX leads up to the discovery thus:

> (A 11) "And when Mordecai, who had seen this dream and what God wanted to do, awoke, he kept thinking about it [εἶχεν αὐτὸ ἐν τῇ καρδίᾳ] and desired to understand in every detail until nighttime [ἕως τῆς νυκτός]. (12) And Mordecai was resting in the court . . . (13) and he heard their schemes . . .

Since there is no gap between the events of vss. 11 and 12, we get the impression that in the LXX Mordecai discovered the plot on the night after his dream. The AT, however, reads:

> (i 10) "And his dream was hidden in his heart, and at all times he sought to understand it. (11) Its verification (ἐπίκρισις) would become clear to him on (ἕως) the day when Mordecai slept in the court . . ."

The AT largely maintains the LXX's wording, including ἕως, which is awkward in the new sentence. But the AT extends indefinitely the time during which Mordecai meditated on the dream. The substitution of "at all times [ἐν παντὶ καιρῷ]" for "in every matter [ἐν παντὶ λόγῳ]" reinforces this change. The redactor also turns vs. 11b into a relative clause, "(the day) in which," again suggesting a longer time-scale. These modifications allow AT i 10–11 to narrate the event prospectively and thus not contradict 2:21 of the LXX, which sets the discovery in the seventh year (see 2:16), rather than in the second (A 1).[77] To be sure, the AT lacks a parallel to LXX 2:21–22, but the redactor was aware of the sequence of events as related in the LXX and made adjustments for them. It is unclear just what is meant by the statement that Mordecai understood the dream's verification or validation (ἐπίκρισις) on the day when he came upon the assassination plot. Perhaps the point is that Haman was embittered by the exposure of his subordinates and came into conflict with Mordecai (i 18), and in this conflict Mordecai recognized the two dragons and saw how the dream's portents would be realized. But this possibility is at most hinted at.

9.3. *Mordecai's importance and value.* At several points the redactor emphasizes Mordecai's value to his king and his people. He first does this, somewhat prematurely, by magnifying the importance of Mordecai's initial appointment in i 17–18 // A 16b–17:

LXX   And he gave him gifts for these things. And Haman son
AT   And he gave him   for these things   Haman son

LXX   of Amadathos the Bougaian   was honored in   the
AT   of Amadathos the /Macedonian/   /before/ the

LXX   presence of the king. And   he   sought to harm Mordecai
AT   presence of the king. And   /Haman/   sought to harm Mordecai

LXX   and   his people because of
AT   and all his people because of his having spoken to the king

LXX   the two eunuchs of the king.
AT   about the   eunuchs,

LXX
AT   for they were executed.

Although the sentence that results from the absence of the word "gifts" is so strange that one might suspect an accidental omission,[78] the further absence of "was honored" reinforces the implications of the first variant and thus confirms its legitimacy. Both changes exalt Mordecai, though rather

---

[77] These observations are based on Moore 1977:178.

[78] Fritzsche adds δόματα καὶ ἔστη after ἔδωκεν . . . τούτων, "and gave him gifts for this. And Haman stood . . ."

prematurely. This is in line with the plus at the end of i 16, which defines Mordecai's new position (which in the LXX is simply "to serve in the court") by adding that he was appointed "to visibly keep all the doors." Since Haman is angered by the execution of the two eunuchs of the palace guard, the redactor may imagine Haman to be the officer of the palace guard (which may indeed be the implication). In that case Mordecai is now placed over him. Then, after Haman rises to preeminence (iv 1 // 3:1), he expects his former superior to bow to him.

Mordecai's value to the king is further enhanced in viii 51 by a small addition—"and Mordecai glorified" [sc. the king]—and by a change from the LXX's passive "is written" (10:2b) to the active "and he wrote" (viii 51). Now it is Mordecai who glorifies the king by recording the latter's prowess. Later, Mordecai's value to his fellow-Jews is heightened by small modifications in viii 52 (// 10:3), which make the verse say that not only was Mordecai beloved, but he also led his people and bestowed glory on *them* (καὶ δόξαν παντὶ τῷ ἔθνει αὐτοῦ περιετίθει for δεδοξασμένος ὑπὸ τῶν Ἰουδαίων κτλ.).

At the same time, Mordecai's modesty is preserved by changing the verb in i 15 from active to passive. Whereas the LXX says that "Mordecai wrote about these matters" (A 15), which implies a certain self-glorification, the new version says that he "*was written*" in the royal records after he revealed the eunuchs' conspiracy.

9.4. *Esther's banquets.* In the LXX (and MT), Esther invites the king and Haman to a banquet that same day (5:4). In the AT (vi 14 = D +), she invites them for the *next day*. The AT's variant here seems to be a deliberate change in the pace of events: since αὔριον appears twice it is probably not accidental. But the reason for the change is obscure. The AT's reading seems to be contradicted by the next verse, in which the king sends for Haman and they go together to the banquet.

9.5. *The circumcision.* The circumcision following the reversal of Haman's decree is radically reinterpreted in viii 49. In the LXX, one evidence of the rise of Jewish power is that gentiles circumcise themselves because they fear the Jews (8:17). (This is the LXX's understanding of *mityahădîm*, "became Jews.") In place of this rather crude notion of conversion, R-AT has the *Jews* circumcising *themselves* (viii 41a). By eliminating 9:1, R-AT turns the gentiles' fear, mentioned in 9:2, into the reason they do not oppose (ἐπανιστάναι) Jewish circumcision (viii 41b), rather than the reason no one resists (ἀντιστά-ναι) the Jews (9:2).[79]

---

[79] Note further that in viii 42 γάρ is removed (from LXX 9:3, "For the governors . . . were honoring the Jews, because the fear of Mordecai came upon them."). This avoids crediting the governors with the gentiles' fear of the Jews (mentioned in the previous sentence) and thus,

The elimination of gentile circumcision could be a cautious response to gentile opposition to Jewish proselytism, an attitude that was always present but became severe at certain periods. For example, the edict of Antoninus Pius (ca. 140 CE) exacted severe penalties from Jews who circumcised gentiles (Avi-Yonah 1984:145). The notion of Jews circumcising themselves, though some have thought it "absurd" (thus Clines, p. 81), makes good sense in the Hellenistic-Roman period (as Clines concedes on p. 189), when hellenizing Jews avoided circumcision while those who practiced it were likely to suffer persecution.

9.6. *Mordecai's and Haman's "naming"* (viii 43). By interlacing new words in the LXX sentence (9:4), the AT produces a quite different sense from the LXX, which for its part preserves only the gist of the MT.

LXX:	AT:
προσέπεσεν γὰρ τὸ πρόσταγμα τοῦ βασιλέως ὀνομασθῆναι	καὶ προσέπεσεν ἐν Σούσποις ὀνομασθῆναι Αμαν καὶ τοὺς ἀντικειμένους
ἐν πάσῃ τῇ βασιλείᾳ	ἐν πάσῃ βασιλείᾳ)
For the edit of the king	And it happened in Susa
was in force, that he	that Haman and the opponents
[sc., Mordecai] be renowned	throughout the kingdom
throughout the kingdom.	were named.[80]

The AT seems to mean that as the Persian officials came to honor the Jews and fear Mordecai (viii 42), Haman and his allies became notorious —"named" as a byword for disgrace. Perhaps the redactor felt that Mordecai's prestige was adequately stated in vs. 42 and now wished to bring out the obverse, namely Haman's disgrace.

9.7. *The etymology of Purim* (viii 49). The AT's explanation of the name of Purim differs from the LXX's while maintaining its wording as much as possible. The LXX says that the holiday was named after "the lots," which, as in the MT, must refer to Haman's lots, since these are the only ones mentioned.

---

indirectly, for the Jewish circumcision. As in viii 30, the redactor is careful to preserve Jewish self-sufficiency in religious decisions.

[80] The verse is ambiguous. Taking "in Susa" as a modifier of "to be named" makes it appear that Haman was named only in Susa, which is puzzling. On the other hand, it is difficult to construe "in Susa" as a modifier of "it happened," because it is unclear why the "naming" of Haman and the "opponents" in the entire kingdom should be restricted to Susa. Apparently the idea is that they became an abomination to government circles.

The AT, however, explains the name Purim (φουραια[81]) as deriving from lots "that fell upon these days as a memorial," implying that they were cast after the event with the purpose of fixing the days of the celebration.

9.8. *The events of Adar.* The redactor has a different notion of what ensued upon Haman's undoing and what occurred in Adar.

In the LXX, Haman's scheme both begins and founders in Nisan, the first month of the twelfth year of Artaxerxes (as the king is called in the LXX): The scribes are summoned and Haman's decree is issued on 13 Nisan (3:12);[82] Mordecai's decree is issued on 23 Nisan (8:9).[83] The fighting breaks out on 13 Adar, eleven months later (9:1). The Jews fight in the provinces on the 13th of Adar and in Susa on the 13th and 14th. The celebrations take place on the 14th in the provinces and on the 15th in Susa.

The AT is much vaguer about the dates of events and does not say when the plot was initiated. R-AT does not supply from the LXX dates absent in the proto-AT—the king's feast in year iii (1:3) and Esther's marriage in year vii (2:16). Thus he maintains (perhaps carelessly) the proto-AT's fixing of 13 Adar as the date set for the pogrom by Haman's lots ("Adar-Nisan" in iv 7; "Adar" in viii 38)—contrary to the LXX's *14* Adar (3:7). However, R-AT uses LXX's 14 Adar in iv 18 (*//* B 6), thus carrying over its inconsistency in this regard. The AT gives no further dates of events, except to specify 14–15 Adar as days of celebration (viii 30, 47). In other words, R-AT makes no attempt to improve the proto-AT's vagueness about the dating or to correct the LXX's inconsistency as to the date of the pogrom.[84] As a result, the redacted AT

[81] There are several spellings of this word in the Greek versions. The correct LXX reading is φρουραι (Jos. *Ant.* XI 295 has φρουραιοι). The other LXX variants are influenced by the Hebrew or Aramaic name for Purim or are corruptions in uncials (Hanhart, p. 101). The best AT reading is φουραια (392). The other spellings—φουρδια (93), φαραια (319) and φουρμαια (19–108) are clearly inner-Greek corruptions (ibid.). As Wellhausen (1903:143) recognized, the reading φουρδια is a corruption of φουραια, which was a correction toward the Hebrew (or Aramaic). Although R-AT did not use the MT, he would certainly have known the Hebrew or Aramaic pronunciation of the holiday's name.

[82] The text says only that the scribes are summoned on 13 Nisan, but since everything is done in a great rush, we may picture the letters going forth that day or very soon afterwards.

[83] The MT gives 23 Sivan for the writing of the counter-decree (8:9). In the Massoretic sequence, events begin in a rush and then slow down inexplicably. Mordecai responds immediately upon the publication of the decree on 13 Nisan (3:12), Esther goes to the king three days later (5:1), and Haman is denounced the following day. Thereupon follows a puzzling delay of over two months before the scribes are assembled to write the counter-decree on 23 Sivan (8:9), but once it is written, it is published in great haste (8:14). The LXX eliminates the first gap while widening the one between the decrees and their fulfillment.

[84] The dating of the planned pogrom in Adar in the Greek tradition is problematic, as the following comparison shows:

vs.	MT	LXX	OL	Jos	AT
3:7	–	14	14	–	13 (iv 7)
3:13	13	–[a]	–	–	–

assumes its own time-frame. This new time-frame may not be an entirely intentional creation, but we can nevertheless describe it as it would appear to a reader acquainted with the AT alone.

For the year of Haman's plot, the only dates in the AT are 13 *and* 14 Adar for the Jews' annihilation (iv 7; iv 18) and 14–15 Adar for the thanksgiving celebration. In the absence of any further dating, the events of this year are most naturally read as a sequence without major gaps. Haman spins his plot, determines the date of execution as 13 (14) Adar, and has the edict published. The counter-plot begins immediately, and within a few days his scheme is stymied. There is no suggestion of a long hiatus between Haman's downfall and the slaughter of the Jews' enemies (viii 44). The first wave of slaughter ensues immediately (viii 20–21), because in the AT the battle is not a response to a pogrom and does not have to await the attack. A second and third wave of slaughter come not long after Mordecai's appearance in glory (viii 39), which for its part seems to occur right after the issuance of the king's letter.

B 6	–	14	14	14	14 (iv 18)
8:12	13	13	14	–	–
E 20	–	13	14	13	–[b]
9:1	13	13	13?	13	–
9:17	13	13[c]	13?	13	–
viii 38	–	–	–	–	13 (viii 38)

[a]Mss 59, the hexaplaric MSS 58 and 583, and OL[L] read the 14th. Its omission in the main LXX tradition may be harmonistic.

[b]AT does *not*, contrary to Hanhart (ad loc.) and the remarks of several commentators, support the OL reading. The AT does refer to 14 Adar, but only as a day of celebration, and mentions the 15th as well.

[c]LXX-S (prima manus) adds the 14th.

In spite of the confusion, the versions do seem to witness to a tradition setting the pogrom on 14 Adar—one partially preserved in the LXX but obscured by incomplete adjustment toward the MT. Fritzsche (p. 87) explains this vacillation as evidence of uncertainty in dating the event and of a lack of a unified redaction. Schneider (1962–63:206–207) argues that the 14th, with the 15th as accessory, was the "more original" date. But his arguments for this are tortuous and require an affirmation of an "historical kernel" preserved in the text of the decrees in the OL-Greek tradition at the expense of the indisputably earlier MT.

In fact, the MT in Esther 9 seems to be reconciling two traditions of the date of Purim by combining them. The chapter is an extended argument for celebrating Purim on two days. Its reasoning entails introducing a second day of fighting, which is done rather artificially in 9:12–13. Hence the dating of the fighting on 14 Adar may indeed reflect a variant practice, though not necessarily a "more original" one. The dating on the 13th in AT iv 7, which was based on neither the MT nor the LXX, shows that R-MT found this tradition in the text he received. Hence the presumably original Greek reading of 14 Adar in various places shows an adjustment, either in the LXX or its vorlage, toward a local tradition. Perhaps, however, no tradition lies behind this dating. Rather, the LXX translator was accustomed to Hellenic celebrations falling on the same day as the battle, and simply adjusted the date of the battles to the date of the Purim celebrations (thus Bickerman 1951:116).

The proto-AT locates the pogrom on 13 Adar; the dating on the 14th in B 6 is taken mechanically from the LXX.

It is not clear when this all happens, except that it must take place well *before* 13 Adar, for Haman's edict had to be distributed throughout the kingdom. In Add E, the king speaks of the danger as past but sees the celebration as lying in the future.[85] This implies that Haman was overthrown and numerous enemies were killed well before 13 Adar. Mordecai writes his first epistle immediately after the king issues his (viii 33-38, proto-AT). For Mordecai too the danger is past. Rather than ordering the Jews to prepare for battle, he tells them to stay home and celebrate. After writing his letter, he appears in glory (viii 38–39), the Jews circumcise themselves, and two more massacres ensue (first of a specified group [viii 43–44], and then of whomever the Jews wish to kill and plunder [viii 46]). Afterwards, Mordecai writes a second epistle instructing the Jews to celebrate "these days . . . the fourteenth and the fifteenth [of Adar]" (viii 47).

On reading the AT alone, then, one would probably picture the events from the initiation of Haman's plot through to the massacres of the Jews' enemies as occurring well before the celebrations of 14-15 Adar.

However the events are to be dated, it is clear that in the AT no *pogrom*—not even a battle—takes place in Adar. The LXX's dating of the battles on 13 Adar (9:1) is omitted. Haman's lots had pointed to 13 Adar, but the scheme does not even reach the point of an attempted pogrom. And although Mordecai says that Haman *had planned* to kill the Jews on the 13th (viii 38), that day need not have arrived at the time he is writing. In the AT, the Jews are not said to be "standing up for their lives"—that issue has been resolved. The slaughter is rather a matter of "punishing" [χολάσαι] the enemies (viii 18). The Jews massacre many of these enemies in viii 20–21—before the king's and Mordecai's epistles are issued—and afterwards they kill another 700, plus Haman's sons, in Susa (viii 44). Then Esther asks permission for the Jews to kill and plunder *whomever* they wish, whereupon they slaughter an additional 70,100 (viii 46). All these actions are a series of punishments inflicted upon the Jews' enemies.

To be sure, the king's epistle (Add E) does speak of future Jewish self-defense, and this might be thought to imply that a day of reckoning still lies ahead (viii 29-30 // E 19–20). But this passage, though staying close to the wording of the LXX, seems to have a different meaning in the AT:

AT	LXX
(29) Let the copy of the epistle be issued in every place	(19) The copy of this epistle [is to be] issued in every place

---

[85] He says that "the All-Ruling One made for them salvation and joy on those days" (viii 30). God's "making" is in the past [ἐποίησεν], for the issue is already decided, but the fulfillment of God's action is yet to come. In other words, by the act of salvation that has already occurred, God has determined that those days will be joyful, but these are not the days on which he *created* their joy. The LXX uses the same form of the same verb for God's action, and there it is unambiguous that both the salvation and the celebration lie ahead.

so that the Jews may act
in accordance with their
own laws and prevail
[ἐπισχύειν] by them,
so that they may defend
themselves against those
who assail (them) in
time of affliction.
(30) And it has been decided
by all the Jews throughout the
kingdom to celebrate the 14th
of the month of Adar, etc.
(See §10.2 for continuation.)

publicly, to allow the Jews to act
in accordance with their
own customs, (20) and to give aid
[συνεπισχύειν] to them,
so that they may defend
themselves against those
who assail them in
(the) time of affliction,

[namely,] on the 13th of the
12th month, that is, Adar, on the
aforementioned day.

The LXX defines the "time of affliction" as 13 Adar; the AT does not (thus I supply the article in translating ἐν καιρῷ θλίψεως in the LXX but not in the AT). Indeed, after Esther's intercession in the AT there is no specific "time of affliction" lying ahead, not even the danger of one. In the AT, the mention of a "time of affliction" sounds like an indefinite reference to whatever tribulation may henceforth befall the Jews. The message is that the Jews' obedience to their laws enables them to withstand future dangers.

The prefix-variant ἐπισχύειν for συνεπισχύειν may serve the change of meaning. συνεπισχύειν means "to assist, join in supporting," with the recipient of the assistance in the dative; cf. 2 Chr 32:3 (translating 'āzar) and Symmachus to Jer 5:31 (translating yirdû; the LXX uses ἐπεκρότησαν). Ἐπισχύειν (according to Liddell & Scott, p. 663b) means "to make strong" and (in the one case quoted there) governs the accusative. But it is also used intransitively, meaning "be or grow strong(er)" (1 Mac 6:6; Luke 23:5). The AT is best understood to mean "and to grow strong" or "prevail" by them, sc. by their laws. In the LXX, then, the sentence means that the gentiles should let the Jews follow their own customs and should also support them in the coming battle. The final clause (introduced by ὅπως) is consequent upon the preceding infinitive, which refers to the aid the gentiles give the Jews. The AT's point, on the other hand, is that the Jews should obey their own laws and be strengthened (or "prevail") by them, so that they can meet whatever trials lie ahead.

9.9. Slaughtered enemies. The LXX names Haman's ten sons, who are executed by the Jews (9:7–10). (Most LXX manuscripts have 10 names; LXX-B has 11.) The AT understands the six slaughtered enemies named in viii 44b to be men other than Haman's sons. The names in the AT seem to be graphic variants, if not deliberate distortions, of the Septuagintal forms of the barbarous-sounding names (which themselves vary in the MSS): Φαρσαν // Φαρσαννεσταιν; (τὸν) ἀδελφὸν (αὐτοῦ) // Δελφων; Φαρνα // Φασγα;

Γαγαφαρδαθα // Φαρδαθα; Μαρμασαιμα // Μαρμασιμ; Ιζαθουθ // Ζαβουθαῖον. The Jews *also* kill Haman's 10 sons (viii 44c). The additional καὶ is significant: Since R-AT has only six persons in the preceding list, he cannot identify the named casualties with Haman's 10 sons. But it is not clear why R-AT does not import all 10 or 11 names from the LXX.

9.10. *Spoil.* In the redacted AT (viii 44)—as in the LXX but contrary to the MT (9:10)—the Jews do take spoil. The LXX, which reads "and they plundered all that was theirs" (sc., the enemies'), undoubtedly lost a negative through copyist error, since it has a negative in 9:15, which speaks of 14 Adar, and there would be no point for the Jews to take spoil one day but refrain the next. R-AT's LXX vorlage too must have lacked the negative in 9:10, for he adds "all that was theirs" at the end of viii 44. This phrase restricts the scope of the booty-taking by making "they plundered" apply specifically to the property of Haman's sons and possibly of the six previously-named enemies as well.

Perhaps puzzled by Esther's petition in 9:13 to "hang" (κρεμάσαι) Haman's dead sons,[86] and having learned from LXX 9:10 that plunder is acceptable, R-AT changes Esther's petition to a request to kill *and plunder* at will (viii 46a).

9.11. *The two days of Purim.* The distinction between Susan Purim and provincial Purim is a major point of interest in the MT, and it is carried over to the LXX. The narrative in LXX 9:11–19 is schematically developed to establish this distinction, which is then carefully enjoined and confirmed in vss. 20–31. This distinction is lost in the AT.

In the AT (viii 46), unlike the LXX (9:13), Esther does not mention a second day of slaughter,[87] but only asks that the Jews be allowed to kill and plunder whomever they wish. The LXX's elaborate reports on the fighting, the body counts, and the two days of respite as the etiology of the two days of celebration (9:14–19) are all condensed into one sentence (viii 46b, based on 9:16b): "And they destroyed 70,100 men." Since R-AT interprets the point of 9:13–19 to be the extension of Jewish vengeance, he shows this to be fulfilled by raising the body-count from 15,000 to 70,100.

AT still has two days of celebration (14–15 Adar: viii 47b), but the redactor has left no historical rationale for the timing, nor has he assigned the days to different locales. In the AT, neither day has its own historical anchor.

---

[86] In the MT the request probably refers to impalement [Hebrew *TLH*] and exposure of the corpses, since it is clear that they are already dead.

[87] In the MT she limits her request to Susa. Though this restriction does not appear in the LXX, the following two verses presume that Susa was the scene of fighting on the second day.

The loss of the Susan/provincial distinction, so important in the MT and the LXX, was very likely occasioned by a lessening of interest. Whereas the MT (and LXX) seems to be sorting out an issue of current contention and offering a compromise between two rival claims as to the correct date of Purim, for R-AT the matter no longer requires argumentation. He makes do with a brief statement that the Jews are to "establish (στῆσαι) these days for song and rejoicing instead of sadness and mourning—the fourteenth and the fifteenth" (viii 47b). R-AT does not distinguish between the two days of celebration. The MT, at least in 9:19, certainly does so, although 9:21, 27, 28 might be understood as enjoining two days' festivities everywhere.[88] The LXX has a different understanding. The Jews living dispersed in the provincial territories (ἐν πάσῃ χώρᾳ τῇ ἔξω) celebrate the fourteenth (9:19a), while— according to a sentence not present in the MT—". . . those who dwelt in the major cities (ταῖς μητροπόλεσιν) celebrate also [καί] the fifteenth of Adar as a joyous holiday, sending portions to (their) neighbors" (9:19b).[89] Although this addition applies the two days of celebration only to Jews in the major cities, it also blurs the distinction between the two types of habitation: on the 14th all are celebrating, while only the city-Jews celebrate the 15th. Without a clear separation drawn in 9:19, the ambiguous statements in 9:21, 27, and 28 are most naturally read as enjoining two days' celebration upon Jews everywhere. R-AT composed an abbreviated version that avoids the niceties and simply states that all Jews are to celebrate the fourteenth and fifteenth of Adar.

9.12. *The people's role.* The AT differs from its predecessors in its notion of how Purim came to be a perpetual and obligatory holiday.

One senses from MT's lengthy, repeated, and argumentative discussion of the institution of the holiday that its status was at first problematic, since it was neither codified in law nor instituted by divine command. The MT's

---

[88] E.g., Paton (pp. 58, 293), who believes that there is a contradiction between 9:21–23 and 9:19 and that this demonstrates different authorship.

The halacha in M. *Megillah* 1:1 distinguishes two different days of celebration. In my view this is correct, because the distinction of localities, sharply drawn in v. 19 as well as in the preceding narrative, shows that the "two days of Purim" (9:27) refers to two separate one-day celebrations. Even a later supplementer (if 9:20–32 is indeed to be attributed to one) would have realized that his own restatement of the celebration would be understood in the light of the distinction drawn in 9:1–19.

Moore (1971:89) thinks that 9:19 is a gloss contradicting 9:21–22 (similarly Meinhold p. 87). But the distinction that 9:19 draws is anticipated in 9:13–18 by the emphasis on the distinctiveness of the events in Susa. As Bardtke observes, the elimination of 9:17–19 would leave the Purim ordinance of 9:20–23 without any basis.

[89] This is omitted in LXX-B (text) as well as in most hexaplaric witnesses but is reflected in Jos. (*Ant.* XI 292) and is almost certainly original in the LXX; see Hanhart pp. 72–73.

response was to relate a process of *confirmation,* designated by the key-word *qayyēm,* "confirm" (see ch. II, §7.4). The holiday is institutionalized through a lengthy and deliberate dialectic between leadership and community. The LXX replicates the MT's detailing of the process, but with the omission of MT 9:30–31a.

Nearly all this process—which is arguably the essence of MT-Esther—has disappeared in the AT. It was never a part of the proto-AT, and R-AT removes it from the material he transfers, skipping almost all of LXX 9:22–31, namely the confirmations and acceptance of the holiday.

In the present AT, Mordecai first writes the Jews to stay at home and celebrate (viii 34; proto-AT); these instructions precede any spontaneous rejoicing. Later he writes them to "keep" (στῆσαι) the 14th and 15th as days of hymns and happiness (viii 47; R-AT). This is an authoritative order and calls for no confirmation or acceptance on the people's part. στῆσαι is taken from the LXX, where it is an etymological translation of *qayyēm.* In the AT it cannot mean "to confirm," since the Jews do not do that. Here it means "to maintain," for maintenance alone, and not a validation of Mordecai's call, is incumbent upon the people.

Since the Jews need not confirm the holiday, they do not (contrary to LXX 9:23) "accept" (προσδέχεσθαι) Mordecai's instructions. By removing most of 9:22a and 23, the redactor splices καὶ προσεδέξαντο to the end of 22b and makes it the predicate of "the poor," thereby excluding the notion that the Jews had the option of accepting—and thus of rejecting—Mordecai's call to institute the celebration (AT viii 48).

The concept of the festival as an injunction from above is not contradicted by Add E, where R-AT has the king report that it was decided (ἐκρίθη) by the Jews to celebrate the 14th and 15th of Adar (viii 30). This verse is not the narrator explaining the origin of the celebration in his own voice, but rather the gentile king's summary of what he sees happening among the Jews. From his perspective, the Jews as a community have come to a decision. He does not realize that this decision was an imposition of authority or that the date was set by lot (viii 49), which is to say, by divine decision.

10. *Ideology*

Some of R-AT's modifications express and promote religious and social attitudes. That is not to say that the redaction is heavily rhetorical—the redactor does not impose fundamentally new religious or political attitudes on the text. Most of the changes, even those that reflect an interpretive difference, are devoid of an ideological slant. Nevertheless, some changes do have ideological weight. Particularly significant are cases where several distinct changes combine to convey the redactor's own beliefs about the holiday, the Jews, and the world. Overall the redactor tends to emphasize the positive, giving affirmative meaning to the elements of the celebration and the events behind it. The following description deals with the ideological innovations directly resulting from the redactor's work, deferring until ch. III (§3) the ideology of the new book as a whole.

10.1. *Attitudes towards gentiles*

The redactor makes the world of the story a less hostile place. Gentiles are not fundamentally inimical to Jews.

In Add A, R-AT does not envision all the nations gathering to attack the "nation of the righteous" (A 6 // i 6). The gentiles are themselves endangered by the forces of evil. There is no simple dichotomy between "every nation" and the "righteous nation." In the AT, Israel's enemies are more clearly circumscribed. There are, to be sure, malevolent nations in the AT (cf. viii 54b), but these are certain nations, not all of them.

The main difference between Israel and the nations consists not in the Jews' righteousness — they are not called the "nation of the righteous" or "the righteous nation" in the AT (contrast LXX A 6, 7). They differ in their *knowledge of God:* Israel knows how to call upon the Lord in time of danger (i 6).

The gentile king is pictured favorably, even more so than in the LXX. R-AT makes the king a monotheist who calls Israel's God the "sole and true God" (viii 27).

In line with this reduced suspicion toward the gentiles, the redactor describes the salvation not as the judgment (LXX κρίσις; F 8) of all the nations but as God's mastery or rule (κυριεύσις) over them (viii 56).

10.2. *The institution of Purim*

The sharpest and most significant ideological shifts by R-AT concern the process that established Purim as an annual celebration. The AT distances the holiday from unpleasantness — the battles of 13–14 Adar and Haman's plot generally —, emphasizes the autonomy of the Jews in the decision to establish a holiday, and removes the dialectic between leadership and community.

In the AT, the bloodshed is not specifically dated to 13 or 14 Adar (see §9.8). Though willing enough to report massacres and even to increase the body-count, the redactor does not allow the killings to determine the dating or nature of Purim. The holiday does not celebrate these killings — which in the AT are royally authorized punishments — or even the respite from them (as in the MT), but rather the earlier triumph over Haman and the defeat of his plot.

The redactor, as noted, removes Haman's taint from Purim by having its date determined not by his lots, but by the Jews themselves. In Add E, R-AT has the king announce (in the continuation of the passage quoted in §9.8):

> And it has been decided by the Jews throughout the kingdom to celebrate
> the fourteenth of the month of Adar and to hold festival on the fifteenth,
> for in them the Almighty made for them salvation and joy. (viii 30)

These days were chosen, as we learn later, by lots cast for that purpose
(viii 49); these may be an earthly counterpart of lots that *God* had cast.

In his interpretation of his dream, Mordecai refers obscurely to two lots
that God made, one for Israel and one for the nations (viii 55) and continues:

> And these two lots came forward at the right time to the hours and days
> [προσῆλθον[90] ... εἰς ὥρας κατὰ καιρὸν καὶ ἡμέρας] of the Eternal One's gain-
> ing mastery (κυριεύσεως) among all the nations (viii 56).

The LXX speaks of the "hour" and "day" in the singular; R-AT changes them
to the plural. What are these "hours" and "days"? They are not specifically
13–14 Adar, since those dates are not mentioned in the AT (iv 7 refers only
to the 13th of "Adar-Nisan," and that was only the date that Haman's lots
designated). Nor are they likely to be an indefinite period during which the
Jews slaughtered their enemies, because κατὰ καιρόν (not in the LXX)
suggests specificity. Most likely, the "hours" and "days" are the *14–15* Adar,
which are here described as the times of God's "gaining mastery." The two-
day holiday is then the celebration of God's rule — *over the nations* as well as
over Israel.

The departures from the LXX in viii 29–30, 41–42 [i.e. the omission of 9:1],
49 (∥ E 19–21; 8:17; 9:26), which are not merely omissions of redundancies,
show that the shift of emphasis from Haman and his plot is deliberate. The
festival is solely God's and Israel's doing. For R-AT, Adar, the month of
celebration, must not be contaminated by association with Haman's lots or
darkened by commemoration of Jewish suffering and peril. Nor can the date
of the holiday be chosen by idolatrous divination. The 14th and 15th of Adar
is solely a time of happiness and success, a celebration undertaken and
defined by the Jews and their God alone.

The autonomy of the Jewish action is further protected by keeping the
king, friendly though he may be, at a certain distance. The redactor accordingly eliminates LXX E 22, in which the king orders the Jews to celebrate
their deliverance as a special day among their festivals. In the AT, the king
merely gives recognition to the Jews' decision.

The Jewish decision does not, however, belong to the community as a
whole. The redactor removes almost the entire passage in which both leadership and community undertake to keep the celebration and confirm it several
times (LXX 9:22–31). In the MT and the LXX, this process is required by the
holiday's uncertain legal status. In those versions, authority is vested in the
community as well in its leadership, and the full and free agreement of both

---

[90] The phrase (κλῆροι) προσῆλθον is difficult. Apparently it implies that the lots were cast in
advance and that what they had decided was realized at exactly the predetermined time.

is needed to validate an innovation such as a new holiday. For the AT, in contrast, an edict from the Jewish national leader (a sort of exilarch) establishes the new practice, with the date being determined by lots that ascertain God's will.

11. *The redactor's treatment of his sources*

By interweaving two texts and modifying them in the ways described above, the redactor has created a new text. We now focus on the nature of that creativity: the type of activity that constituted it (§11.1), the limitations of such redaction (§11.2), and the redactor's attitudes toward his texts (§11.3).

11.1. *Type of redaction*

R-AT created the AT primarily by *supplementation*, that is, by drawing material from a donor text to fill in gaps perceived in the parallel receptor text.

Supplementation should be distinguished, at least in theory, from *expansion*, in which a redactor (or a series of scribes and redactors) *creates* the additional material that is worked into the receptor text. This is a common and well-recognized practice, discernible, among other places, in MT-Samuel and Jeremiah (though some MT pluses might be truly Jeremianic). A fairly certain example of expansion is the MT of the David and Goliath story in 1 Sam 17–18 (as described by Tov 1985a). Here the shorter LXX text allows us to extract an earlier version from the expansions, which do not in themselves form a continuous narrative. LXX-Esther is also expansionistic in this sense, at least for Adds B-F (Add A may first have existed independently of Esther; see §9.1.7).

Supplementation should also be distinguished from *conflation*, in which two parallel versions are interlaced in such a way as to preserve the essentials of both (as happened, according to classical source-analysis, in the Flood story). Supplementation, by contrast, makes use of *some* material from the donor text to "correct" presumed gaps in the receptor text without trying to represent the donor text in its entirety.

As a supplementer, R-AT was perforce a copyist, transferring material from the LXX into the MS he was working on. Talmon (1975) has shown that the same techniques used in the formative stages of literary creativity continue to influence manuscript transmission in its later stages, down to and including simple copying. These techniques are (1) stylistic and textual interchangeability of words; (2) stylistic metathesis and textual inversion, and (3) stylistic and textual conflation.

Since R-AT was a copyist as well as a redactor (as all redactors probably were), it is not surprising that his work has much in common with manuscript transmission (see Table VI). Two of the features Talmon lists, (1) interchange-ability of words and (2) textual inversion, are prominent in R-AT's work. As for (3) conflation, there may be conflations of the LXX and proto-AT in miscellaneous verses, but in the absence of an independent witness to proto-AT it is impossible to verify this. Other modifications of the sorts made by R-AT appear in manuscript copying as well: additions, omissions, transpo-sitions, non-synonym interchanges and (not tallied here) minor grammatical changes.

Inasmuch as R-AT was also a redactor, creating a new version of the Esther story from earlier materials, it is not surprising that his interventions are far more extensive and bold than in most manuscript copying. Whereas most minuses in such copying are unintentional, most of R-AT's are deliberate and rarely explicable as mechanical lapses. His pluses, though mostly minor glosses and fillings of the sort that appear in manuscript transmission, are often complete sentences communicating new ideas and attitudes. He is situated near the middle of the continuum running from mechanical repro-duction to creative authorship.

11.2. *Rough spots*

The resulting AT text is not quite smooth and consistent. A careful exami-nation reveals contradictions and difficulties at certain points of the narrative.

11.2.1. In the LXX, 9:24 mentions Haman's lots, and 9:26 refers back to them as the reason for the name of Purim. The AT (viii 49a), using the LXX's wording, says, "Because of this [διὰ τοῦτο] these days were called Phouraia." But R-AT has eliminated Haman's lots from this passage (when he omitted almost all of 9:22–25) and so has deprived this sentence of a prior reason to which διὰ τοῦτο can refer.

11.2.2. In the LXX, Add E appropriately gives in full the text of the decree that has just been issued. The AT imports the text of the decree from the LXX, although in the AT none has been issued. The redactor artificially splices the king's letter into the preceding text by means of the statement "And he wrote the following epistle" (viii 22). This royal epistle is a counter-decree and unnecessary by the proto-AT's presuppositions; it consequently lacks an integral role in the redacted AT as well. Moreover, the narrative logic is flawed because the Jews have already begun slaughtering their enemies "in great number" (viii 20), and there is no point in having the king only now order his subjects to ignore Haman's demands. The redactor does, however, avoid a gross contradiction by removing the king's reference to the specific date on which the Jews will be attacked (E 20).

11.2.3. The king's statement in viii 30 (Add E), that the Jews have decided to celebrate 14 and 15 Adar, is premature, since they so decide only after Mordecai calls upon them to do so, in viii 47b. Seeking to change the meaning of the days mentioned in Add E from battle to celebration, the redactor retrojects the decision anachronistically.

11.2.4. The Jews kill Haman's sons in viii 44 (in a redactional section), even though according to viii 37 (proto-AT), Haman's "house," which surely includes his sons, has already been executed (διαχεχειρίσθαι).

11.2.5. The understanding of the *river* in the interpretation of Mordecai's dream cannot be reconciled with the role of the river in the dream itself. In Add A (i 7), the river grows out of the little spring (identified as Esther in Add F: viii54 // F 3) and is a source of salvation. In Add F, however, it represents hostile nations (viii 54b). Perhaps the redactor was puzzled by the LXX's lack of a symbol for the gathering nations and so created one by transferring ποταμός from an earlier sentence in the LXX (F 3) ("The river is Esther, whom the king married"). When R-AT reaches Add F, he reworks *the Septuagint's* Add F with little attention to his own version of Add A. However, the awkwardness of the construction in viii 54 (ποταμὸς τὰ ἔθνη . . .) may point to a textual problem within the AT.

11.2.6. There is also a contradiction *within* the proto-AT: viii 37 says that Haman was hanged at the gates of Susa, yet the king earlier agreed to have him hanged in his own courtyard (viii 12–13).[91] This contradiction may be a slip on the part of the original author, but it may also have resulted from the interference of the redactor, who possibly imported "at the gates of Susa" from E 18 (into viii 28); see §5.3 (j).

The cause of all these incongruities and tensions, except for the last-mentioned item, seems to be that the redactor is concentrating on whatever section he is currently transcribing, focusing especially on the material he is importing from the LXX. Since he takes the proto-AT for granted while scrutinizing the LXX to see what is lacking, the latter is what holds most of his attention. He is attending to the contents of the LXX more than to the details of the receptor-text or the coherence of the end-product. Evidently the new text's literary virtues were not as important as its completeness.

The rough spots are important. The redactor did not smooth over them, and neither should we. Recognition of the literary and logical tensions in the redacted AT may counterbalance the tendency, strong though not always

---

[91] It would be harmonistic to posit that Haman's house was next to the gate. Even if it were, "at the gate" would not be a natural way to describe a private courtyard.

deliberate — among both redaction and literary critics — to ascribe to redactors too high a degree of control over the literary movement and logical organization of the text.[92] This tendency, as J. Barton has observed (1984: 57–58), can result in the "disappearing redactor": the more one reveals the redactor's artistry in producing a simple and coherent text from diverse sources, the more one reduces the evidence for the existence of the sources. But the redactor under study here is far from disappearing behind his work, because he does not achieve, and does not seem to be striving for, the sort of coherence, consistency, and organization that literary scholars deem vital qualities.

A redactor who is supplementing one text from another or merging two texts is likely to leave behind traces of his activity: contradictions and tensions, non-functional narrative gaps, overlaps, awkward transitions and the like — features of the sort that made it possible to distinguish the Pentateuchal sources. The artistry of a redactor must be evaluated in terms of goals appropriate to the particular redaction, such as the maximal preservation of traditions, the harmonization of different versions of the "same" stories, and the communication and validation of new ideologies in old vehicles.

11.3. R-AT's goals and his attitudes towards his texts

We can deduce R-AT's goals from his procedure and his achievement. Since his primary activity was to supplement the receptor text, he clearly felt that it lacked something. His work, then, is most appropriately described and evaluated in terms of *completeness*. Rather than employing microanalysis to detect *Stichwörter*, word-patterns, motif sequencing, hierarchic designs, and the like, we should look at what the redactor himself obviously cared about. We should give our attention first to the gross features of the new work: the broad religious concepts supplied in the lacunae that *he* perceived in the receptor text, the new ideology communicated by the new array of components, and the factual and conceptual substance produced by changes in wording.

Even though the redactor's procedure of supplementation was largely mechanical, it is fair to assume that he recognized and intended the major effects that the combination produced. For example, since he thought it necessary to add the prayers of Add C to Mordecai's and Esther's other

---

[92] To give one example among many: R. Alter, who has had a considerable impact on studies of the Bible as literature, almost always seems able to find aesthetic and thematic structuring — formal symmetry, *Leitwörter*, and the like, in almost any narrative. When he cannot find it, he maintains that literary coherence is present but hidden. For passages that "seem to resist any harmonizing interpretation," he suggests two possibilities: that transmission and editing could sometimes lead to "intrinsic incoherence" *or* that "the biblical notion of what constituted a meaningful and unified narrative continuum might at times be unfathomable" because of our temporal and cultural distance from the texts. Alter prefers the latter alternative (1981:133).

actions, he had an image of the two protagonists as pious Jews and wished to bring that quality to the fore.

Observation of R-AT's working procedure allows us a glimpse into not only his religious ideology, but also his attitudes toward the *texts* he was working from and toward. The proto-AT is the text being redacted. This is what he takes as his basis, working the LXX into it and, as far as we can tell, rarely altering its wording. (Alterations would probably, though not necessarily, show greater conformity to the LXX.) R-AT is therefore creating a *version of the AT*—a supplemented AT rather than a supplemented LXX. The AT is authoritative and is to be transmitted; it is not enough simply to make another copy of the LXX.

On the other hand, neither is the proto-AT self-sufficient. It tells the truth but not the whole truth. The redactor looks to the LXX to fill in the gaps in the proto-AT. So the LXX too is authoritative, and a book of Esther that lacked significant material present in the LXX would be inadequate for this redactor. In fact, the greater authority was not the receptor text but the donor text, for *it* is the standard of adequacy, and *its* ideology is, for the most part, what the redactor ends up imposing. The redacted AT is the result of the interplay between two versions that are authoritative yet have not attained a degree of fixity that precludes adjustments in either.

The redactor omits material from the Septuagintal transfers far more often than he adds to them (see Table V). The sparsity of additions to the transfers suggests a redactor who hesitates to "create" material, to add large innovations to authoritative text, but who rather seeks to mine an authoritative source. He will add words and sentences as necessary to make the receptor text conform to his idea of the holiday's meaning and development. He also introduces new ideas (though he might not have recognized their essential newness) by using the wording of the LXX, sometimes by cutting-and-splicing the donor text. I assume that this latter technique is not a game,[93] but reflects a serious attitude toward the text—namely, the conviction that the material of the donor text is authoritative and that a new idea gains in stature by using its words as building-blocks. But this is a device, not a rule; the redactor certainly felt free to substitute synonyms and even non-synonyms.

Synonym substitution is very common in both redaction and textual transmission. Sometimes the synonyms update or simplify the text; often, however, they have no apparent motivation. Non-synonym substitution is less conservative and shows that to some extent even the material of the text—its wording—was fluid.

The redactor's imprint is visible in all the redactional sections, but not in the same way in each; no single section has the most occurrences of all kinds of change. AT-end, where omissions are most frequent, has fewer additions

---

[93] Readers of *Mad* magazine will recognize the game of reversing the meaning of a text by selective quoting.

and phrase-transpositions than most of the other sections. Adds B and E, which are very conservative in additions and omissions, have more transpositions of both kinds. Add A, which is high in additions, synonym substitutions, and phrase-transpositions, is low in omissions, non-synonym substitutions, and word-transpositions. Add F is very high in additions and omissions but very low in the other kinds of change. Adds C and D, as well as D +, tend toward the middle in all types of change. One gets the picture of a redactor whose willingness to make changes is counterbalanced by a hesitation to disturb his donor text too much, so that when making many changes of one sort, he reins himself in on changes of other sorts.

Omissions in particular throw light on the redactor's mentality. The extent of the omissions in AT-end is striking; in fact, however, AT-end is not the area of greatest omission. We may say that the redactor omits *most* of the LXX, leaving out everything but the larger part of the Adds, D +, and AT-end. One might expect that in the transcription of a canonical text additions would be more frequent than omissions, because the former do not diminish the sacred text, but only supplement it with supporting material. After all, a generally valid working principle of text criticism holds that a leaner text is closer to the original; this principle is usually believed to apply, for example, to 1 Samuel and Jeremiah. The redacted AT shows that a redactor could omit much of the material of the donor text.

In evaluating the redactor's changes we should, however, remember that they are not actually within the LXX itself. The transferred material is no longer the LXX, but part of a new text, the AT. The LXX, as the authoritative Greek Esther, could not have been so readily remolded in the service of a new ideology. The proto-AT, on the other hand, which by the first century CE had at most marginal status within canonical literature, could more easily be transformed so as to express the redactor's own notions and purposes. Yet the proto-AT too must have had a recognized position in the literary tradition, for the redactor chose to build upon it instead of writing his own version from scratch. Rather than ignoring the proto-AT as an inadequate, deviant text, the redactor thought it best to "correct" it, bringing it into conformity with the canonical book. He was thus coordinating two authoritative texts of a canonical book without nullifying either.[94]

The way the redactor extracts and reworks material from a text he treats as authoritative shows that he sees himself neither as a transmitter of the Septuagintal Esther nor as the creator of a new book of Esther. Rather, he seeks to create a recension of the AT that moves closer to the LXX without displacing it. Both tell the story of Esther, and the AT only needed some help to do so adequately. The redactor could "omit" text at will, because doing so means

---

[94] Sandmel, citing the Apocryphal Gospel of Hebrews and Philo's and Josephus' recasting of Abram's sojourn in Egypt, states that "while canonization can act to crystallize tradition, it does not fix it beyond change" (1961:110).

simply not using everything available, and one may always extract material from a sacred text or quote part of it. In other words, for R-AT, the LXX is truly treated as a *source*. It is available to be mined as necessary, but what *is* extracted is not to be too deeply altered. The AT is to be *aggadah*, interpretation through retelling.

In this chapter I have examined what R-AT did to his sources, in particular to material from his donor text, the LXX. The question still remains as to what he *produced* by these labors. The description of the new text will be deferred to ch. III, where I will compare the redacted AT with the redacted MT.

II

THE MASSORETIC TEXT OF ESTHER
AND ITS REDACTION

1. *Reconstructing the literary history of MT-Esther*

The Massoretic book of Esther, brief though it is, has struck many scholars as the creation of different people from different times. Some scholars believe they can isolate earlier components within the Base Narrative itself (chs. 1–8). More frequently, critics have excavated the Aftermath of the story (chs. 9–10), for layers of additions and glosses. Redactional issues—how and why components were assembled—have rarely been discussed. The notable exception is Clines (1984), who sought to trace the history of the Esther story step by step from hypothetical earlier stories to the MT (and to the LXX) and to ascertain the main intentions of each redactor who participated in this complex process.

Redaction criticism requires at least partial isolation of the source materials the redactor used. In the case of the AT, the existence of the LXX made it possible to separate two main constituents, and to inquire into how the redactor combined them (ch. I). For the MT, on the other hand, none of the donor texts is extant, so redaction criticism cannot proceed so securely. Yet we do not have to rely solely on internal criteria (contradictions, repetitions, variations in style, incongruities, and the like), because the proto-AT provides an external control. While the proto-AT is not a *source* of the MT, it does show us a collateral version of the Esther story. This external vantage-point enables us to ascertain, by a sort of triangulation, the main components of the tale underlying the MT version. This aid, together with internal criteria for identifying different levels of authorship, will help uncover the scope and nature of the redaction that produced MT–Esther, though with more conjecture and less precision than was attainable in the study of the AT redaction.

To use the AT in attempting to trace the formation of the MT is undoubtedly a bold, if not precarious, maneuver. After all, the AT exists only in four medieval Greek manuscripts. Yet the premises justifying this procedure are reasonable, namely: (a) The proto-AT can be extracted from the current form of the AT. This, I believe to have shown, can be done with some confidence (ch. I, §§2.2–10; 3).

(b) The proto-AT is not a recension of the LXX, but an independent version of the story. The arguments in ch. I §2 have made the case for this theory.

(c) The proto-AT is a translation of a Hebrew text, as was established in ch. I (§2.2, 9, 10). And since the proto-AT was written in Hebrew, it was certainly a Jewish work.

(d) The proto-AT is not a recension or midrashic reworking of MT–Esther, for it is too distant from the MT and omits themes that would have been important to a Jewish redactor — above all the establishment of Purim and the forms of its observance.

(e) As a Jewish work, the proto-AT must have been composed *prior* to MT–Esther, or at least prior to the time the latter attained widely recognized canonical status, because the proto-AT ignores some of the Massoretic version's central concerns that were also important to Jewish practice. The MT and the proto-AT are too similar to be construed as two unrelated compositions, yet the proto-AT does not derive from the MT.

It is far more difficult to establish just what their relationship is. Clines usually treats the proto-AT as a direct ancestor of the MT, but greater caution is required, since much might have changed in the proto-AT subsequent to its divergence from MT. It is safer to approach the proto-AT as a collateral relative of the MT.

The proto-AT's manifest similarities to the MT indicate that neither version has departed radically from the common ancestor, proto-Esther. But just how far away are they from the shared background? In other words, which of the proto-AT's *differentia* were present in proto-Esther? My use of the proto-AT assumes that the major *additional* themes in the MT (discussed below) were more likely absent in proto-Esther and added by R-MT (just as they were later added by R-AT to *his* receptor text) than to have been present in proto-Esther and systematically excised in the AT tradition. If, however, the proto-AT itself was indeed the ancestor of the MT, that would only strengthen the hypotheses of the present chapter. For brevity, I will speak of proto-AT as the background of the MT-Esther; this is shorthand for speaking of proto-Esther as attested in the proto-AT.

2. *Strands: the earliest components of the Esther Story*

Several scholars have claimed to be able to extricate various earlier stories or traditions that are interwoven into MT–Esther. Clines (pp. 130–38) has summarized their theories and effectively refuted most of them while incorporating elements of others into his own source division. There is no need to cover that ground again.[1] Moreover, the considerations adduced below argue against all proposed variants of the two-source theory.

---

[1] Lebram (1972) argued that an Esther *tradition* was expanded by a Mordecai tradition and Purim legislation, as well as by several redactional additions. Gerleman refutes this theory in detail in the introductions to most of the units of his Esther commentary.

Clines, in a modification of an analysis suggested by Cazelles (1961), distinguishes two hypothetical sources, a "Mordecai source" and an "Esther source" (Clines 1984:115–38). The Mordecai source was a success story that told of a conflict between two courtiers and of Mordecai's personal victory and rise to the highest office in the empire. The Esther source was a deliverance story that recounted how a Jewish woman saved her people from destruction. Clines does not convince himself that these sources once existed separately, but claims that *if* they did, they were probably as he describes them.

Such source divisions of the book of Esther are able to identify doublets (e.g., two gatherings of virgins, two royal banquets), and even to group passages into two or more narrative sequences that *could* have been independent stories. This does not, however, constitute an argument for source division, since the doublets are nowhere contradictory, and the distinction between the strands is not reinforced by differences in style and conception. The presumed sources are at most two thematic developments within the plot.

Another weakness in this separation of narrative strands is that clear echoes of the Joseph story—in phraseology, motifs, and formal-structural features—appear throughout both of the posited sources of the story. It seems far-fetched to assume that two authors, the one of the Esther source and the other of the Mordecai source, were each influenced by the Joseph story—and each one by different parts thereof. If, on the other hand, we were to set aside the passages dependent on the Joseph story by positing that they were introduced by the MT redactor, there would not be enough left of the earlier narrative to comprise two recognizable tales.

The material in Clines' two sources and the echos in the phraseology of the Joseph story are as follows, with the cases of specific dependency given in brackets[2]:

> Esther source: 2:2–4 [Esth 2:3–4 // Gen 41:34–37]; 2:5–11; 2:12–18 [Esth 2:12 // Gen 50:3 (?); Esth 2:18 // Gen 43:34]; 3:6b–15 [Esth 3:10 // Gen 41:42]; 4:1–7a, 8–17 [Esth 4:16bβ // Gen 43:14b]; 5:1–8; 7:1–8; 8:3–14 [Esth 8:6 // Gen 44:34]; 8:17.

> Mordecai source: 2:19–23; 3:1–3, 5; 5:9b–11, 13–14 [Esth 5:10 // Gen 43:31; 45:1]; 6:1–13 [Esth 6:7–11 // Gen 41:42–43]; 7:9–10a; 8:1–2 [Esth 8:2 // Gen 41:42]; 8:15–16.

---

[2] For the correspondences between the Joseph and Esther stories see Rosenthal (1895), Gan (1961), and Meinhold (1975, 1976). The latter two pointed out numerous correspondences in motifs and themes, and these too are found in both hypothetical strands. Significantly, nothing in ch. 9 echoes the Joseph story, another fact pointing to a different origin for this chapter.

Redactional or outside the sources: 1:1–22 [Esth 1:3a // Gen 40:20aβ; Esth 1:21 // Gen 41:37]; 3:4 [Esth 3:4 // Gen 39:10]; 3:6a; 4:7b (wĕ'ēt pārāšat hakkesep); 5:9a, 12; 6:14; 7:10b; (Esth 8:1–2 intertwines the two sources).

Moreover, the generic and structural dependencies of the Esther story on the Joseph story, as described by Gan (1961) and Meinhold (1976), extend through the entirety of Esther 1–8 and show that Mordecai and Esther *taken together* fill a role parallel to Joseph's.

Even if sources such as described by Clines and others did exist, they were too distant from both the proto-AT and the MT to bear directly on the interpretation of either version. The Esther story (or, strictly speaking, the proto-Esther story) would still be a literary innovation, no more constrained by its sources than, say, Shakespeare's *King Lear* was by *The True Chronicle History of King Leir*, to which it owed its plot line, or by Sidney's *Arcadia*, to which it owed its subplot and concept of tragedy. Construction of a narrative from earlier plots is clearly authorship, not redaction.

3. *Layering: additions to the primary level of MT-Esther*

More to the point is the possibility that MT-Esther developed by localized supplementation and reworking of an earlier form of the story. We may call that form the primary text—the major narrative block whose authorial unity is accepted as the starting point. For most scholars, the primary text is the narrative, 1:1–9:19. In other words, when additions are proposed, this is the base to which they are thought to have been added. However, as Clines has shown, the movement of the narrative takes a sharp turn at 9:1; hence we cannot take it for granted that the connection of 9:1–19 to the first eight chapters was original.

I shall proceed by examining the interrelationship of the components of the Aftermath (9:1–10:3), which various commentators have assigned entirely or in part to secondary stages of development. This analysis will, I believe, establish the basic unity of the Aftermath, after which the relationship of the Aftermath to the Base Narrative (chs. 1–8) can be considered.

3.1. *The Aftermath as a whole* (9:20–10:3)

Many commentators regard 9:20–32 (with or without 10:1–3) as a supplement added to *the* book of Esther, which they take as ending at 9:19. Others assign only parts of these passages to later hands.

> *Views on the originality of 9:20–10:3*: Critical commentators of the nineteenth and twentieth centuries have commonly assigned 9:20–10:3, or parts thereof, to a later stage in the book's development. The argument is based on the preception of incongruities

and contradictions between that unit and the rest of the book (see Paton 1908:57, Eissfeldt 1966:511). If this is correct, the Esther story was not originally the etiology of Purim.

Paton (pp. 57–60) argues that 9:20–10:1 was *earlier* than the narrative proper (1:1–9:19) and quoted from the "Chronicles of Persia and Media" mentioned in 10:2. But there is no particular reason for supposing that these chronicles actually existed or that if they did, they would have shown much interest in the holiday of Purim.

Bardtke, who holds that the book was composed from three earlier traditions (a Vashti story, a Mordecai story, and an Esther story), ascribes 9:20–10:3 to the author of the present book of Esther (pp. 249–52 and *passim*). At one point (p. 385), Bardtke speaks vaguely of two sources in the report of the Jews' defense and the institution of the Purim festival. But the sources he describes in his introduction (pp. 249–52) extend only to the end of ch. 8. This, as well as his exegesis of chs. 9–10, seems to indicate that he places the composition of the concluding units later than the three individual source narratives but concurrent with the composition of the present narrative.

Meinhold (1983a:12–14) regards 9:20–28 and (subsequently) 9:29–32 as later insertions, which required certain revisions in 9:1–18 and 3:7; he considers 9:19 a later gloss. He thinks it possible, however, that the author himself inserted some passages in the Esther tale.

Clines regards all of 9:1–10:3 as a series of supplements, namely the ending (9:1–19), Mordecai's letter (9:20–28), Esther's letter (9:29–32), and the encomium on Mordecai (10:1–3).

There are two main lines of argument on behalf of attributing the constituents of 9:20–32, in whole or in part, to later supplementers: incongruity with earlier material and redundancy. The latter argument is not very powerful, for authors as well as editors can be repetitive. (Redundancy is significant for source analysis only when it coincides with non-functional stylistic differences.) Incongruity is the more valuable criterion in isolating stages of development, but the incongruities appealed to should not merely be *differences*. Even in a unified work, one passage may naturally differ from the others in purpose, focus, and tone. In fact, if there are *no* differences, the passage is superfluous, and there is no more reason for an author to have added it than a redactor; either may have been responsible for a superfluity. An example of difference without incongruity is the one Clines observes in 9:20–32, namely that "the focus has moved . . . from the spontaneous celebrations following the successes of the thirteenth (or fourteenth) of Adar (vss. 17ff.) to a regulated, agreed, institutionalized celebration . . ." (p. 162).

The focus has indeed moved, but that does not prove that the passage represents a later stage in literary history.

One argument used in separating stages of authorship in 9:20–10:3 — though it is actually of little value in this case — is the claim that its diction is distinctive. Paton (pp. 59–60) lists words that appear in 1–9:19 but not in 9:20–10:3, as well as words that appear in the latter but not in the former (the second list is potentially the more significant). But these lists prove nothing, since most of the words peculiar to 9:20–10:3 are required by the subject-matter of the passage; e.g., *'ebyônîm* "poor," *'iyyîm* "islands," *dôr*, "generation," *mišpāḥâ* "family." Nothing in the events of the earlier narrative called for these particular words. There are some words that might have occurred earlier but did not (e.g., *mišneh* "viceroy," *yāgôn* "misery"), but these are too few to prove different authorship. Conversely, the argument for unity based on *similarities* in diction (such as Bardtke makes with regard to 10:1–3) has little force. A later scribe would have been influenced by the book he had just read and could easily have used the vocabulary and style of the narrative in producing an addition.

B. Jones (1978) argues for single authorship of the entire book on the grounds that certain phrases and motifs of the narrative recur in its ending and are constituents of literary patterns. Clines (pp. 60–63) summarizes and refutes Jones' arguments. In essence, some of these supposed patterns are accidental by-products of recurrent phrases. Jones calls these patterns "approximate inclusios" when they occur at both the beginning and the ending of the book, and "synthetic linear progressions" when they do not. But, as noted, a redactor would have known the primary text and adopted some of its vocabulary and imagery and may even have created patterns deliberately. An argument from design must reveal a pattern that begins to develop in the primary text and that would be truncated without the conclusion provided by the disputed passage.

I will try to show that the component passages of the Aftermath function well in context and do not contradict the earlier narrative or the other parts of chs. 9–10. The most significant argument for single authorship is that a passage in question is *required* by material on which it is manifestly dependent. Such mutual dependency not only eliminates an argument for disunity, it constitutes positive evidence for unity of authorship. This argument, however, works at only a few points in the passages under discussion.

3.2. Mordecai's epistle (9:20–28)

At the very least, Mordecai's letter and its popular confirmation are presupposed by 9:1–19 and cannot be later than that unit.

9:1–19 lays the ground specifically for the *two-day* duration of Purim. The report of the fighting on 14 Adar serves no other function. The dynamics of the story-line do not necessitate Xerxes' offer in 9:12 or Esther's request in 9:13. The Jewish victory is already decisive, the body-count already impressive (vs. 12). The Jews do not *need* another day. To be sure, another day makes the revenge more thorough, but if thoroughness were the goal, the author could be expected to give a second day to the provinces as well, or simply to increase the body-count of the thirteenth. (The latter move would not, of course, be noticeable in itself, but it would obviate the need for a second day of battle.) Hence the main point of 9:11–19 is to explain the two days of the celebration. To be sure, an etiology appeared already in vs. 19, but the significance of the two-day theme, given such prominence in 9:11–18, is surely not exhausted in vs. 19's brief and flat explanation for the two days of the holiday—a holiday not yet introduced or identified.

One argument made for dissociating 9:20–28 (Mordecai's letter and its response) from 9:1–19 is that it enjoins the sending of gifts to the poor (9:22) although this act was unmentioned when the merrymaking was reported in 9:17–19 (Clines, pp. 166). But the celebration regularized in 9:22 and 31 is not an exact replica of the spontaneous rejoicing following the victory. Rather, Mordecai is proposing customs appropriate to an institutionalized re-enactment of that response.

One might argue that these considerations can at most show that *9:11–32* is essentially monolithic and that they do not disprove the possibility that this block is later than 9:1–10. But 9:1–10—even when followed immediately by 10:1–3—would not constitute a suitable ending to the book, jumping as it does from the Jews' victory to Mordecai's glory, with no mention of the victory celebration. While such celebrations might be omitted in a book that told only of Mordecai's victory and ascension, with 9:1–10 present the Jews have been introduced as a force to be reckoned with, the force that defeats the enemy, and their response is still awaited. Even in the proto-AT, where Mordecai and Esther alone secure the victory (the Jews merely punish their enemies *after* the victory), Mordecai calls upon the people to celebrate their salvation (viii 33–38). This provides more than a parallel, for the presence of viii 33–38 in the AT shows that even prior to the formation of the MT the tale did not end before the equivalent of 9:17, i.e. the rejoicing of the victors.[3]

---

[3] Defending the originality of 9:20–32, Berg (1979:42) observes that in light of the importance of the motif of feasting in the narrative, it would be surprising if the Scroll did not end with some mention of Purim and its banquets. But while it is true that the feasting motif in MT 9:20–32 develops naturally and effectively from the earlier chapters, its extension into ch. 9 is not required by its use in chs. 1–8. In any case, if a Jewish celebration were needed to round off the feasting motif, the spontaneous celebrations in 9:17–18 could have filled that role, just as Mordecai's simple call to celebrate does in proto-AT (viii 34). *Purim* feasting is not a necessary extension of the feasting motif. It does seem, however, that R-MT gave that motif greater emphasis by adding the feasting by Haman and the king after the issuance of Haman's decree (3:15). The MT redactor integrated the Purim deliberations into the earlier narrative by extending the feasting motif into the Aftermath on the basis of a slim hint in AT viii 34.

3.3. *The historical retrospective* (9:24–25)

The retrospective in Mordecai's epistle summarizing the events of Haman's plot and downfall is often considered a later addition to the epistle because it diverges at several points from the narrative it purports to encapsulate.[4] Those who view all of 9:20–32 as supplementary (see above) commonly take 9:24–25 as further evidence of this. Yet even if the historical retrospective were an addition to Mordecai's letter, that would say nothing about the place of the letter as a whole in the book's development. Nevertheless, these verses too are probably original.

These are the main arguments commonly used for separating 9:24–25 from its context:

(a) Vs. 24 says that Haman threw lots to "harry" or "confound" the Jews (*lĕhummām*), but this is only loosely true. The lots were intended to ascertain the best day to destroy the Jews, not to affect them emotionally.

(b) In ch. 7, Xerxes did not react against Haman's plan, but against a personal offense. The historical retrospective makes the king look like a clear-thinking, exemplary proponent of justice; the bumbling, putty-like Xerxes of the tale is scarcely recognizable in this picture. Moreover, the king did not say that Haman's scheme should "rebound . . . on his own head," nor did he order the execution "in [?] writing" (*'im hassēper*—a difficult phrase).

(c) The historical retrospective, as Clines observes, minimizes the roles of Mordecai and Esther (p. 165). (The degree of minimization depends on *who* or *what* "came" before the king—Esther herself or "the matter"; the suffix of *bĕbō'āh* can be taken either way.)

(d) The retrospective identifies the salvation entirely with the moment of Haman's overthrow, ignoring the crucial counter-decree, which was (according to ch. 8) essential in averting destruction. Nor is mention made of the battles of Adar, as if the crisis had been solved by the king's condemnation of Haman (as was indeed the case in the proto-AT).

---

[4] Although Hoschander (1923) considers the passage "an almost literal quotation from the Letter of Mordecai" (p. 265), he also believes that the MT contradicts the earlier tale at many points and therefore "could not have been handed down correctly" (pp. 266–67), whereas the LXX, lacking those contradictions, preserves the correct version (pp. 268–70). In fact, the LXX's version probably resulted from harmonistic presuppositions similar to Hoschander's.

Paton takes the differences as evidence that 9:20–10:3 as a whole was derived from an earlier source (specifically, the Chronicles of the Kings of Persia and Media [pp. 58–59]). Bardtke (p. 394) argues that the differences are due to the summary character of 9:24–25. But such discrepancies as do exist do not seem to be by-products of condensation.

Counter arguments:

As for *lĕhummām,* although Haman's immediate purpose in casting lots may not have been to "harry" or "confuse" the Jews, this was the effect of the plot and so could be described as the long-range purpose of the lots. Furthermore, *HMM* often connotes *deadly* confusion (e.g., Exod 14:24; Josh 10:10; esp. Judg 4:15 [*wayyāhom . . . lĕpî ḥereb*). The word was probably chosen as a pun on the name Haman, perhaps as a way of reinforcing the play of "Purim" on *pûr.*

I believe we are to understand the retrospective as drawn from Mordecai's epistle. The retrospective is cast in the form of "erlebte Rede," not direct quotation; it conveys Mordecai's perspective but not his exact words. It gives the reason why the Jews took upon themselves "what Mordecai had written to them" (9:23). Such a statement would be quite appropriate in Mordecai's epistle, because the call to inaugurate a new holiday needs more than just a reference to a victorious battle. Mordecai would have to appeal to the entire episode of danger and salvation — just as the book of Esther itself does — to convince the people that the recent events demand perpetual commemoration.

It is true that 9:24–25 is not a precise reprise of the events related earlier, and the differences are not due to condensation alone. They arise because the passage summarizes the story from a different viewpoint. Its purpose is not to retell the tale, but to show Mordecai at work as a skilled courtier and protector of the Jews.

Mordecai, speaking in a public letter in his role as vizier, gives the credit to his king, not to himself or his protegée. Thus he transforms the king's outburst in 7:8 into a deliberate judgment on Haman for plotting against the Jews. The king has recently revealed his new self-image as protector of the Jews by declaring that Haman was impaled "because he had assaulted the Jews" (8:7), though that was by no means Xerxes' motive in 7:9. Mordecai, continuing to display the subtlety and tactical skills he has already demonstrated, publicly places the king in that role in 9:24–25. Mordecai flatters the king into adopting attitudes favorable to the Jews by speaking as if he already possessed them. To be sure, the summary does present Esther and Mordecai as more passive than they are in the Base Narrative, but it thereby reflects the way Jews must operate in the foreign court: they must make the ruler do their will thinking it is his own. This is exactly the approach Mordecai and Esther have been taking since ch. 4. Moreover, vs. 25 accords with the Base Narrative in situating the real victory in the events of Nisan.

The statement that the king gave his command "in writing" again shows Mordecai fully implicating the king in *Mordecai's* strategy: *'im hassēper* must refer to Mordecai's decree (8:10–13), which he now couples with the king's command — given three months prior to that decree — to kill Haman. Mordecai wrote his edict "in the king's name" and wants it perceived as originating with the king. Thus the summary does not ignore the counter-decree but presents it as a direct expression of the king's anger at Haman. In other words, this historical retrospective is exactly what a canny vizier would produce for public consumption.

The proto-AT provides further evidence for the originality of 9:24–25. It too includes a historical retrospective in Mordecai's epistle (quoted above, ch. I, §5), which says that Haman had plotted to destroy the Jews but has been hanged and his household executed. This item supplies the essential elements of 9:24–25, except for the Purim etymology.

3.4. Esther's epistle (9:29–32)

Esther's epistle is sometimes assigned to an even later stage than Mordecai's. Meinhold (1983:93) says that 9:29–32 is an addition whose purpose is to include fasting among the rituals associated with Purim. Moore (1971:95), too, considers it later than the rest of ch. 9, arguing on the shaky grounds that the passage is lacking in the AT and OL and has a somewhat different form in the LXX. Clines (pp. 166–67) regards Esther's letter as a separate appendix that emphasizes the role of the community in determining its liturgical life and shows the festivities to be a reversal of grief.

In fact, the epistle contains nothing inherently new. If the text had skipped those verses (as the proto-AT does), little of substance would really be lacking. The attitudes Clines ascribes to the epistle echo ones heard earlier: the insistence on communal "confirmation" of the holiday and the definition of 14–15 Adar as days of respite from hostility. Esther's epistle adds nothing to these.

Nor does the epistle innovate a fast, for 9:31 does not *prescribe* fasting, but only describes the *way* in which the community obligated itself to celebrate Purim.

Comment on 9:31b:

The phrase *dibrê haṣṣômôt wĕzaʿăqātām*, "matters of fasting and their laments," is usually construed as prescribing a fast in conjunction with the holiday, to commemorate either the Jews' fast (4:3) or Esther's (4:16). Yet this phrase, regardless of when it was added, does not fulfill the purpose ascribed to it, namely to teach that fasting before Purim is henceforth an obligation. Such a purpose would require having Esther or Mordecai *enjoin* a practice and spell out some of its specifics, whereas fasting is merely mentioned incidentally in a subordinate clause. Even by the usual translation, the verse refers to a practice already established and known and mentions it simply as a point of comparison: the Jews confirmed the celebration of two days of Purim *just as* they had earlier taken fasting upon themselves. But we are not told earlier that any of the parties wrote to "confirm" the practice of fasting, so the supposed comparison is otiose. Evidence for a practice of Purim fasting is quite late, and the Fast of Esther, held on 13 Adar, is probably of medieval origin and based on this verse (Schwarz 1923:192–96). In any case, this remark about fasting and lamentation is too off-hand to be the point of the passage.

A better interpretation may be suggested on the basis of Abraham Ibn Ezra's explanation: "The Jews confirmed for themselves the rejoicing in the days of Purim just as they had confirmed for themselves and their descendants fasting in the days of their mourning when the city [of Jerusalem] was broken open and the Temple was burnt. [The Jews did this] because the prophet [Zechariah] had not commanded them to fast . . ." (Ibn Ezra is referring to Zech 8:19, which mentions fasts in the fourth, fifth, seventh, and tenth months.) Ibn Ezra recognizes that the phrase in question simply compares the Purim undertaking to certain public fasts in regard to the *manner* of obligation. Such fasts were not commanded by the Torah or a prophet, but were voluntary commitments on the part of the community. The nineteenth century Jewish commentator Malbim, following Ibn Ezra's interpretation, explains that the point of the comparison is to show that one can legitimately undertake such obligations as a type of vow without claiming that they originate in the Torah. A vow, we might add, cannot be imposed by religious authorities, but must be freely undertaken by individuals or the community as a whole.

The only weakness in Ibn Ezra's interpretation is that "the matter of fasting and their laments" is too vague a formulation to point specifically to the fasts mentioned in Zechariah. Instead, it refers generally to any communal fast that can be proclaimed before or after a disaster (thus Schwarz, 1923:197–98). Esth 4:3 and 16 provide examples of communal fasts, but these are not the "fasts" designated in 9:31. Those verses refer to one-time, spontaneous outcries, which one cannot say were "confirmed," whereas 9:31 refers to the introduction of permanent practices. Accordingly, the comparison is a broad one, describing the voluntary institution of permanent fasts in general. We should translate 9:30–31 thus: "And letters were sent . . . to confirm the observance of these days of Purim in their set times, just as Mordecai the Jew and Queen Esther had confirmed for them, in the way that they [sc., the Jews] confirm for themselves and their descendants matters of fasting and the accompanying laments."

The second epistle's redundancy does not show it to be a later addition; indeed, redundancy is its point. The importance of one confirmation reinforcing another has already emerged in Mordecai's epistle. Esther's confirmation is a natural, though not necessary, extension of this concern. Thus the innovation is not in the contents of the letter, but in its authorship. The second epistle goes beyond the first by bringing Esther, the heroine and reigning queen, into the communal dialogue. The author of chs. 1–8 — more so in the MT than in the AT — brings out Esther's growing independence and authority. Compare AT viii 15, in which the king gives Haman's property directly to Mordecai, with MT 8:2b, in which Esther is rather artificially made the intermediary between the two men in the transfer of the property. Esther's letter also continues this trajectory. There is less of a motive, on the other hand, for a *later* scribe to append Esther's confirmation, since Mordecai — not Esther — was considered the religious leader, and his authority would have sufficed in later generations.

Excursus on the text of 9:27–32
It is difficult to evaluate the bearing of the versions on the history of this passage. Its absence in the AT is just another of R-AT's many omissions from the LXX in this chapter and is irrelevant to the formation of the MT. The LXX does not represent MT 9:30–31aα (through *kaʾăšer*) and handles MT 9:31b quite differently (rendering *zarʿām* as τῆς ὑγιείας ἑαυτῶν and reading καὶ τὴν βουλὴν αὐτῶν for the MT's "matters of fasting and their outcries"; this is perhaps a paraphrase). All of MT vs. 32 is represented, though rather loosely. But even when its paraphrastic technique is taken into account, the LXX does not seem to have had *haššēnît* (vs. 29) or *dibrê haṣṣōmôt wĕzaʿăqātām* (MT vs. 31) in its vorlage. The omission in the OL (MSS c and m) of LXX 9:31 (MT 9:32) as well as of MT 9:30 (already lacking in the LXX) says nothing about an earlier state of the text, because the OL abbreviates throughout the book, omitting no less than 20 verses in ch. 9 (along with 10:1). Loewenstamm's attempt to trace the steps from a short original text (closer to the LXX) to the MT (1971) is too tortuous to be convincing.

If there are any later developments within 9:20–32, they are probably to be found in certain glosses that introduce Mordecai and Esther into both this epistle and the preceding one.

Problems with the present Hebrew text have given rise to several emendations; the difficulties are: (1) Vs. 29a is apparently contradicted by vs. 32, according to which it is Esther's word alone that confirms the Purim practices. (2) It does not make much sense for Esther and Mordecai to confirm their own confirmation. (3) MT vs. 31aα has Esther and Mordecai issuing the original epistle, while according to vss. 20–22, Mordecai did that alone. (4) There is little point in confirming a second letter *in* the second letter.

For these reasons, most modern commentators (e.g., Paton, Moore, Gerleman, Bardtke) excise the words "and Mordecai the Jew" from vs. 29, making this epistle Esther's alone. (Consequently, the verb *wayyišlaḥ*, "he sent," at the start of vs. 30 must be emended to *wayyiššālēhû*, "there were sent" or *wattišlaḥ*, "she sent.") Next, they remove "and Queen Esther" from vs. 31, since the earlier letter was Mordecai's alone. Another change worthy of consideration, though rarely suggested, is to omit "second" from the end of vs. 29, with the result that "this epistle" refers to the previously mentioned one, i.e., Mordecai's (vs. 26). The reconstructed text reads:

"And Queen Esther, daughter of Abihayil, conveyed in writing all the authority necessary to confirm this Purim epistle. And letters were sent to all the Jews in the one hundred twenty-seven provinces of Xerxes' kingdom—words of peace and faithfulness—to confirm the observance of these days of Purim in their set times, just as Mordecai the Jew had confirmed upon them, in the way that they confirm for themselves and their descendants matters of fasting and the accompanying laments. And the declaration of Esther confirmed these matters concerning Purim, and it was written in a document."

The emended text is logical, but if we accept it we must explain how the present illogical text came about. In the case of "Queen Esther" in vs. 31 and "Mordecai the Jew" in vs. 29, we may surmise that a later scribe wished to double the authority behind each letter. As for the addition of "second" in that verse, perhaps a scribe did not know which letter was meant by "this epistle" and added "second" as an explanatory (though not very helpful) gloss. Gerleman suggests that a scribe thought that "this letter" was the object of "wrote" rather than of "confirm," and so believed that the addition of "second" made sense.

These are major emendations, all conjectural. The versions do not help one way or the other, because they either lack the passage or differ too much to aid in the reconstruction of the Hebrew. The only argument on behalf of the emendations is that they produce a much neater text: Esther writes a letter to confirm by her authority the validity of Mordecai's epistle.

3.5. *The epilogue* (10:1–3)

The account of Mordecai's subsequent glory is an appropriate culmination to the narrative strand that tells of Mordecai's personal struggle and rise to power. His clash with Haman had developed into a national crisis, which has now been settled. But the narrative tension within Mordecai's own story has not been resolved, nor would such a resolution make sense prior to the national salvation. Mordecai's exaltation in ch. 6 foreshadowed his victory and his subsequent glory, but that was not yet his true victory, because he did not actively fashion it, but received it by good fortune, and moreover it did not materially advance the Jews' cause. For full justice to be achieved, not only must Haman and his scheme be defeated and Mordecai rise to his enemy's position (as he did in 8:2), but Mordecai must fill the position successfully and permanently, and this happens only in the closing verses of the book. This completion is not essential; it is lacking in the proto-AT. But it is a literary improvement, not an awkward appendix tacked on uselessly.

There are two main aspects to Mordecai's role: service to his monarch and service to his people. Previously these had remained separate, spontaneous, and episodic. This unit unites them and makes them permanent. Having proved his value in both regards, he is now indefinitely, and ex officio, his king's benefactor and his people's protector.[5]

Though I consider the epilogue original, I am not convinced of the particular connection that D. Daube (1946) draws between the epilogue and the narrative. He interprets Xerxes' tax as a peaceful substitute for the revenues he would have gained by bribery and plunder had Haman's plot succeeded. But the text hints at no connections between the two acts, as if the tax were compensation for the king's losses, and in any case Xerxes could have levied a tax in addition to taking Haman's bribe, had he so wished.

This tax[6] may, however, be connected (by reversal) with an earlier act of Xerxes, his granting of "(tax) relief" (if that is indeed the meaning of *hănāḥâ*) in honor of Esther's coronation in 2:18. No direct connection is made, but levying a tax is the opposite of giving tax relief (Ehrlich). One message of 10:1, in light of this connection, is that not only does Jewish success benefit the king's other subjects (Esther's coronation gave rise to a tax relief), but Jewish advancement is somehow (*post hoc ergo propter hoc*) good for the royal coffers. A similar belief motivates Gen 47:13–26, in which Joseph, after saving the Egyptians, subjects the entire land to the king's direct ownership and imposes a 20% tax. Yet although the motif of Esther 10:1 has a parallel in the Joseph story, it is not an echo of that passage, for different vocabulary is used and Mordecai is not said to have masterminded the taxation. (Perhaps the author did not want to press the point because he was not eager to have a Jew blamed for taxation.)

I have argued that chapters 9 and 10 are a unit. It remains to ask about their relationship to the rest of the book.

---

[5] The transposition of the usual order of the phrase "Persia and Media" in 10:2 is not evidence for different authorship; compare the transposition of "her people and her kindred" in 2:10 and 20.

[6] Elsewhere in BH, *mas* means "corvée." In Rabbinic Hebrew it means tax. Either sense is possible here, but the latter is preferable because of the unlikelihood of assembling forced laborers from distant islands (though a hyperbolic statement [thus Meinhold] is, of course, possible). We may also compare Herodotus' statement about the powers of taxation of Darius I: ". . . as time went on, more [revenue] came in from the islands and from the peoples in Europe as far as Thessaly" (III 96). In any case, even if *mas* means "corvée," a corvée is a form of taxation.

4. Is the Aftermath by a different author?

Clines has vigorously and perceptively argued for a sharp separation between 1–8 and 9:1–19 (taking 9:20–10:3 as a further series of supplements). He claims that the original Esther story (after the combination of the hypothetical "sources") was the proto-AT, which he defines as ii 1–viii 18, minus the Adds. To this narrative foundation an author added the theme of the irrevocability of Persian law, the conspiracy of the eunuchs (2:21–23), and some minor items, while omitting religious statements. This reworking produced what Clines calls the "proto-Massoretic story"—in other words, MT chs. 1–8—which reaches its climax and conclusion in Mordecai's counterdecree and his appearance in glory (8:9–17). Apparently the MT redactor reworked some details and phraseology as well, but Clines, quite correctly, refrains from reconstructing the minutiae of this process.

If Clines is right, chs. 1–8 constitute the essential story of Esther, and 9:1–10:3 is a series of additions motivated by concerns and informed by attitudes quite distinct from those of the earlier chapters. The literary and moral level of the book was, in Clines' opinion (pp. 39–49), lowered by the splice with 9:1–19, though supplements in 9:20–32 toned down the militarism that the first addition had introduced.

I accept the thesis that chs. 9–10 were created in a manner very different from the earlier chapters (at least chs. 1–7); however, 9:1–19 is not a *later* addition. A bond, both integral and authorial, links the Base Narrative to the Aftermath. (I have already given my reasons for not subdividing the Aftermath.) I will justify this seemingly paradoxical description of the relationship between the two major blocks of the story by describing the lines of harmony and tension between them, once again proceeding in dialectic with Clines' fruitful work.

4.1. Validity of the arguments for identifying 9:1–19 as a later addition.

Clines argues that 9:1–19 is a later addition to chs. 1–8. Although I accept his position in part, I believe that some of his arguments obscure the literary congruity between the two blocks and thus blur both their literary history and present meaning. Analysis of the supposed discrepancies will show that ch. 9 does indeed have a different prehistory from most of the book. Nevertheless, the Aftermath is not incompatible with the Base Narrative, but, on the contrary, is required for its fulfillment.

4.1.1. What is the point of the battles of 9:1–18 after the neutralization of Haman's decree?

According to Clines, the major discrepancy in the MT (he calls it a "logical narrative weakness") is that the conflict between the two decrees, crucial to

MT chs. 1–8, is ignored in ch. 9. From the standpoint of the dynamics of the plot, the story concludes in 8:17, when the second decree "denatures" the first (p. 39; cf. 28–29).

In fact, however, the fighting in ch. 9 does presuppose Mordecai's decree (8:11–13) as well as Haman's. The second decree allowed the Jews to defend themselves. Without this license they would have had to defy the might of the state, for they would be taking up arms against a royal decree—and that in an empire obsessed with rigid maintenance of law. Without Haman's decree there would have been no attack, without Mordecai's no defense.

The Aftermath's report of Jewish victory is necessary in the MT, for it could by no means be taken for granted that no one would dare assail the Jews now that they were allowed to defend themselves. They were still a scattered minority and vulnerable to massed assault, and their enemies still had the right to attack them.

4.1.2. Defense or aggression?

The second decree gave Jews permission to defend themselves against armed attackers and to destroy them. Esth 9:1–19, according to Clines (pp. 39-40), misunderstands that decree and reports an extensive massacre of antisemites initiated by the Jews.

On the contrary, 9:1–19 understands Mordecai's decree quite well, relating the logical outcome of the clash of the two decrees and presupposing the tale as related in the MT. The Jews do not instigate the fighting in ch. 9. The description of Adar 13 as the day the Jews' enemies hoped to gain mastery over them (9:1) makes sense only if the enemies were planning to attack. Moreover, the enemies are defined by the fact that they "sought to harm them" (9:2), not by their status as heathen or as adherents of a certain party. The verses in question do not say just what actions the enemies took, but we can hardly conclude from this silence that their "seeking to harm" the Jews consisted merely of having inimical intentions. This "seeking to harm" the Jews took the form of the licensed attack. Moreover, the image of the Jews "gathering" (9:2, 15, 16, 18) to "make a stand for their lives" ('āmōd 'al napšām; 9:16) is that of a body forming for defense, not a mob hunting down individuals it considers hostile. Nothing distinguishes the action carried out in 9:1–11 from the one envisioned in 8:11.

To be sure, the Jewish reaction went beyond the demands of immediate survival, just as in the Second World War the Allies went beyond rebuffing the Japanese invasion in the Pacific Theater. Such actions are in response to aggression and are part of an overall defensive strategy—or, at least, are undeniably perceived as such by the powers that carry them out and their sympathizers. The Jews' actions in 9:1–19 are within the scope of the license of self-defense granted in 8:11, which authorizes them "to stand up for their lives."

4.1.3. Does the Aftermath misuse phrases learned from the Base Narrative?

Clines says that the "the fear of the Jews" in 8:17 implies religious awe, an enlightenment conducive to proselytism, whereas to the less subtle author of the Aftermath (in 9:2) it indicates mortal dread of Jewish might (pp. 40–42).[7]

In actuality, the object of fear is Jewish military power in both cases. Religious awe is not the only motive for conversion.[8] Fear of danger, and not only spiritual enlightenment, can bring about conversion—as it did to the Idumeans and as it has done often enough in the history of Christianity and Islam, as can the wish to join a more powerful group. In the Esther story, it was the "fear of the Jews" that inspired these people to become Jewish. "Fear" (*pahad*) does not refer only to fear of God or religious awe—see its use in Ps 27:1; 78:53 (verb); Ps 31:12; Job 21:9; Esth 9:2 (noun); and often. "Fear of the Jews" is not religious awe any more than is the "fear of the Jews" in 9:2 or the "fear of Mordecai" in 9:3, which was inspired by Mordecai's growing importance. Of course, the foe might recognize that an unnamed power is on the Jews' side. Haman's advisors and wife reveal such a fear of the Jews in 5:14 (though the term *pahad* is not used). But though they may sense a supernatural power somewhere in the background, this is hardly a matter of "enlightenment" or sensitivity to the numinous, nor is it distinguishable from dread of superior military power. To the extent that a gentile awareness of a divinity supporting the Jews is indeed in mind in 8:17, it may be intended in 9:2–3 as well. Even so, the immediate cause of the gentiles' anxiety is not God but the Jews themselves.

---

[7] Similarly, Dommershausen (1968:110) regards this emotion as awed fear before the God who protects this people so wondrously.

[8] *mityahădîm* (8:17), a denominative from *yĕhûdî*, "Jew," may mean either "became Jewish" or, as Ehrlich suggests, "gaben sich aus für Juden" (the hithpael often has the sense of "present oneself as," "pretend to be" something [GKC §54e]). Ehrlich argues that conversion motivated by fear of death would violate the principles of Judaism. However, people ready to convert for fear of death would not scruple to violate the principle that conversion be uncoerced, a principle that in any case was formulated only in later times. John Hyrcanus, after all, did not hesitate to convert the Idumeans by force of arms. Moreover, what could it mean in practical terms to say that many of the peoples of the land "gave themselves out to be Jews"? There was no distinctive Jewish dress they could wear as a disguise (if there were, Mordecai's colleagues would have known he was Jewish without his telling them in 3:4). The gentiles might have declared themselves to be Jewish, but (as Bardtke points out) Jews from the same town would have known that they were lying. The action of the gentiles is thus to be understood as joining the Jewish people. Neh 10:29 refers to "everyone who separated himself from the peoples of the lands [to follow] the law of God" (using the same term of the heathen, *'ammê hā'ărāsôt*, as here).

4.1.4. Where do all the antisemites come from?

Contrary to Clines (pp. 42–46), it is not the case that in the Base Narrative Haman is the *only* enemy of the Jews whereas in ch. 9, 75,000 enemies appear from nowhere. In the early chapters too the Jews have enemies, but they lurk in the background. Mordecai's insistence that Esther hide her Jewishness reveals some apprehension on his part, some foreboding of a danger that may threaten Esther as a Jew or the Jews as a people. Moreover, the first decree's *license* for a pogrom could be effective in exterminating the Jews only if there were already many enemies willing and able to carry it out. The enemies emerge from the background when it is appropriate for them to do so, on the day of battle.

The Aftermath is therefore the natural and necessary continuation of the Base Narrative. Clines is right, however, in insisting that the dramatic tension slackens in 8:17, with the Susans' rejoicing and Mordecai's glory. The conflict broke out between individuals, was played out among individuals, and in ch. 8 was essentially resolved by individuals. The essence of deliverance—the possibility for the Jews to control their own fate—lies in the issuance of Mordecai's decree. The Aftermath reports the working-out of the victory secured earlier. By the end of ch. 8, the tension has abated but the story is not complete.

4.2. The scope of R-MT's source

Though chs. 9–10 are not later "additions" to the story, it is true that those chapters had a different literary prehistory from that of the Base Narrative. Significant evidence for this distinction is the fact that the proto-AT contained very little corresponding to MT chs. 9–10. In fact, it had little corresponding to ch. 8 either.

The MT parallels the proto-AT fairly closely through 7:10, the equivalent of AT viii 14. The relation of the rest of the MT to the proto-AT is much looser. Some notable divergences:

(a) For the MT the crucial device of salvation is Mordecai's counter-decree. The proto-AT lacks this, simply having the king give Mordecai the power to annul Haman's edict.

(b) The MT tells of the massing of the Jews' enemies and the battles with them. The proto-AT refers to the *punishment* of Esther's foes, which is carried out when the mass of Jews are already safe.

(c) The MT reports widespread conversion of gentiles, the proto-AT does not.

(d) The MT describes the Jews' confirmation of the holiday. In the proto-AT, the Jews do not initiate or establish a holiday; rather,

Mordecai proclaims an immediate, apparently one-time celebration of the deliverance, with no mention of Purim, not even its date. (e) The MT carefully distinguishes between the battles in Susa and those in the provinces and correspondingly requires two days of celebration. The proto-AT knows of no such distinction. (f) The MT reports on Mordecai's success in the following years (ch. 10), the proto-AT does not.

All these MT pluses are additions to the proto-Esther narrative. It would be far-fetched to suppose that these elements were once present in proto-Esther, then omitted by the redactor of the proto-AT while being adopted by the redactor of the MT. After all, the additional features in the MT augment the honor of Mordecai and his fellow Jews and justify subsequent religious practice. Once these features were present in the Esther tradition no one would have been likely to remove them, nor is it reasonable to suppose that they were present in the proto-AT and later replaced by material from the LXX. If R-AT had before him an approximation of LXX chs. 9–10 in his receptor text, there is every reason to believe that he would have preserved it, as he did elsewhere to the proto-AT material paralleling the LXX.[9]

Furthermore, most of these additional elements do not fit well with the narrative dynamics of the proto-AT. One indicator that the proto-AT did not know of true battles in Adar is that the Jews' enemies, including Haman's sons, were slaughtered in viii 20–21 and so were not available for a battle. Likewise the report of the slaughter there does not make a Susa-province distinction that would prepare the way for a two-day holiday. Moreover, a public confirmation process would have been inappropriate in the proto-AT, where Mordecai simply commands the Jews to hold celebration (viii 33–38). In the proto-AT, a report of the communal give-and-take would have introduced a sudden and unmotivated "democratization" of communal organization.

In sum, most of the substance of chs. 9–10 was not available in R-MT's source.

4.3. Qualitative differences

Another significant, though subjective, argument for the distinction between chs. 1–8 and 9–10 is the difference in literary quality. Chapters 1–8 constitute a skillfully shaped, dramatically paced story, whereas ch. 9 — when

---

[9] R–AT did accidentally overwrite material in D +, but that consisted of just a few verses whose formulation had no ideological importance. Morever, had proto-AT reported the battles and the institution of Purim, those passages would have followed the proto-AT material in viii 21 and viii 38, rather than following redactional material. Thus they would not have been so easily overwritten. In the case of D +, in contrast, the overwriting occurred *after* a redactional supplement (Add D). The redactor was copying Add D and just kept going for a few verses, probably unintentionally.

judged as narrative—is stilted, schematic, and devoid of subtlety in character portrayal. Clines considers the Aftermath "striking for its poor construction, its inferior narrative development, and its logical weaknesses" (p. 39). This judgment is too harsh, because 9:1–19 has a different purpose from the preceding narrative, namely to show how the events of Adar issued into the new festival. The chapter is analytical rather than narrational, more interested in explaining events than in reporting them. Nevertheless, the narrative is still in progress, and what happens to the style is largely *required* by the new purpose. The Aftermath is the conclusion, if not the climax, of a tale told until now with high drama and sensitivity to characterization. Suddenly the drama goes flat; events play themselves out mechanically. Particularly clumsy are Xerxes' renewal of his now-standard offer, which seems to come from nowhere, and Esther's request for another day of fighting in 9:13, which is not motivated by the preceding narrative.

This change in style and literary quality might support a claim of different authorship, but it does not prove it. We may compare a similar shift in Richard Wright's *Native Son*. Parts I and II are an intense, dramatic, concrete character-study. In part III (the lawyer's speech), we are faced with a rambling ideological preachment. In Esther, too, the Aftermath prepares for and expounds an ideological program. The endings of both books seek to put the earlier story in a broader framework and may claim to hold the primary message of the book as a whole, but in both it is the psychological insight and dramatic pace of the preceding narrative that enthralls the reader.

5. R-MT's treatment of his source

The redactor uses his donor-text differently in ch. 9 from the way he did in chs. 1–7 and even in ch. 8, where the momentum of the narrative still dictated the shape of the denouement. But ch. 9 is not a *later* addition—any more than ch. 8 is. That is not to say that the book of Esther is a "unity" as this term is commonly used, meaning that one person created it all. There is indeed a unity, but one compounded of two stages in the history of the text. A single redactor shaped the entire MT by adapting and supplementing the Hebrew proto-AT, or—to be cautious—proto-Esther, their common forerunner. In chs. 1–7 this author-redactor is closely reworking an older story, most of it ready to hand. In ch. 8 he continues the narrative, but now treats his source much more expansively. In ch. 9 he is composing a new ending with a liturgical purpose, building upon only a few hints supplied by his source. The MT is a unity insofar as a single redactor has imposed his will and his intentions on an earlier text.

Until ch. 8, the MT follows the proto-AT fairly closely. At this point R-MT more actively expands, reshapes, and reorganizes the underlying text. A comparison of the MT with the proto-AT shows approximately what R-MT did in these chapters, though we cannot assume that the proto-AT is identical to the source he used.

AT	MT
viii 13b) The king removes the ring from his [probably Haman's] hand, and Haman's life is sealed with it.	8:2a) The king removes the ring that he had taken away from Haman and gives it to Mordecai.
14a) The king remarks that Haman wanted to kill the king's benefactor,	(lacking)
14b) but Haman did not know that Mordecai was Esther's relative.	8:1bβ) Mention of their relationship.
viii 15) The king summons Mordecai and gives him Haman's property.	8:1, 2b) The king summons Mordecai . . . and gives Esther Haman's property. She puts it into Mordecai's custody.
(lacking)	8:3) Esther begs the king to remove Haman's evil.
16a) The king asks Mordecai what he wants.	8:4) The king stretches out his scepter to Esther.
16b) Mordecai requests annulment of Haman's decree.	8:5–6) Esther requests annulment of Haman's decree.
17) The king appoints Mordecai vizier (so that he can cancel Haman's decree).	8:2a) The king appoints Mordecai vizier.
(Cf. 33b: Mordecai receives permission to write what he wishes.)	8:7) The King notes his past benefices to the Jews. 8:8) He allows Mordecai and Esther to write what they wish.
	8:15) Mordecai appears publicly in full regalia, and Susa rejoices.
(Cf. 34: The Jews are instructed to celebrate.)	8:16) The Jews celebrate.
	8:17) Heathen convert out of fear of the Jews.
(viii 16a resembles the wording of the king's abrupt offer in 9:12b.[10])	9:11–12) The king learns of Jews' successes, admires them, and asks Esther what more she wants.

----

[10] viii 16a: καὶ εἶπεν αὐτῷ, Τί θέλεις; καὶ ποιήσω σοι. 9:12b: ûmah šĕ'ēlātēk wĕyinnātēn lāk ûmah baqqāšātēk 'ôd wĕtē'āś.

18) Esther asks permission
to slaughter enemies
19a) and to kill Haman's sons.
19b) The king agrees.

20) She (?) smites enemies
in profusion.

21) The king agrees to
have men killed and hanged.

(lacking)

(lacking)

(lacking)

33a) A proclamation about
these things is issued in Susa,
33b) and the king
empowers Mordecai to write
as he wishes.
(lacking)
34a) So Mordecai sends a letter,
sealing it with the king's ring,

34b) telling Jews to stay at
home and celebrate a festival.

35–38) His letter says that
Haman plotted to kill the
Jews, but he was hanged and
his household executed.
(lacking)
(lacking)

(lacking)

(lacking)

9:13a) Esther asks permission for
a *second* day of slaughter,
9:13b) and to hang Haman's sons.
9:14a) The king agrees.
9:1–5) The Jews stand up to their
enemies. Officials give them aid.
They smite enemies in profusion.

9:6–10) Jews kill 500 in Susa
and expose the bodies of Haman's
sons.
9:14a) The king agrees (sc. to
a second day of slaughter and
the execution of Haman's sons).
9:15) The Jews fight in Susa on
the 14th.
9:16–18) Summary of events of the
days of fighting and respite.
9:19) Etiology for two-day
celebration.
8:14b) The law is issued in Susa.

8:8a) The king empowers Mordecai
and Esther to write as they wish,

for a royal edict cannot be changed.
8:9–13) Mordecai signs and seals
the letter with the king's ring,
allowing Jewish self-defense.
8:14a) The runners go forth . . .
9:20–22) Mordecai writes the Jews
to institute and confirm
the festival.
9:24–25) His letter tells how
Haman threw lots to destroy the
Jews, but his plot was foiled
and he and his sons were hanged.
9:26) Etymology of Purim
9:27–28) Purim confirmed for all
generations.
9:29–32) Esther's letter and
confirmation.
10:1–3) Epilogue

The proto-AT, and thus probably proto-Esther as well, had little to correspond to most of the events and actions of chs. 8–10. These are paralleled,
but only vaguely, in viii 18–21 (the background of 9:1–17) and viii 33–38 (the

germ of 9:20–26), and thus probably present in proto-Esther. R-MT's re-worked version of Haman's rage and scheme (ch. 3 // AT ch. iv) sets in motion a story that required more extensive development in ch. 8, and ch. 8 in turn required a development of the Aftermath. The MT never existed *without* chs. 9–10, just as it never existed without ch. 8.

In ch. 8, R-MT expanded material narrated in 67 words in the proto-AT (in the parallel passages as listed above) into 347 words in the MT. In chs. 9–10 he expanded material narrated in 134 words in the proto-AT into 595 words in the MT. (In this comparison of Hebrew words with Greek, only the ratios are significant, not the actual word count. The presumption is that the extent of material in the proto-AT is roughly proportionate to that of the parallel material in proto-Esther.) The proportions are: AT : MT :: 1 : 5.2 in ch. 8 and 1 : 4.4 in chs. 9–10. In other words, R-MT is *less* expansionistic in chs. 9–10 than in ch. 8. On the other hand, he introduces more new themes into the latter two chapters. All in all, the redactor does not treat ch. 9 fundamentally differently from ch. 8. Both sections are expansions of passages in proto-Esther, and both are required by the premises of the MT, though not those of proto-Esther (insofar as the latter can be extrapolated from the proto-AT). The counter-decree in Esther 8 is clearly necessitated by Haman's decree in ch. 3, given the assumption of the immutability of Persian law. Ch. 9 too is, as argued above, a natural and necessary development of premises introduced by R-MT into his new version.

6. R-MT's new themes

The major MT innovations are (1) the assumption of the inalterability of Persian law; (2) the expansion of the battle reports; (3) the Purim etiology; (4) the second day of fighting and celebration; and (5) the epilogue (10:1–3). One *lack* that is just possibly an MT innovation is (6) religious language, absent from the MT but present in a few passages in the proto-AT.

6.1. The inalterability of Persian law

The notion that once a law was issued in Persia it could not be altered is unparalleled in the proto-AT; in fact, it is excluded by the ending, in which the king agrees to annul Haman's edict. R-MT introduces this important theme. While he states it explicitly only in 1:19 and 8:8, that is enough to make it the chief constraint upon Esther and Mordecai's strategy. Since Mordecai's decree becomes the means of neutralizing Haman's, it becomes necessary to expand the counter-decree and also to make its wording and the details of its issuance match, almost exactly, those of the first decree.

The inspiration for this theme probably came from proto-Esther, in a passage found in proto-AT iv 10b, where the king says, "Write to all the countries, and seal (it) with the ring of the king. For there is no one who will reject [ἀποστρέψει] the seal." The point in the proto-AT is that no one, at least none of the king's subjects, would dare repudiate a royal decree properly sealed, not that the decree is inherently irreversible.[11] But R-MT seems to have understood this statement to mean that Persian royal edicts can never be repealed.

It is most unlikely that this notion was present in proto-Esther and omitted by the proto-AT. A redactor would be unlikely to systematically remove this notion, especially once it was validated by Daniel 6.

6.2. The punishment of the Jews' enemies

In the proto-AT, the Jews punish their enemies with the king's permission. They are in no apparent danger, and since they are carrying out a royal warrant, their success is presumably guaranteed by the army. R-MT expanded the battle report and made the fighting a life-or-death matter of Jewish self-defense. Though his report of the clash lacks vividness and tension, he still makes it clear that the Jews are defending their lives.

In the MT's telling, Haman's decree proscribed the Jews in a way that could only be counteracted by a decree allowing them the right of self-defense, and this in turn calls for an account of their success.

6.3. The etiology of Purim

R-MT's main innovation was the use of the Esther story as the etiology of Purim. The MT prepares for the association of Purim with the Esther story by glossing Haman's lot as pûr in 3:7, then appending the battle narrative in 9:1–19. This bridges the way to the legal matters of 9:20–32, which include the etymology of Purim.

There is no hint of a Purim etiology in the proto-AT, not even at the point where Haman casts the lot. But the proto-AT, and thus probably proto-Esther, does offer something from which R-MT could shape such an etiology, namely viii 33–38, in which Mordecai urges an immediate, apparently one-time celebration. The relation of this celebration to 14–15 Adar is vague, as is the chronology throughout the proto-AT. Mordecai does refer to 13 Adar as the day on which Haman planned to kill the Jews, but he does not suggest that a festival should be held the *next* day. R-MT converted Mordecai's call for thanksgiving into an appeal to the Jews to "confirm" the celebration of Purim.

---

[11] If ἀποστρέφειν implied absolute irreversibility, then Haman's decree too would be inalterable and Mordecai's decree could not cancel it. Rather, the proto-AT has the king saying that no one would dare reject *his* decree, not that no royal decree can ever be changed, not even by the king. In the MT, one of the points of the Vashti story is to demonstrate that Persian royal decrees bind even the king.

6.4. *The second day of fighting and celebration*

The proto-AT does not allocate two days to the fighting or the celebrations. The MT adds a second day of fighting in Susa (9:11–15). This has no literary motivation, but only lays the foundation for inaugurating a two-day holiday. The two-day duration receives great emphasis in the confirmatory letters (9:20–32), as if this was at stake no less than the validity of the festival itself. The redactor seems to be justifying and regulating an existing practice. He may have found a hint of the Susan day of battles in a proto-Esther equivalent of viii 21a: "And in Susa the king made an agreement with the queen to kill men." To be sure, these men are hanged, not killed in battle (viii 21b). But since this agreement "in Susa" is apparently distinct from the king's earlier license to the Jews to punish their enemies (viii 20), this second, Susan, agreement might have provided the inspiration for the introduction of a second day of fighting in Susa, so as to explain the celebration of 15 Adar practiced in certain localities.

6.5. *The epilogue*

The epilogue with its praise of Mordecai (10:1–3) is absent from the proto-AT and probably was lacking in proto-Esther as well. Its function is to cap off Mordecai's story by telling of his continuing honor.

6.6. *Religious language*

It is arguable, though very uncertain, that R-MT *removed* religious language from his source (as Clines, pp. 107–112, claims). The religious passages in the proto-AT could just as well be additions to proto-Esther with easily understandable and well-paralleled motivations. The religious statements in v 4b–5, vii 1, and possibly vii 22b (ὅτι ὁ θεὸς ἐν αὐτοῖς) are (as Clines recognizes; pp. 109–112) taken from the LXX with only slight changes. References to heathen gods in iv 7 and vi 23 (the latter dependent on the former) may well be original, but (contrary to Clines) they are not "religious language," for such references make no statement about God's control of events and could have no religious significance for the redactor. Religious language appears also in v 9, 11; vii 17; viii 2; and viii 34. These phrases could have been introduced during the transmission of the AT's predecessors or during translation. To be sure, they are well-integrated into their sentences, but since there is an obvious motive for adding them, I can see no reason to prefer the hypothesis that R-MT removed them.[12] The excision of religious statements would be a far more radical act than simply not writing them into a story to

---

[12] Clines suggests this hypothesis cautiously on p. 112 but in absolutes on p. 152 ("it is impossible to deny that the pre-Massoretic story had some such references").

start with. It would be a bold *theological* statement, but one that would require some guidance or clarification beyond what is offered by MT-Esther. Nothing in the book is suggestive of an ideology that would require such a radical modification of the source. Whether or not the various references to chance and reversals of expectation really do point to divine providence as so many commentators have argued,[13] the MT neither denies nor affirms divine providence, though 4:14 does seem to allude to it obliquely.

6.7. Minor items

A few minor statements and motifs absent in the proto-AT may have originated with the MT, though this is very uncertain, since the absences might also be explained as AT omissions. The expansive treatment of the beauty regime in 2:10–15 might be R-MT's contribution. On the other hand, the proto-AT's shorter version could be a condensation within the AT tradition, since the details add little to the development of the plot line. The eunuchs' plot in 2:21–23 might be R-MT's innovation—or it may have been present in proto-Esther and displaced by R-AT because it appears in Add A and would thus be redundant here (as it is in the LXX).

7. The literary and ideological implications of R-MT's changes

With the adaptation of proto-Esther and the addition of the Aftermath, a very different work was created. To describe this work is to retell the tale of Esther. R-MT appropriated the Esther story and made it serve his own ends. The Esther story is now narrated from the perspective of someone generations later who reveals how historical events led infallibly toward the liturgical practice of his own times.

I will focus on the major thematic contributions of R-MT and ask how they supplement and reinterpret the earlier Esther story, as reconstructed with the help of the proto-AT.

7.1. The theme of immutable law has several consequences. One result is a much tauter, tenser story in chs. 1–8. Instead of a crisis that can be solved simply by prevailing upon the king's will, there is now a legal crisis, a puzzle that must be solved even when the king is won over and whose solution requires risk and bloodshed.

The result is that both heroes are raised in independence and significance, for the drama does not end with the king's acquiescence. He retires from the center of the drama and leaves Esther and Mordecai to confront the principles of Persian law—yet to do so without violating them.

---

[13] Including Clines 1984:155 and Fox 1983:298–303.

7.2. Greater cleverness is demanded of Mordecai in the MT's version. Not only must he get Esther to approach the king and entreat him on behalf of the people, he must compose the utterance that delivers the people from a crisis that the king cannot solve. He becomes not only a beneficiary of royal favor but the power behind the throne, the true author of the text that will save the Jews. Seen from another direction, the king becomes Mordecai's mouthpiece. Mordecai's rise to power is confirmed by his magnificent public appearance after his victory, a personal victory that resonates in rejoicing and festivity among the Jews (8:15a, 16–17a) and in a mixture of happiness (8:15b) and fear (8:17b) among the gentiles.

Mordecai becomes not only the savior of the people but also their spiritual leader. This feature is present in the AT but greatly heightened in the MT. It is Mordecai who seizes upon the spontaneous celebrations and undertakes to import them into the festival calendar. He writes the Jews in his own name—all writing until now in the story has been a royal prerogative—to urge the conversion of the two days of respite into a permanent liturgical institution. In the proto-AT, in contrast, he only instructed them to rejoice at what had befallen them.

7.3. R-MT also augments Esther's status and independence considerably. She progressively rises in stature throughout chs. 2–8. In 8:2 she, rather than Mordecai, is given Haman's property and transfers it to Mordecai's steward-ship. Her role now goes beyond begging the king to spare her people and asking him to punish the Jews' enemies. Along with Mordecai, she is given the authority to write whatever they think will neutralize Haman's decree (8:8). (It is, however, Mordecai who actually does the writing in 8:10.)[14] Esther also becomes a shaper of military strategies, asking the king, apparently on her own initiative, to permit a second day of slaughter in Susa and to expose (*TLH*) the bodies of Haman's sons (9:14–15).[15]

Esther's dignity reaches its height when, speaking in her royal authority and in her own name, she validates the decision to establish a new holiday (9:29–32). She is no longer Mordecai's adjunct, but an independent force in the Jewish community. Her word (*ma'ămār*) is the final seal on the Purim compact. The emended version of 9:29–31 (see §3.4) gives her greater independence in issuing the second epistle. The unemended MT sets her equal to Mordecai in the issuance of *both* letters, since vs. 31 retrojects her participation into the first communication as well. In either case, the author of the present passage seeks to strengthen Esther's role. The once malleable,

---

[14] As in 8:2, the author seems to want to give Esther *prerogatives* that he does not picture her exercising.

[15] They were executed on the thirteenth. She is asking that their bodies be exposed, apparently in order to dishearten the opposition.

nervous little beauty (see 2:15 and 4:11), who has already become savior of her people, has grown into one of their two leaders and an authority to her own and all subsequent generations.

7.4. The Jewish people also gains stature. The addition of the immutable-law motif makes them an active player in the drama, for it means that the crisis that originated in the royal court cannot be finally resolved there. Instead of the Jews being the passive beneficiary of Mordecai's machinations as in the proto-AT, they must guarantee their own salvation by their own deeds. The obstacle to be overcome is the Persian law itself, and not only certain hostile Persians; hence gentiles and gentile law cannot rectify the situation. In the final analysis—when their leaders have done all they can and the imperial administration can help no more (except insofar as Persian administrators individually give aid)—then the Jews must "stand up for their lives" (9:2).

The battle reports of 9:1–18 bring the Jewish nation to the fore. Earlier the people could only echo their leaders' distress and await the outcome (4:3, 16a); now they must deliver themselves. Their leaders have made salvation possible, but have not carried it to fulfillment. The nation must finally redeem itself; it must forge its own destiny. Individual Jews with access to power must do their all to influence the holders of power. They also must maneuver cleverly and bravely within the alien polity. And leaders—not institutional leaders but individuals who find leadership thrust upon them—must join the people both to meet present crises and to shape the future. The people, for their part, must respond to this leadership and, if need arise, confront their enemies in bloody battle.

The foremost use of the people's authority is in the creation of permanent communal practices. As Clines observes (pp. 165–66), the holiday of Purim derives its validity—which is problematic in the absence of rooting in biblical law—from two sources: the formal authority of Mordecai and Esther and the intrinsic authority of the community. The people have certainly strengthened their authority by their victory in battle. Now Mordecai calls upon them to employ it.

The key-word of 9:20–32 is "confirm" (*qayyēm*): the popular celebration is converted into a permanent and obligatory practice through a process of confirmations and reconfirmations. The verb *qayyēm* means "confirm," not "command." Thus the ancient legal gesture of taking off the shoe was used "to validate (*qayyēm*) any matter" *after* the bargain was made (Ruth 4:7). Esther 9:27 and 31 use this verb to report that the Jews made the Purim celebration binding upon *themselves*. In Ps 119:106 the verb is used of keeping a vow and in Ezek 13:6 of fulfilling a prophecy. In all these cases, it refers not to the incipience of a legal action or condition, but rather to the formalization or fulfillment of a decision or a previously declared intention.[16] "To

---

[16] In Ps 119:28 the verb means "support" or "keep alive," a different sense but in line with

command" obviously cannot be the verb's sense when describing how the Jews took the obligation upon themselves in Esth 9:27 and 31. Hence *qayyēm* refers not to the imposition of one's will on others or to the prescription of new ordinances, but rather to the fulfillment or regularization of a decision or an existing intention.

At the call of a leader who has earned moral authority, and in response to the events reported to it, the community undertakes certain observances and makes them binding on their descendants (9:20–28). Then all this is further validated by the authority of another leader, the queen (vs. 32). Through this dialectic the Jewish nation rises to its true place among the characters of the drama. The author—as R-MT is in this passage—portrays the Jewish people as a united body. Though dispersed throughout the world, they act as a community: they weigh arguments and interpret events, come to decisions, and take upon themselves and their descendants obligations as they see fit. A historian of religions might speak of practices rooting themselves in the people and only later being interpreted as religious obligations (such may indeed be the true origin of Purim). In such cases, the moment of decision is diffused among numerous individuals, who may enter into the practice with little thought of its higher significance. In Esther 9:20–32, however, the entire people makes a conscious decision to institute a practice in accordance with the interpretation of their acknowledged leader. Such a process, assuming an alert and responsive interaction between people and leadership, was probably an ideal more than a historical reality. But it is a bold, visionary ideal, a vision of the Jews as a *demos* without territory.

The concept is exemplary and didactic. It is a counter-ideal to the law of the Persian (i.e., gentile) realm. In that realm, all formal power derives from the office of king. His decision, even when it is a silly or murderous whim, creates a law so constrictive that he himself is helpless before it. Others may borrow the royal power if they are granted its symbols. Or they may exercise authority by manipulating the person in whom this authority is invested. But the legal order (in reality closer to a *disorder*) that issues from this process of legislation is beyond anyone's control and holds the entire empire by the throat. Thus does legal absolutism become anarchic and deadly.

The Jews, in contrast, arrive at decisions through a dialectic of proposal, assent, and validation. Mordecai and Esther speak from a position of authority, legal and moral, but they do not simply impose this on the Jews. They

---

its legal usage. In Dan 6:8, the Aramaic *qayyāmâ* means to establish or put into force a unilateral royal ordinance; here too it denotes the maintaining or implementing of an existing command. The exact intent of the sentence is not clear. The officials say that they have "taken counsel" to *qayyāmâ* the king's ordinance (*qĕyām malkāʾ*) and to *taqqāpāʾ* ("strengthen," "enforce"?) the prohibition. Thus *qayyāmâ* (inf.) does not mean to initiate the injunction but rather to carry it into effect, because it does not refer to the king's issuing the prohibition but rather to the way the officials treat a command the king has issued.

do not write their Purim epistles "in the king's name" or "seal them with the king's signet." Such a unilateral imposition would be a shaky basis for a practice lacking Mosaic sanction. The ordinance might pass away with the persons who commanded it. A communal decision, reminiscent of the one at Mount Sinai, "We shall do and hearken" (Exod 24:7)—but this time without divine participation—endures as long as the nation that so binds itself.

True authority resides in the Jewish community, without whose joy the spontaneous celebrations would not have occurred and without whose confirmation the practice would not have become law. Mordecai is alert to communal practice. *That* is the origin of the holiday: he extracts the holiday from the people's spontaneous activity. They are to repeat "what they were the first to do" *(hēḥēllû la'ăśôt* [9:23], cf. the verb in Gen 9:20; 10:8), thereby determining their future practice "in accordance with the days in which the Jews had respite from their enemies" (9:22).

By this confirmation the practice becomes as durable as a Persian law *(wĕlō' ya'ăbôr;* 9:27) and reflects a social unity that the mighty law of the Persian empire does not. Persian law led to two days of bloody strife. The result of Jewish legislation is that all Jews in all places and in all ages (note the extraordinary emphasis on unity in vs. 28) uniformly celebrate the peace and joy that followed upon their struggle for existence, and they symbolize their solidarity by exchanging gifts of food. The book's ideal is democratic in requiring the consent of the governed, but it is not anarchic, for communal practice is interpreted, encouraged, and guided by the leadership.

7.5. The redactor made the Esther story the etiology and justification for the celebration of Purim. In spite of much speculation, we do not know the historical origin of Purim. Very likely it was foreign, as suggested by the Babylonian derivation of its name (from *pûru,* "lot"[17]). The holiday seems to have originally been independent of the events described in Esther. The absence of any connection to Purim in the proto-AT is the primary evidence for this. Beyond that, R-MT seems to be deliberately and artificially shaping the story to explain the practice. The second day of battle certainly serves no purpose other than to explain and justify an existing custom of celebrating two different days. (The Susan practice is then artifically extended to all walled cities.) The strained Purim etymology (which is R-MT's alone) also suggests an effort to link the holiday with the tale.

The Purim etiology (and not the exciting narrative or its ideology) is the essence of MT-Esther. Rather than call it an "addition" to the book of Esther, we should think of the rest of the book as a prelude to *it.*

---

[17] Lewy 1939b.

8. R-MT's use of his donor-text

Although we cannot know for certain just what R-MT did to the wording of proto-Esther in chs. 1–8, it is clear that it provided him with only vague hints from which to create what became chs. 9–10. In those chapters, the redactor becomes an author. In that capacity he is less skilled than in forming the primary narrative. Dramatic momentum gives way to bland statement of facts and rather tedious restatements of legal procedures. While this new style can be explained in terms of the purposes of the concluding chapters, there is little doubt that vividness is lost and narrative logic weakened as we move from ch. 8 to ch. 9.

R-MT musters the Esther story to a new purpose by making it a *hieros logos* explaining and justifying the holiday of Purim. He seeks to propound a new ideology and uses his donor text as a vehicle for it. The purpose of all of the primary narrative, most of which derives from proto-Esther, is shifted, as it is made to serve as preparation for the establishment of the holiday in ch. 9.

Whereas R-AT served his texts, bringing one expression of the tradition into conformity with another, R-MT *used* his source text, making the tale the vehicle for a new ideology. He shifted the central purpose of the story from exemplary and inspirational to institutional and normative, without, of course, doing away with the former functions.

III

THE RESULTS OF REDACTION

1. *The final forms*

When describing the redactors' ideologies (ch. I, § 10; ch. II, § 7), I focused on passages and features identifiable with a specific redactor. In this chapter I broaden the scope to a comparison of three Esther stories in their entirety—the proto-AT, the AT, and the MT. For the latter two texts, the redactors produced two stories that expressed more than the ideas and attitudes they were adding to their receptor texts.

It is impossible to know to what extent the meaning and form of a composite text is controlled by the redactor's literary intentions and to what extent it is the unintended by-product of other factors, some of them non-literary and non-ideological. Undoubtedly, a highly intrusive redactor can approach authorship. But many details of composite texts were not intended by the author, the latest redactor, or any other participant in the creative process, but arose as the accidental by-product of combining disparate texts. Accidents do happen, even in literature, even in fine literature. Almost certainly accidental are the fissures and tensions visible to a detailed scrutiny of the composite Esther texts, particularly in the case of the AT.[1] These rarely serve any purposes that can be reasonably imputed to the redactor, and an interpreter would need an excess of ingenuity and harmonistic zeal to come up with literary functions for them.

In the case of the Esther books, the redactors were responsible for choosing and reshaping most of the material that makes up the present texts, but they were not the creators of the greater part of it, either in outline or in wording. This is especially so in the case of R-AT, whose working procedure was largely mechanical and less deliberately tendentious, but even the Massoretic redactor adopted more than he wrote.

Nevertheless, it is reasonable to assume that the redactors were aware of the broad, fundamental features of the texts they were producing and that they found nothing in the new texts that violated their beliefs or sense of

---

[1] Since R-MT was composing, and not just transferring, his new material, he was more able to give it a more organic connection to the base text than was R-AT. The unevenness in the MT is stylistic rather than factual or conceptual.

order. After all, they could have omitted material and made extensive changes in the base text, so non-interference too is a choice determining the text's form. Having spent much time and at least some thought on their texts, they would have recognized the central messages of the texts they put together. Furthermore, accomplished redactors might carry forward motifs, patterns, and microstructures from the base text into new areas, making the literary structure of the new text a natural extension of the old. Hence an analysis of gross structures and major concepts of the new texts can—insofar as it succeeds—describe the intended results of redactional activity and not merely accidental phenomena.

2. *The proto-AT*

The proto-AT was the basis for R-AT's work and was probably not too distant from the text R-MT began with. The proto-AT offers a salvation tale with no divine intervention. It is not strongly religious, in spite of the references to God, which were possibly (though probably not) original[2] and, in any case, were certainly present in the form of the proto-AT used by R-AT. (*His* practice was to use Septuagintal locutions for introducing religious statements.) God is given at most a supporting role in the deliverance. The most telling verse is that which most directly implicates God in the course of events: "If you neglect your people, not helping them, God will be an aid and salvation for them, while you and your father's house will perish" (v 9). In other words, God serves as a back-up to human help, entering history only if humans fail. Esther is not perceived as an agent of God's salvation, but as an alternative to it. Yet God *is* in the background, ultimately guaranteeing Israel's preservation, but also demanding that individual Jews meet their responsibility in the moment of crisis and punishing those who fail to do so.

The proto-AT assumes that it is a Jewish duty to respond to national danger and explores human potential to do so. The solution it offers is Jewish *influence*. Jews become influential by being valuable to the crown, through loyal service as well as personal attractiveness to the king.

Dangers are localized and solutions are specific. The power of the state is essentially reliable. Though it may be deflected from its proper course by lies and deceit, it has mechanisms for correcting itself. The practical problem is how to reach the king, the guarantor of stability who stands at the source of power, who can then be expected to restore the order.

The existence of the mass of the Jewish people depends on others: their enemies, their friends, and, above all, a small number of well-placed Jews. Salvation is invested in individuals who arise sporadically and spontaneously to meet the need. These are judges without charisma, raised up by circumstances without the appointment, support, or compulsion of divine

---

[2] See above, ch. II §6.6.

inspiriting. Salvation prevails as the heroes' courage, cleverness, and influence are reinforced by the enemy's stupidity. The Jewish people, other than these heroes, are spectators of the unfolding of their fate. Beforehand they bewail the danger; afterwards they observe the miracle and—upon instructions from their leader—rejoice in it.

3. The AT[3]

R-AT brought to the fore the sacral dimension of the tale. In the proto-AT, God stays in the background, insuring Israel's safety and receiving their prayer and lamentation. In the AT, religion comes into the foreground, and God's plan is the dimension in which the true meaning of the crisis and salvation is to be sought.

In the AT, salvation is only apparently the fruit of personal influence and sagacity; in reality it is the culmination of a drama scripted by God. That drama is the terrestrial recapitulation of a conflict between cosmic good and cosmic evil. The outcome has already been resolved in a supertemporal reality—a "hyperreality" where archetypal cosmic forces clash, as they always have and always will, until the day of God's final victory and uncontested reign. God may encode this hyperreality in visible, symbolic drama and communicate it to the wise man. In this way, the initiate—both the wise man within the text and the reader above it—perceives the end given at the beginning. Time itself is subverted, as time-bound events—the realities visible to most people—are exposed as epiphenomena of processes in a higher reality. Thus the dramatic tension is invested in the details of events, not in their outcome. The initiate wonders how the hyperreal drama will manifest itself on earth, not how it will conclude.

Before the event, the wise man may receive a symbolic preview of the earthly drama to come (Add A), and afterwards he can decode the cosmic drama by an interpretation that maps its items against earthly events (Add F). However, unlike most dream interpretations (such as those of Joseph and Daniel), Mordecai's (Add F) deciphers events in the past rather than the future. Mordecai did gain some prior insight into the dream when he happened upon the eunuchs' plot (i 10-11), but this awareness hardly revealed the particulars of the events in store. These could be matched up with the dream only after they had come to pass, when Mordecai could think back and recognize that all the dream's details had been realized (viii 54). Thus the usual function of mantic exegesis, "to provide a meaningful correlation between what is seen in the present and unseen in the future" (Fishbane 1985:444), is not in operation here. Rather, Mordecai correlates what was unseen in the past with what has recently become visible. The purpose of

---

[3] The following remarks apply by and large to the LXX as well, since the ideology of the AT is now dominated by the Adds transferred from the LXX.

this interpretation is not to give a message about the future, but to *give meaning to the past* by setting it in the context of a higher reality. The decoding of the dream serves to interpret temporal phenomena, and this interpretation then forms a matrix in which future crises are to be understood.

The individuals facing the crisis must act their part in the drama. Their task demands proper attitude no less than appropriate action. Thus they turn to God in prayer, in which they justify the purity of their motivations and behavior as well as seeking God's help (Adds C-D). National existence at the moment of prayer was not truly in jeopardy, for Israel's deliverance is written into the cosmic plan. Human decision alone is left open. As in Daniel 6–12 and in apocalypse generally, the drama is meant to test the Jews' faith, not their actions.

Although victory is the Lord's doing, human actors are still involved — the same ones as in the proto-AT. But the relative importance of their roles shifts against the backdrop of the cosmic drama.

The king is treated respectfully in the AT, more so than in the proto-AT. By soul-searching and political moralizing in Add E (viii 23–24), he demonstrates his basic rectitude and ascribes the near-disaster entirely to the excessive trust he placed in his right-hand-man.

Mordecai and Esther maintain their centrality in the palace intrigue but attain a further level of importance. Mordecai's role, as the manifestation of one of the dragons, is to present himself for battle with the other dragon. It is significant that the dragons do not actually fight, and so the good dragon cannot be said to win the battle. The crucial point of this engagement is not Mordecai's victory but his willingness to challenge evil; this is prerequisite to God's intervention. Salvation is initiated by Israel's prayer and accomplished by means of the small spring, which somehow issues into (but is not to be identified with) the mighty rivers that punish the powerful. This small spring, we later learn, is manifested in Esther, but she is — as the symbolism shows — the *means* of salvation, not its author.

The true heroes in the AT are the people of Israel, for in the cosmic drama it is their outcry that turns the tide against the dragon of wickedness (Add A, i 7). The outcry in hyperreality will be replicated in earthly reality before Esther acts on their behalf (v 11). Esther tells Mordecai to call a service (θεραπείαν) and pray (δεήθητε) at length, which they presumably do (v 11). Salvation rests on faith, the faith of the Jewish people as a whole; the specific heroes are merely individuals chosen for particular roles in the drama.

The outcome is really dependent on the response of the onlookers, i.e., Israel. In the communal outcry, Israel is acting out a response that, as Mordecai's dream revealed, it would, and thus *must*, act out. Thus the outcry too was determined in advance, outside the visible dimension of human events. Effect circles back into cause.

At the same time that the redactor shifts the true drama to a higher plane of reality and gives the people of Israel the crucial role in salvation, he also extends the significance of events from the national to the universal. Humanity in its entirety, we learn, has a stake in the salvation of Israel. When the nations were imperiled and prepared for war, Israel's outcry to God (i 6) was the key to deliverance (i 7). *Knowledge of God* is the requisite for universal deliverance, and Israel alone possesses that. In the AT (unlike the LXX), Israel is the intercessor for all humanity, while the nations are ignorant of the means to salvation (i 6). Israel's victory prefigures the day when both they and the gentiles, each with its own lot and own fate, will come under God's rule (viii 55).

When the crisis has passed, the Jews, still not privy to Mordecai's insights, witness the culmination of the deliverance drama, whereupon they reaffirm their Jewishness by circumcision (viii 41). They celebrate their deliverance and give praise to God (viii 34, 58). Then they forever re-enact their celebration — not their deliverance — before God (viii 59). This celebration, being predetermined by God and communicated by lots, is detached from temporal events and thereby dehistoricized.

The festival thus directs the people's thoughts to the higher reality and becomes emblematic of the ongoing drama of salvation in Jewish history. In the AT, the story looks forward as well as back. Since the horrors of history will recur, its triumphs must be *made* to recur through re-enactment — not of the triumph itself but of the Jewish response to it. This re-enactment adumbrates the eschaton, as each year the Jews experience anew, in memory and in prospect, the respite and joy that attend the defeat of evil.

4. *The MT*

R-MT, building on a story similar to the one preserved in the proto-AT, did not expand the religious dimension of the drama. Indeed, he may have pushed God even farther into the background. Mordecai's statement in 4:14 still seems to assume that God is the guarantor of salvation, since there is *something* assuring that deliverance will come from some source — if not from Esther then from another. But God's presence is misty. Although the people and Esther fast and lament, presumably directing their words toward God, the author avoids saying that God was the intended audience or that he heard them. The people are acting out their role, but neither they nor the reader ever knows if the communication was completed or if it changed the outcome.

Many interpreters have strained to find God at work in the background. He may indeed be there, but the background of a drama is often where *unimportant* entities are relegated to. God is not an actor in the events of the book. His absence from the foreground is clear and noticeable and should not be ignored, but the meaning of this absence is unclear. It is not to be read as a denial, a statement that God does not control the course of history, for a deliberately atheistic assertion would demand direct statement and would not allow for even allusive reference to providence, such as we have in 4:14.

Nevertheless, the decision to keep God's role obscure and well in the background does assert the sufficiency of human powers in effecting salvation.

The determined secularity of the book is not atheistic but humanistic. It is almost an act of bravado, an insistence on the adequacy of the intrinsic powers of the most powerless of peoples, as if to say: see what we the people, though weakened and scattered, can accomplish by our personal strengths — determination, suppleness of response, cleverness, loyalty, and beauty! (Piety, observe, is not among them.) Indeed, even a woman trapped in a court of macho males nervous about their powers can carry the burden of deliverance. A woman of the Persian harem, emblematic of the exiled Jewish people in her lack of power, living in a stranger's domicile in complete dependency on the whim and favor of others — such a woman can, by dint of courage, womanly charms, and nimble wit, bear the weight of national existence on her shoulders and give the nation the opportunity to redeem itself.

The alignment of human forces in the MT differs from that of proto-Esther. The state is not inherently a source of moral order, nor the king a reliable corrective to perversions of justice below him. The state does hold the *potential* for moral order simply by virtue of its power to restrain anarchic desire and behaviors. But the MT shows little confidence in the reliability of that power. The gentile law is a morally neutral mass that cannot be dislodged but only circumvented, whether for better (as by Mordecai and Esther) or worse (as by Haman). Since the law is immutable, it must, when the need arises, be subverted from within.

A personal appeal to the king no longer suffices to resolve the crisis, for there is a momentum in events beyond his control. He cannot be relied on to ensure the just order, even when he is persuaded to try. Like the Persian law, the king is a neutral entity, or at best a vaguely well-intentioned one that must be manipulated. He is doltish and malleable. Even after his good-will is secured, when he finds himself at an impasse he is not willing to put much effort into solving the crisis — one for which he shares (but does not acknowledge) much of the blame. The MT reserves the ultimate deliverance to the Jewish people in its entirety: individual initiative is preliminary to national self-redemption. And this, in turn, is the basis for the establishment of the holiday through the interplay between leadership and people.

The nation is called upon to celebrate its redemption and consents, covenanting itself and its descendants to a perpetual communal observance. The celebration strengthens communal cohesiveness. Both the sharing of joy and the exchange of "portions" welds Jews together in friendship. The portions do not constitute charity: the poor are *included* within the fraternal exchanges rather than being singled out for benefactions. The "portions," meaning gifts of food, are a way for everyone to involve everyone else in their merrymaking, to invite others in to their private banquets, as it were, thereby extending the household to include the entire community.

Future celebrations will replicate the ancient respite from danger and bloodshed. As in the AT, the holiday in the MT becomes emblematic of the ongoing drama of danger and salvation underlying all of Jewish history. This festival hints at the eschaton, the age of unbroken Jewish brotherhood and unending respite from the strains and dangers of history. But devoid of clear guides such as Add F, the MT does not point to this overtly. The MT refuses to promise supernatural or superhistorical salvation; temporal joy must suffice. Neither the festival nor the history behind it is an actualization of a higher reality. Earthly events are reality in its fullness.

IV

MODELS FOR REDACTION CRITICISM

In the first three chapters I analyzed two instances of redaction and sought to understand their methods, motives, and ideologies. In this chapter I consider redaction more abstractly, asking about the application of the results of the earlier chapters to the question of the validity and practicality of literary-historical criticism.

The source and redaction critic of the books of Esther can work with external as well as internal witnesses to the history of composition. In the case of the AT, the external witness, namely the LXX, makes it possible to reconstruct the earlier stage with a fair degree of objectivity and confidence. In the case of the MT's development, the external witness — the proto-AT — is less helpful, because we do not know how closely it resembled R-MT's source (sc., proto-Esther). Furthermore, the relation of the MT to its source must be established by a series of arguments (see ch. II, §1), none of which is as solid and quantifiable as those that identify R-AT's work. Nevertheless, proto-AT *is* a witness to the prehistory of the MT, and as such provides some external criteria to trace its development.[1] Can these cases of redaction serve as models for literary-historical analysis of other texts?

Models can not constrain interpretation, for one can never know *a priori* how appropriate they are; they can only be suggestive, and their relevance is assessable only in the application. When we can associate certain textual phenomena with the processes that produced them, we may look for similar phenomena elsewhere and ask whether they too are best understood as results of similar processes.

To evaluate the Esther redactions as models, we must ask just how effectively one could use *internal* criteria — which are all we have for most texts — in sorting out the layers of the Esther texts. If this method produces results in agreement with the findings that were based on objective criteria, the texts studied here can serve as *models* and be employed in compositional studies

---

[1] Objective criteria do not necessarily produce certain or even correct results. Objectivity means that the data can be witnessed by all observers, however they may interpret them. Subjective data, such as variations in literary quality, inner tensions in the ideas and attitudes expressed in the text, and even most contradictions — though they may be quite accurate and significant — are dependent on the individual observer's responses, interpretations, and attitudes.

of other texts. The internal criteria can be used with greater confidence. If they are not effective, these texts can only be *examples:* they can demonstrate that processes such as described here did occur in ancient Jewish literature (no small gain in itself), but they will not provide criteria for use in diachronic study of other works.

1. The AT

1.1. Excavating the AT

Knowing, as we do, just what R-AT did to his base text, at least in the redactional sections,[2] we may ask to what extent source criticism could analyze the AT *without* the help of the LXX (or the MT).

Add A could easily be recognized as secondary by internal literary criteria, for it makes Mordecai appear too soon and reach prominence prematurely: at the very start he is an "important man" (i 1), and he quickly gains a high position in the court (i 16). Moreover, the dream slackens the tension of the story and dulls its vivid character-portrayal by turning the personae into symbols of cosmic processes. Furthermore, the dream does not completely fit the events it predicts (nor does it do so in the LXX).

Incongruities between the dream and the story:
(1) The cosmic dimensions of the dream-drama are disproportionate to the scale of the clash in the tale itself, where the conflict begins and is resolved among a few individuals in the court. In the dream, all nations are in terror because of the cataclysm — the cries, turmoil, earthquakes, thunder — whereas in proto-AT, no one outside the court is aware of what is taking place until the crisis is resolved, and then only the wicked have anything to fear.
(2) In the dream, a little spring rises up when the Jews cry to God, and then grows into a mighty river, which apparently becomes great rivers, which consume those who are held in honor. This image does not accord with the way Esther enters upon her task and it overlooks Mordecai's role in motivating her. Furthermore, it makes her the means of a universal punishment of the haughty, not of national salvation.
(3) In the dream the two dragons clash and *then* the nations are in terror, the Jews cry out, and salvation ensues. In the story, in contrast, first one of the "dragons"— Haman — creates a danger to the other, then there is an outcry, and only then do the "dragons" clash.

---

[2] The possibility that R-AT excised short passages from the proto-AT cannot be excluded, though it is unlikely, since the main thrust of the redaction is to supplement the proto-AT rather than to correct it. There were almost certainly no major excisions, since the narrative of the proto-AT proceeds without noticeable lacunae (see ch. I, §8).

Since the dream in Add A can be identified as secondary on internal grounds, it follows that its interpretation, Add F, is secondary as well.

Adds B and E, too, might be recognized as secondary. To be sure, their most striking peculiarity—a florid, intricate style—could be justified as an attempt to imitate the air of a Ptolemaic royal edict (as indeed it is). But even apart from style, Add E in the AT has little integral connection with the narrative (even less so than in the LXX), and the wisdom and monotheistic piety ascribed to the king seem out of character with his behavior elsewhere. Furthermore, the king's permission to ignore the first decree comes too late in the AT (viii 20), and his declaration that the Jews have decided to celebrate 14-15 Adar (viii 30) is premature and unrelated to the preceding narrative.

Add C is not manifestly secondary. Its portrayal of Esther and Mordecai is not sharply incongruous with their portrayal in the proto-AT. This Addition is, however, much more concerned with prayer and supplication than most of the AT (especially once Adds A and F are removed), and a critic might suspect it of being a pious interpolation. Furthermore, Esther's interest in the Temple (v 22b) and in dietary prohibitions (v 27) have no echo in the rest of the narrative.

Neither is Add D obviously secondary. Admittedly, Esther is far more frail and obsequious in Add D than elsewhere, but this difference might also be accounted for by the circumstances described in this context, namely the dangerous intrusion she is about to make into the throne room.

AT-end *was* recognized as secondary—by Torrey (1944:14–15) and Clines (1984:78–84), who argued the case on literary grounds. To be sure, they did have the MT and LXX available for comparison, but they did not use that comparison to make the point. Rather, they made their case by literary considerations internal to the AT. (They could not use the MT, since the passage diverges significantly from it, while parts of the proto-AT approach it fairly closely.) Clines' basic position is that the "literary logic" of the AT falls apart after viii 16. The subsequent narrative, he argues, is not coordinated with what precedes, and its literary quality is markedly inferior. While I do not consider all of Clines' arguments valid (ch. I, §5.3), and while I define the scope of AT-end differently, I think that on the whole his literary criteria (pp. 82–84) succeed in showing that AT-end belongs to a different stage of development than the proto-AT.[3]

---

[3] The persuasive arguments are these (using Clines' numbers): (11) The king's solicitous question in viii 45 is poorly motivated, since there is no reason to think that the Jews were in any danger at that point. (12) Esther's request in vs. 46 for permission to slaughter more enemies seems to presuppose an invitation to make a request (as elsewhere in the book)—but the preceding verses have no such invitation. (13) Mordecai writes that the Jews should keep "these days" (vs. 47)—but the preceding context has nothing to which this can refer, nor does it lay the basis for celebration on both the fourteenth and fifteenth of Adar. Clines observes that the AT here "seems to be a rather unintelligent abbreviation of a longer account of the institution of the festival" (p. 83). (15) The AT does not relate the lots cast for the festival to Haman's casting of

On the other hand, some redactional changes in the receptor text could never, as far as I can tell, have been identified without the existence of the donor text. We could not have detected the isolated Septuagintal borrowings scattered throughout the AT (indeed, there may be others that I have not identified). These, however, have little effect on the overall message. More significantly, we could not have recognized any of the changes the redactor made *within* the Septuagintal material in the course of transfer, and these internal changes often express the redactor's ideology. The redacted form does convey the redactor's ideology, but if we lacked an external source for comparison, we could estimate only approximately the degree to which this message was his own contribution.

Assuming for the moment that we could by internal criteria isolate the Adds and AT-end as secondary and identify them as taken from a "source," what could we say about the character of that source, in other words, about Septuagintal Esther, if it were not extant? We would certainly conclude that this source was more religious, for it places far more importance on divine control of history, on the heroes' spiritual stance, and on the theological import of events. These conclusions would be correct, though in this case we would be misled into thinking that these features were distributed throughout the donor text, whereas it was the *differences* between these blocks and the rest of the text that made them candidates for transfer. The dream would certainly give us a distorted notion about the nature of the conflict between Haman and Mordecai.

I conclude, therefore, that the criteria traditionally used in literary-historical criticism could identify most, though not all, of the redactional blocks in the AT. This could succeed even without reliance on analysis of diction (which, it seems, would be of little help here, especially given the diverse origins of the Adds and the rest of the LXX.[4] Some of the contradictions discussed in ch. I (§11.2.1–4) would point in the direction of the correct analysis, namely: the loss of the etymology of "Phouraia," the awkward placement of the king's second decree, the king's premature statement that the Jews have decided to celebrate 14–15 Adar, and the "second" killing of

---

lots. [This is not, however, a literary flaw, but an ideological difference.] (16) In vs. 52, Mordecai is said to have succeeded king *Xerxes*; elsewhere in the AT the king is always *Assuēros*.

To this we may add that the continued, massive slaughter of the Jews' enemies in vs. 46 is pointless after the punishment of "great numbers" of enemies in vs. 19–20, and after Mordecai has already sent out letters instructing the Jews to stay home and celebrate. Also, the report of the killing of Haman's sons in vs. 44 is otiose, since they were executed some time earlier (see vss. 19, 37). In the present text, vs. 44 reads as an awkward retrospective note.

[4] The best argument for the diversity of the Adds is offered by R. Martin (1975), who demonstrates that Adds B and C were composed in Greek, whereas A, C and D are translations from Hebrew or Aramaic, and F was either composed in Greek or translated freely from a Semitic vorlage. Furthermore, there are no cross-allusions among the Adds, except that A and F, B and E, and probably C and D are paired.

Haman's sons in viii 44. One inconsistency, however, might confuse the issue by leading the source critic to separate material *within* the redactional level, namely the difference between the function of the river in the dream and in the interpretation (ch. I, §§9.1.4; 11.2.5). This inconsistency may reflect the prehistory of the donor text, not the layering of the AT. The analysis would be further confused by the inconsistency concerning the place of Haman's execution (ch. I, §11.2.6), which belongs to the receptor text. In other words, the tensions and awkwardness that are clues to redaction can also appear *within* the work of an individual author or redactor, although, I assume, they are less frequent and blatant in the latter.

Unaided literary-historical criticism, therefore, could produce correct if incomplete results. The arguments for the identification would not be equally decisive for all units, and we could not recognize the smaller transfers or the alterations within the transferred passages. The greatest gain from the exercise would be the largely accurate reconstruction of the receptor text at a stage prior to its supplementation.

1.2. *Redaction by supplementation*

The AT provides a model of one type of redaction, namely *supplementation* — the transfer of material from a donor text in order to fill in gaps perceived in the receptor text. There are various cases where this process is presumed to lie behind the MT, and some cases where it is undoubtedly at work in the formation of the LXX. One demonstrable instance of large-scale supplementation is the hexaplaric filling-out of the OG of Job with material from Theodotion.[5] In general, all hexaplaric supplementation of OG minuses is redaction of this sort. The difference between this case and the AT is that in the former the borrowing was mechanical copying, whereas in the latter it was more flexible and tendentious. Moreover, the supplementation of the OG was governed by an external standard of sufficiency — the MT — which was not so for the AT. R-AT's work had in it features of authorship; Origen's did not.

In the course of supplementing the receptor text, R-AT *abridged* material taken from the donor text, particularly in AT-end. A parallel to this technique is the Codex Vaticanus of Tobit, which abridges the text-form that was to later appear in the Codex Sinaiticus. The Vaticanus is essentially interested in the moralistic message of the story and omits much dialogue and other details that do not contribute to this directly (Zimmermann 1958:39–41, 127–29).

The formation of the AT resembles that of the source JE in the Pentateuch,

---

[5] The original Greek translation of Job lacked about one-sixth of the Hebrew text. Origen supplied the missing material from Theodotion's translation. For the history of research on the topic see Dhorme 1984:cxcvi–ccvi and Orlinsky 1957. Dhorme (1984:ccii) lists the verses absent in the OG.

according to classic source criticism. When **E** is extracted from JE, the remaining text, J, forms a document possessing narrative continuity as well as a characteristic style, ideology, and literary shape. This is the receptor text that was supplemented from E.[6] The character of E, the donor text, is much harder to determine; the E sections do not form a continuous, sequential narrative, nor is their style distinctive. There are features that tend to distinguish it from J, but there is not much to indicate stylistic uniformity within the E sections themselves. Any attempt to describe the "E document" on the basis of the segments taken from it must be compared to an attempt to extrapolate LXX-Esther from the redactional supplements in the AT.

2. The MT

Would anything of the MT's redaction history be recoverable without the aid of the proto-AT? To answer this we need not speculate, since many scholars actually have been probing the redaction of the MT, and the effort has had 200 years to prove itself. (In the following I must assume the validity of my own earlier conclusions, though I consider them less firm than in the case of the AT's redaction.)

The answer is not clear-cut. My own view is that the entire MT of Esther is a reworking of an earlier source, with relatively minor changes in chs. 1–7 but major ones in chs. 8–10. This source lacked the major themes of chs. 8–10 or held them only in embryo. No other critic has come to quite this conclusion, though other theories have shared some of its assertions, in part for the same reasons. Clines, as noted, placed chs. 9–10 at a later stage of the book's development, thus recognizing the same two layers in the text's history (and, of course, influencing the direction of my own thinking).[7] The commentators who argued that 9:20–32 is a later addition to the story (defined as 1:1–9:10; see ch. II, §3) — and this was the very first move in the literary-historical study of Esther — had much the same perception. They recognized that the report of the establishment of Purim is not organically connected with the narrative. (Esther 9:19 does describe the holiday, but not by name, nor does it *establish* the holiday the way 9:20–32 does.) The story proper seems self-

---

[6] According to the hypothesis of Volz and Rudolph (1933), E never existed as an independent source. According to the classical theory, it was a continuous document that provided material that was worked into J.

Numerous scholars have followed and advocated the classical source theory. The most careful and thoroughgoing presentation of the arguments on its behalf is Carpenter and Harford 1900. Still valuable is the influential introduction of Driver 1967 (1891). The classical critics spoke of the combining of the J and E sources but always recognized that E, as it stands in the Pentateuch (or Hexateuch), is incomplete, and that J provides the narrative frame for the combined source JE.

[7] Although he makes use of the proto-AT in reinforcing his conclusions, he first argues for the separation of chs. 9–10 on literary grounds (pp. 39–49).

contained, and the epistles give the appearance of being grafted onto it. The artificiality of the lots/Purim equation gives 3:7, as is widely recognized, the quality of a gloss, a rather forced attempt to make the story serve as the etiology for the holiday. Wellhausen severed the holiday's origins from the Esther story, associating them instead with a new-moon festival (1902:145). Meinhold also recognized two main stages in the development of the MT: the story and the establishment of Purim (1983a:13). He saw that the addition of the Purim epistles in 9:20–32 entailed revision of 9:1–4 and 9:5–28. This separation reflects an awareness that the battle reports of 9:1–18, at least in their present form, are shaped with 9:20–32 in mind, and if the Purim letters are later than the Base Narrative, so are the battle reports as they now stand. Moreover, Meinhold suggested that 9:19 is a later gloss and that the practice of Purim was originally independent of the book of Esther (ibid.). Again, the general literary criteria used by these scholars and others in the identification of diachronic layering were *not* illusory, and are in part supported by comparison with a parallel text (the proto-AT). Still, they are inadequate, for the greater the literary skills of the redactor, the less effective the criteria that detect his presence. But not every redactor seeks to cover his tracks, and, moreover, objectives other than literary may govern redaction.

Are there other cases in the Bible of redaction comparable to R-MT's work? There are a few redactional appendices at the ends of books (e.g., the historical material in Jer 52, the instructional poems in Prov 30–31, and possibly the appendices in 2 Sam 20:23–24:25[8]), but none of these shifts the purpose of the preceding text the way Esth 9–10 does. We may compare the Chronicler's recension of Samuel-Kings, though his intervention, both verbal and thematic, was more profound.

The value of the redaction of MT-Esther lies in alerting us to a range of devices in a redactor's toolbox: rewording, insertion of new themes without disturbing the story line, the creation of a new ending by expansion of minor themes in the donor text, and the appropriation of a base text for a new purpose by the addition of an appendix.

My experiment has suggested that unaided source criticism of the AT and the MT could provide some, but only some, of the results made possible by the comparison of parallel sources. The tools are effective but not powerful.[9]

---

[8] 2 Samuel ends with various lists, short narratives, and poems that interrupt the story of David's life and do not belong to the Deuteronomistic history proper or the earlier material it incorporated. These appendices are not a continuation of the preceding narrative, but it is disputable whether they were added to a completed book of Samuel (Hertzberg 1964:415–16; Noth 1981:124–25, n. 3; et al.), or were inserted before the division between 2 Sam and 1 Kgs (McCarter 1986:17, noting that the "Lucianic" MSS of the Septuagint divide at a different place, before the equivalent of the MT's 1 Kgs 2:12).

[9] Tigay (1982:248) came to a similar conclusion about Morris Jastrow's 1898 source criticism of the Gilgamesh epic based solely on the late version. Berlin, however, counters that, insofar as he succeeded, Jastrow was using his knowledge of similar elements in other texts, not

Another implication of the experiment is to show that too much has been made of the importance of contradictions in the study of composite texts. Contradictions are only one means of discriminating among compositional layers; they are not the essence of redaction. Their absence does not prove single authorship, nor their presence multiplicity. (They become more significant when combined with other indicators, such as ideology, style, and diction.) Works by single authors can be quite ragged and self-contradictory— sometimes for literary ends, sometimes out of carelessness, sometimes because the contradictions are too trivial to worry about. Furthermore, redactors can, probably without great difficulty, cover their tracks, if they are so inclined.

---

proceeding by unaided source criticism (1983:133–34). S. Kaufman (1982) similarly doubts that it would have been possible to reconstruct the sources of the Temple Scroll without the existence of those sources (i.e., the Pentateuch).

V

ON READING REDACTION[1]

Having considered two cases of redaction and their bearing on the practice of literary-historical criticism, I turn to redaction generally, offering some thoughts on the nature of redaction as an artistic process and as an object of reading.

1. *The literary significance of redaction*

There is a continuum of redactional intervention from trivial to major. At the one end are restrained editors who are one step away from being copyists. They allow themselves (not always consciously) to introduce modest "corrections," minor glosses, and synonym-substitutions. They are comparable to copy-editors, who subordinate themselves to the author's words yet sometimes, deliberately or not, override authorial intentions.

At the other end of the continuum we find aggressive redactors who reduce, rephrase, rearrange, recombine, and supplement the receptor text, sometimes intending only to serve the author's goals, sometimes deliberately going beyond them. They may appropriate the text and turn it into a very different work. Of the latter sort was Ezra Pound, who cut, reshaped and radically revamped T. S. Eliot's "The Waste Land."[2] Or Nahum Tate, who strove to burnish Shakespeare's "Heap of Jewels, unstrung and unpolisht, yet so dazzling in their Disorder," while "Newmodelling" the plays and remedying "Quaintness of Expression."[3] Or Edward Aswell, who abridged and restructured Thomas Wolfe's outpourings to make them publishable and (as he saw it) readable — and left scholars to debate whether Wolfe's novels are indeed his own.[4] Such editors usually (I would surmise) believe that they are *helping* the author by making the text more readable, acceptable, and

---

[1] I am grateful to Professor Stuart Lasine of Wichita State University for reading and carefully criticizing a draft of this chapter.

[2] Eliot was pleased with the revisions and believed that the poem in its final form was the best thing *he* had done so far; Ackroyd 1984:117–20.

[3] From his preface to his version of King Lear, 1681.

[4] See, most recently, Field 1987.

accessible, thereby drawing out the potential of the original. But all are to some degree constructing a new work.

Redactors use various means to achieve a more accurate and complete expression of the "same" thing, yet inevitably create something different. In this sense redaction subverts canon while serving it.

If the redactor's role in the creative process can be so great and its effects so pervasive, certainly it should not be discounted or ignored. Toward the second, more active, end of the continuum (which alone will be our concern in the rest of the discussion), the redactor becomes a type of author, but one working with greater constraints than a (relatively) free creator—who also operates under a range of constraints. The problem then is how to give the work of such a redactor the kind of reading appropriate to this activity.

It is, of course, possible and legitimate to read a compound text as a monolith, even if in actuality that meaning thus discovered never resided in any individual consciousness. To do so, we take the text that resulted from a multiplicity of decisions (and accidents) as if it were the expression of a single author. This is the way we usually treat modern texts, however extensively edited; and traditional readers, along with most readers without academic expertise, have always approached the Bible in this way. Even in scholarly literary analysis, this is the best primary perspective, since it accords with the conventions of most texts and with the intentions of most editors. But must literary analysis stop there? Can we also read a redacted text *as* a redacted text, attending not only to the "final form"[5] but to the redaction itself? Is there a way of reading redaction as a special *mode* of literary creativity?

Recent scholars of biblical literature have almost always viewed the latest stage of a text's development as the only valid object of *literary* study. They have commonly insisted (with some impatience) that interpretation exclude questions of the text's past and avoid "excavation," which is thought to fragment the text and, in any case, to fall short of producing firm results. See, for example, M. Sternberg's notion that "over two hundred years of frenzied digging into the Bible's genesis" have produced paltry, contradictory results (1985:13). R. Alter more graciously allows excavative scholarship "its place as a necessary first step to the understanding of the Bible" (1981:13–14).[6] Still, this concession pictures *his* kind of analysis as a more advanced stage in the

---

[5] See the caveat in the Introduction, p. 4.

[6] To pursue the "excavation" analogy (which is often brandished in reproaching source criticism), we can note that many great works of ancient architecture would be lost or obscured without excavation. Excavation does not destroy their aesthetic values, it restores them. And in literary-historical excavation, unlike archaeological excavation, the integrity of the surface is in no way marred. Literary scholars who scold source critics for "fragmenting" the text act as if the canonical text ceased to be available thereafter.

investigative hierarchy, indeed, identifies that kind of analysis with "under-standing the Bible," and values other activities only insofar as they facilitate *it*. Literary analysis is confined to interpretation of the texts "as they actually exist" (Alter 1987:4). Indeed, it has become virtually a *Gattungsformular* to set up an opposition between diachronic and synchronic approaches and, while conceding the validity of both, to identify *literary* readings exclusively with the latter.[7] Variations on this theme are to be found in the major works of biblical literary scholarship starting with R. Moulton (1896:iv) and con-tinuing, most notably, with M. Weiss (1984:ch. 1), R. Alter (1981:12–14), A. Berlin (1983:111–34) and M. Sternberg (1985:14–23). All of them set "exca-vative"/"external"/"source-oriented" inquiry on one side of a methodological divide and "literary"/"internal"/"discourse-oriented" inquiry on the other. If historically-oriented literary criticism cannot be invalidated, it can still, it would seem, be banished from respectable company.

This segregation is neither inevitable nor desirable. And here let me emphasize: I am not disputing the value, or indeed the primacy, of synchronic reading. Literary critics such as those named above have immensely en-riched our understanding of the Bible and our appreciation of its art. I am rather advocating that critical reading itself be enriched by an awareness of the text's inner history. I see four main reasons why "literary criticism" should embrace both perspectives.

(1) An eclectic approach provides more tools for interpretation, and we need them all. There is no reason why a literary scholar cannot roam back and forth between synchronic-literary and diachronic-historical explanations, selecting and combining them in whichever way accounts for the data most fully with least tortuosity.

That is not to say that synchronic interpretation and source analysis can or should coexist in harmony. They frequently offer competing explanations for the same phenomena. Shifts of perspective, attitude, and style, as well as outright self-contradiction can be accommodated under literary rubrics, such as point-of-view, frame breaks, ambiguity, irony, voice, and indeter-minacy (which can account for anything); or they can be explained as the seams between different developmental layers. How, for example, shall we account for the differences between the historical summary in Est 9:24–25 and the story proper? Should we ascribe them to literary purposes — reading

---

[7] A strong declaration of a common doctrine is that of G. Tucker, in his foreword to D. Robertson's *The Old Testament and the Literary Critic*: "Historical issues concerning ancient Israel or the biblical books themselves are [in this book] steadfastly and intentionally ignored. . . . [The literary critic] does not ask how the story came together, or who Moses was, but takes the story as it stands and asks what role Moses plays in it, what the tensions and resolutions of the plot are" (1977:viii). Indeed, redaction criticism is a willful shirking of duty: "And certainly an attempt to solve structural or conceptual difficulties by relegating parts of the text to later redactors is a way of avoiding the interpretive enterprise" (p. 7). Even if the solution is right?

the summary as a public communication that formulates events in a way that will secure the king's favor (my explanation[8])? Or should we allocate the different viewpoints to different persons—viewing the summary as a later scribe's misunderstanding? There is no inherent reason to prefer an approach such as mine in this passage simply because it treats the text "as is." If my interpretation (or the like) is wrong, then the text "as is" is not the only one worthy of reading and probably not the best one.

In seeking to account for literary phenomena, each approach uses up data the other needs for itself. From one point of view, this is the problem of "the disappearing redactor," nicely described by John Barton:

> The more impressive the critic makes the redactor's work appear, the more he succeeds in showing that the redactor has, by subtle and delicate artistry, produced a simple and coherent text out of the diverse materials before him; the more also he reduces the evidence on which the existence of those sources was established in the first place. (1984:57)

Conversely, the artist can be diminished, or at least redefined, when elegant explanations of leitmotifs, image patterns, and rhetorical structures must overlap blocks of material combined, but not composed, by a redactor. Such explanations do not coexist comfortably with the hypothesis of composite-ness.[9] Yet however uncomfortable each approach may be with the other's company, neither should be given inherent priority. The availability of competing options increases the possibilities for credible interpretation. The relaxed eclecticism of Clines' study of Esther, for example, strengthens both its literary and its historical arguments, for neither approach need be made to solve all problems.[10]

(2) Literary-historical criticism respects the text as a *means of communication*. It enables us to hear the voices of the individual authors and redactors who created the composite work; and all creativity is (contrary to a current belief) ultimately individual.[11] The fact that we can never extricate the

---

[8] Ch. II, §3.3.

[9] For example, in Alter's discussion of Gen 38, the Tamar story (1981:5–12), which he seems to recognize as an interpolation in the Joseph narrative (p. 10), he points out that the "narrator" contrives an ironic play on the kid (*gĕdî ʿizzîm*) of Judah's pledge and the goat (*sĕʿîr ʿizzîm*) whose blood had fooled Jacob (Gen 37:31). But mention of the kid must have already been present in the Tamar story, for if the redactor had inserted that motif deliberately as an allusion to the goat of 37:31, he would have used the same term. The creation of an ironic echo of kid and goat was almost certainly not the redactor's motive for interpolating the Tamar story in the Joseph story. If that were indeed the motive, we could only be amazed at the fundamental thematic significances that fortuitously resulted from the insertion of one story in another merely on the basis of a tangential verbal similarity. But it is, in my view, more reasonable to ascribe such connections not to the author's or redactor's creativity, but to the interpreter's.

[10] That is not to say that his conclusions are *right*; no methodology, pure or mixed, can guarantee truth. But my disagreements with him are on specifics.

[11] See J. L. Battersby's eloquent *apologia* for the supremacy of the individual's intention in literary communication in "The inevitability of professing literature" (1988). In sum: "Codes and

individual contributions confidently or completely from the collectivity is no reason to despair of the attempt to do so or, even worse, to decide that it is not worthwhile.

To be sure, source critics may sometimes be rescuing redactors against their will, so to speak—subverting their achievements by recovering them. If so, perhaps the enterprise may be justified as a sort of deconstruction, but one aiming (via redaction criticism) at a *re*-centering of the meaning— though now in a multiplicity of texts.

Literature enables the solitary—and exciting—communion from one person to another across the centuries. Literary scholarship should facilitate this communication, not obscure it. By searching for and attempting to hear the individual creators of a composite work we are participating in the act fundamental to language and literature: "[T]he underlying reason for writing is to bridge the gulf between one person and another" (W. H. Auden).[12] We are doing what most authors and most readers think they are doing, and if this effort is a delusion, it is a most fruitful one, one that makes literature possible.[13]

(3) Aesthetic clarity can be enhanced by recovering artistry obscured by later accretions.[14] The great nineteenth century critics were aware that "excavation" often brings to light, rather than (as the accusation goes) obscuring or atomizing literary integrity and artistic excellence, and they realized that these qualities had sometimes been blurred by the redactors, whose skills and motivations were doctrinal more often than literary.

(4) There is currently a special social imperative to integrate literary history into the literary study of the Bible. Powerful religio-political interests are attempting to impose an anachronistic reading of biblical texts on the public school curriculum. By an egregious misapprehension of genre, fundamentalists would have biblical creation myths (alone of all creation myths) repackaged in pseudo-scientific rhetoric and taught in science classrooms as biological and geological theory. As a consequence of the fundamentalist clamor, the broader public is often led to believe that this is the right way

---

conventions make writing possible; writers make codes and conventions behave" (p. 69).

[12] Taken from the epigraphs to part II of W. Booth's *The Company We Keep* (1988:156). In ch. 6 of that book, Booth discusses this one-to-one relationship viewed as "friendship." Note also the quote from Descartes: "the reading of all the great books is like conversing with the best people of earlier times . . ." (ibid.).

[13] From the historian's standpoint, too, it is (as Halpern [1988] emphasizes and demonstrates) essential to retrieve the voice of the individual redactor, to ask about the redactor as a person. Only thus can we understand and evaluate the redactor as a historian, for this inquiry removes him from an historical and social void. "In a void, any or all of the historian's reports could be arbitrary and unbased—and his convictions conjure up suspicions that the evidence for them is concocted. In his social setting, however, the historian is answerable to the expectations of his contemporaries (see Polybius 31.22)" (Halpern 1988:30).

[14] A fine example of this is McEvenue 1971.

to read the Bible. Given the political impact and goals of this distorted hermeneutic, critical scholars have, I believe, an obligation to foster the literary-historical perspective in research (at least affirming its significance if it is not congenial to their own interests) and to convey this perspective to their students and the general public. We should teach the historical-critical approach not as an antiquarian exercise of interest only to dusty academicians, but as a means to deeper understanding and appreciation of what the living text can communicate to the modern reader.

Frankly, I see no great need for one more "unitary" reading of Genesis that scolds Bible critics for slighting the literary unity of the primeval history and demonstrates how it is structured in an intricate chiasm or whatnot. There *is*, however, a need for lively and ongoing source-critical and tradition-historical study of this material. Such study would advance scholarly and public understanding of just what kind of text the primeval history is. It would show how the text arose through a process of fluid and extended development, how it encompasses various and even incompatible viewpoints, and how its various components promulgate different theological-political goals and attitudes. It is not only Genesis that requires this treatment; the entire Bible should be read with an eye to its developmental—which is to say, human—dimension.

The results of literary-historical scholarship are not esoteric. They can and should continually be introduced to the public by means of popular publications, high school and college teaching,[15] and, in my opinion, even in homiletics and religious-school textbooks. The purpose is not indoctrination but exposure. And it is not enough to say that scholars believe that the Pentateuch is composed of four sources and then proceed to show why that doesn't really matter. The historical complexity of biblical literature *does* matter,[16] and students should learn why. Revealing the rough-edged humanness and historical rootedness of the Bible will enhance its interest and relevance.

---

[15] James Ackerman's pioneering book on Bible instruction in secondary schools does not avoid literary-historical issues. He defines his course as a literary approach, and for him this includes "... tracing the development over many generations of these passages of literature before they were written down" in order "to show how Israel's early literary traditions were formulated to give further expression to her faith" (1967:xv).

[16] Many advocates of Bible-as-Literature teaching would not even bother with the first step. In a handbook on secondary school Bible teaching, T. Warshaw, Ackerman's frequent collaborator, carefully avoids "commitment either to the two-source theorists or to traditionalists" (a false either-or) and consistently pursues a synchronic, largely New Critical, analysis (1978:35 and *passim*). "Teachers of literature," he advises, "would also do well to accept the text as it now exists rather than worry about its provenance. The business of a secondary class is literary criticism, not literary scholarship" (p. 94)—a dubious and unfortunate distinction. Similarly, in introducing an anthology for use in the teaching of the Bible as literature, K. Gros Louis includes among his "most basic assumptions" the assertions that "[t]he literary critic assumes unity in the text" and that "[t]he literary critic assumes conscious artistry in the text" (1982:14–15). But if you assume it you will, of course, find it.

There is no need to expect unanimity of results among Bible critics any more than among evolutionary biologists. But the results of mainstream critical scholarship should be brought before the public with pride of accomplishment—for these *are* real accomplishments, by no means inconsequential or (in essence) outdated. The introduction of the historical-critical perspective into the schools—which being critical, *does* belong there—would, of course, meet with strong controversy, but that would show that Bible scholarship still has something vital to say.

2. Redaction and hermeneutics

The developmental perspective has not been entirely outside the purview of recent literary study. There have been significant efforts to trace the inner history of texts not only in order to isolate the historical components but also to recover the messages of the various levels and to observe their interaction. A major step in this direction is M. Fishbane's study of inner-biblical exegesis (1985), which, while not taking a specifically "literary" approach, focuses on the presence of later voices commenting on their predecessors (often in immediate contiguity) and lays a theoretical basis for understanding this process. Fishbane also shows how conventions or formulas sometimes mark a sentence as commentary.

A few specifically literary studies do combine a diachronic perspective with sensitivity to the literary and rhetorical characteristics of the texts studied.[17] Clines (1984) examines the dynamics of expansion of the Esther texts, viewing each stage of development as a coherent literary statement, a distinct "Esther story" with an intent and emphasis of its own.[18] In a chapter on "composite artistry," Alter describes the redactors' artistry and purposes in some biblical narratives. Alter's is a thoughtful contribution to redaction criticism, though it seems always on the verge of undoing itself by showing that the redactional seams are only "seeming contradictions" or merely violations of "our notions"[19] of narrative unity. Though fully receptive to the possibility of textual compositeness, he seems uneasy about the redaction-critical enterprise, as if it were something one does as a last resort to save a text from charges of "intrinsic incoherence" or being "the confused textual patchwork that scholarship has often found."[20] A systematic and productive

---

[17] The following paragraphs only give some examples of this approach and are not meant to be comprehensive.

[18] 1984:139–74. Like the critics of the nineteenth century, Clines is aware that an understanding of narrative dynamics is not a rebuttal to literary-historical criticism but a prerequisite for it. And unlike modern practitioners of literary criticism he does not invariably find perfection in the "final form" of every text he subjects to literary scrutiny.

[19] Not mine.

[20] Alter 1981:133. There are passages in the Bible that "seem to resist any harmonizing interpretation." Such uncooperative passages might, Alter believes, lead one to conclude either that

attempt to introduce developmental considerations into literary analysis is D. Damrosch's *The Narrative Covenant* (1987). Damrosch emphasizes the bearing of genre transformation (and not just genre identification) on the interpretation of biblical texts and calls for a "dynamic reading" that is aware of the text's genetic complexity without losing sight of its canonical shape.[21]

I would further inquire into ways that multiple, sequential voices *interact* — and not only tell their own stories — within a single work. I see no reason why attention to form and expression within a text's development is inherently less "literary" than a synchronic criticism or why a scholar of literature should ignore diachronic readings or even relegate them to the other side of an academic divide. A literary critic who strives to produce a richer, more adequate — indeed, *truer* — reading can approach the text from both perspectives separately and together. Source and redaction criticism become part of the interpretative process, alongside analysis of structure, thematic patterns, interplay of voice, and the like. Appreciation of a landscape may, after all, include attention to its geology. The validity of any such reading will depend on the success of the diachronic analysis, whose results will inevitably be provisional, but synchronic interpretation too requires postulations, hypotheses, and arguments that do not always win assent.

The reconstruction of the earlier forms of a text is, of course, uncertain and will never attain consensus, but that is true of any literary interpretation. Diachronic reconstruction at least offers the *theoretical* possibility of certainty, because *something* happened to produce the book, and if sufficient data were available we could have certain knowledge of the process. Textual meaning, on the other hand, is not even theoretically stable, and no accumulation of facts can or should fix it in place.

Certainly from the standpoint of the *reader's* activity, a text's development need not be excluded from its meaning. Even when a redactor intends his contribution to be read as an inseparable part of the original — which is not always the case — a critical reader (and not only a historical critic) may choose to override that intention and ask about the redactor's purposes in modifying

---

transmission and editing could sometimes produce "intrinsic incoherence" *or* that "the biblical notion of what constituted a meaningful and unified narrative continuum might at times be unfathomable from the enormous distance of intellectual and historical evolution that stands between us and these creations of the early Iron Age" (1981:133). Alter prefers the latter alternative, which is, of course, self-justifying: when we find coherence, that shows we understand the biblical artistic norms; when we do not, that is because we lack that understanding.

[21] A. Berlin offers the intriguing assertion that, in addition to the synchronic poetics that she pursues, "there *is* diachronic poetics. Just as one is able to write a historical grammar, showing grammatical changes over a period of time, so one ought to be able to write a historical poetics, showing the changes in structure and discourse that a text may undergo" (1983:111). She does not pursue this further and says that it is probably beyond the capabilities of current Bible scholarship. This may be so, but the gathering of data such as undertaken in Tigay's anthology (1985), his Gilgamesh study (1983), the present monograph, and a few other works, makes such a poetics conceivable.

the earlier work. After all, even a synchronic "literary reading" of a sacred text—especially narrative—is, to some degree, going against the grain, for it applies rhetorical or aesthetic norms to what the author would have us take as reporting of raw fact in a form dictated by the events themselves.[22] The refusal to subordinate one's reading entirely to the text's directives is the essence of *critical* scholarship.

Once awareness of diachronic complexity is present, a strictly synchronic approach requires a willed naiveté—perhaps a good initial heuristic tactic but certainly not an adequate one. Such an approach taken exclusively yields a reading less rich and complete than one sensitive to the dialectic among the multiple voices in the text. An orientation to the reader's response should ask how the earlier readers would have received the new form of the text in *its* historical and canonical context.[23]

When we consider a text from the standpoint of authorial intention, we must undoubtedly begin with a synchronic reading (of the canonical form or of any other stage we believe we can isolate and choose to read), unless we find indications that the redactors themselves sought to indicate the composite nature of the text. In some cases there may be conventions that alert the reader to earlier levels of the text and thus signal that its compositeness is supposed to be recognized. For example, Targum Sheni to Esther proceeds by quoting lemmata from the Bible in a fairly literal Aramaic translation and extending them by aggadic material dealing with issues and historical events sometimes quite distant from those of the Esther story.[24] We are thereby invited to read the Esther story in counterpoint with these other matters, not merely to submerge the older text (i.e., MT-Esther) in the new one. The author-redactor of Targum Sheni certainly does not intend us to read that version as *the* book of Esther. Still, such cases are undoubtedly rare. Usually, an author-redactor who incorporates earlier sources (rather than referring to or quoting them) intends the new text to be read as a unity, without regard

---

[22] J. Kugel (1981, 1982) argues that a *literary* analysis cannot claim intrinsic validity, because the identification of the Bible as literature is not called for by the Bible itself. Kugel asks, rhetorically: "would not a rhetorical analysis of Muzzey's classic high school history textbook, or the U.S. Constitution, or any of the other analogues I have cited, be urging us to read these documents in a way fundamentally different from that in which they were intended to be, and normally are, read?" (1982:328). The answer is yes, but we may gain much from overriding that intention—an understanding of how high school text books create and promulgate cultural myths, for example.

[23] S. Boorer (1989) shows how different "diachronic readings" of Genesis-Kings produce different "final readings" of the same text, and argues that these are likely to be different from a synchronic reading of that text. Applying Ricoeurian hermeneutics, she argues that the "self" of the interpreter is modified by appropriating the "way-of-being-in-the-world" projected by each diachronic level, and thus encounters the final form differently from one who encounters that form alone (p. 205). In other words, knowing the different levels in a work affects the way we read it.

[24] For an authoritative translation and study of Targum Sheni see Grossfeld 1991.

to its inner history. While a reader can override that intention, the unitary perspective can claim to be (literally) authoritative and the best primary— though not the exclusive—stance for a reading. Yet even in the absence of conventions or other deliberate signals of a text's inner history, a diachronic awareness may sometimes be faithful to the redactor's intention.

The AT is such a case. R-AT could not expect the LXX to disappear just because *his* version of the AT was now available for others to read. Moreover, unless he had—and knew he had—the only copy of the proto-AT, he could not have realized that his version would eventually dislodge the older text from memory. Even if he had hoped that his own text would become the authoritative version of the story, he was not perpetrating a "pious fraud," pretending to promulgate the sole and original version of Esther. He could not have expected his readers, or at least not many of them, to view his version as *the* book of Esther, as the sole textual authority by virtue of being (as far as they knew) the "final" form of the text. Rather, he would have expected them to regard his AT as a *response* to both the LXX and the older AT, as an expansion and retelling of these—in the same way that the author of Targum Sheni of Esther intended *his* readers to view his translation. The interplay among the different voices of a redacted text, then, may well belong to the authorial intention, and those who consider this the locus of interpretation should include it within their field of vision.

The concept of *intertextuality* is the key to reading the compositeness of composite texts. I find particularly suggestive the concept of intertextuality advocated by Harold Bloom (who calls it "influence").[25] There are, of course, caveats: Intertextuality in Bloom's sense is uncertain as a general principle of poetic creativity; it was in any case formulated specifically to describe the motive forces in Romantic poetry. Also, Bloom is speaking of an author's relation to authors of *other* texts. Nevertheless, the concept of intertextuality, as envisioned by Bloom, has validity for the relationship among authors *within* a single composite text.[26]

When a text's development is recovered, the dialectic between an author— or redactor—and his precursors presses on reading with a special immediacy. The fiction of textual autonomy cannot even be *imagined* to apply to a redactor's work, for redaction cannot exist by itself. It is absolutely dependent for its existence on its context—a context it creates in order that it might itself exist. To be precise, a redaction does not actually consist in the resulting text, but in the complex of *changes* that produced it. In other words, the redaction

---

[25] See especially *The Anxiety of Influence* (1973); also *A Map of Misreading* (1975). J. Culler (1981:107–111) provides a useful critique of Bloom which relates his ideas of influence and misreading to the semiotic concept of intertextuality; also helpful is the interpretation of (inter)textuality by Leitch 1983:129–63.

[26] My use of Bloom is, in Bloom's sense, a "misprision" (specifically, in Bloom's terms, a "clinamen"); but Bloom has taught that the history of reading proceeds by such "misreadings."

does not reside in the word ποταμοὶ, which has replaced ταπεινοὶ in i 8, but rather in the *replacement* of ταπεινοὶ by ποταμοὶ. Similarly, R-AT's redaction of the LXX's chs. 9–10 is not to be identified with the AT verses corresponding to those chapters (viii 41b–52), but with the numerous acts of substitution, excision, transposition, and addition made in the LXX material as it was being interwoven with the proto-AT.

While every work of literature resides in the intertextual space of its literary culture, redaction has a more concentrated, compressed intertextual space of its own — namely, the redacted text itself. Indeed, redaction is the epitome of intertextuality, with the later text both incorporating its precursor and living upon it symbiotically, thus, in a sense, destroying it in order to create something new from its parts. Redaction thereby holds within itself "the complex movement of a simultaneous affirmation and negation of another text."[27] The oedipal struggle between author and precursor, which Bloom so vividly describes, is intense in redaction and very relevant to its reading.[28]

3. *Intertextuality in the Esther books*

It is difficult to estimate the status proto-Esther would have had for R-MT; but, if we accept the thesis that the redactor was supplementing and reshaping an older tale, it is likely that he expected his readers to know the earlier version as well as the new one. A version that reached the MT redactor would not have been known to him alone. Indeed, a widespread knowledge of the older version would have encouraged the readers of the new version to accept its authenticity. They would have been familiar with the story of Mordecai and Esther and thus more inclined to accept the historicity of the tale as told by the MT. (This is important, because the author of 9:20–32 bases Purim's claim to validity on the presumption of the story's historicity.)[29]

To a reader aware of the parent version, the MT's retelling argues against giving too much credit to gentile government, since the legal system that endangered the Jews proved unable to rectify itself. The original readers were asked to revise their notion that individual leadership alone saved the nation; ultimately it had to redeem itself. Most important, the retelling reveals that the old deliverance story, with its brief mention of celebration, held within it *all along* the rationale for the Purim festival.

---

[27] Kristeva 1969:257; see Culler, 1981:107.

[28] Damrosch (1987:304) observes that sometimes "the later author really wishes to *suppress* the earlier source, or at least to co-opt it and impose on it a structure and emphasis that guide the reader toward a new perspective in preference to the old." In fact, strictly speaking, the redactor *always* suppresses the older text, at least for the reader of the new text. Even when the redactor intends for the older text to be recognized, it is filtered through the new text and is thus to some degree subordinated to it. But the critical reader need not accede to the suppression.

[29] That is not to say that the book does record actual events, but only that it *claims* to do so.

The creative struggle is most evident in the AT. Even as R-AT serves the proto-AT by preserving and completing it, he is *opposing* it. At the very start he overrides his receptor text by presupposing the protagonists' victory while wresting it out of their control. By prefixing the dream of Add A to the tale of the struggle he shows the victory to be predetermined and not truly the result of their own efforts. Victory is the Lord's! The redactor reinterprets human heroism, converting it from lonely initiative into confident piety by having the protagonists declare their dependency on God's will in long and humble prayers. R-AT also strips terrifying temporal events of their substance by subordinating them to a determinative hyperreality. In all these ways he is undermining his receptor text, not only elaborating it.

The dialectic in the AT is actually tripartite, for the redacted AT has two immediate precursors, the proto-AT and the LXX. Although R-AT aligns himself ideologically with the LXX, he is also re- (and mis-) reading that version, in the ways I described in ch. I (§§8, 9, 10). In the apparently pointless synonym-substitutions and transpositions within the borrowed LXX material (ch. I, §§8.1, 3), we glimpse the "anxiety of influence," the "fear of being *flooded*," that Bloom sees as the core of modern poetic consciousness.[30] The very lack of inherent significance in these changes allows the redactor to signify that he is an originator, a partly-free operator in the interstices of textual space—doing so above all where he is most slavishly dependent on his donor text. (In passages where he effects many substantive changes, he makes fewer insignificant ones.) Such changes, present throughout the biblical text, are often dubbed "stylistic" because we have no other explanation for them. Yet they are more than that: they are acts of aggression as well as love.

By the new conjunction of materials, R-AT is saying: When you see Jews struggling and scheming for Israel's existence, realize that their manifest story—such as that told by the old text—is incomplete. The full story must reveal first the supernatural drama and, second, the spiritual one. R-MT is saying: When you see individuals standing alone in the breach against foreign hostility, realize that their efforts are actually preparing the way for the exercise of *communal* power, both martial and legislative. Know further that episodic deeds of deliverance are not mere flashes in the dark night of exile, but bright lights that are ever renewed in annual celebration and that thereby augur the final salvation of Israel.

---

[30] Bloom 1976:57 and *passim*. According to Bloom, this phenomenon becomes central only in post-Enlightenment poetry. But it has a powerful forerunner in the Egyptian lament of Khakheperre-sonbu (early 19th century BCE), who bewails the difficulty of finding something truly new to say: "Had I unknown phrases, /Sayings that are strange, /Novel, untried words, /Free of repetition; /Not transmitted sayings, / Spoken by the ancestors! . . . I wring out my body of what it holds, /In releasing all my words" (Lichtheim 1973:146).

The revisionary move taken by these two redactors is precisely what Bloom calls the "tessera," the link between poet and precursor:

> In the *tessera*, the later poet provides what his imagination tells him would complete the otherwise "truncated" precursor poem and poet, a "completion" that is as much misprision as a revisionary swerve is. (1973:66)

The notion of "antithetical completion," which usually serves as a trope for an author's (not always conscious) attitude, in the case of redaction assumes spatial, substantive form.

By changes both stylistic and ideological, redactors achieve the victory of the living. Even while remaining anonymous and (in sharp contrast to the Romantic poet) usually lacking a persona in the text,[31] redactors assert themselves by arrogating their predecessors' voices as vehicles for their own thoughts. This is not necessarily a sign of poetic "strength," as Bloom defines it ("Poetic strength comes only from a triumphant wrestling with the greatest of the dead, and from an even more triumphant solipsism"; 1975:9). R-AT, at least, was a minor figure, working by rule and creating little that his texts did not already offer. But he, too, produced a "misprision" of his precursors. Both he and R-MT thrust themselves into the process of canon, usurping older, authoritative texts as vehicles for intruding their own presence into sacred tradition. Seeking to join canon, they subverted it.

Only in later times, in ways not necessarily predicted by the redactors, were the proto-AT and proto-Esther to disappear, obscuring the history and, in part, the meaning of the surviving works. But a reading that deadens the tension between the stages of development is not complete, for that tension too, and not only the harmonies that may also have arisen in the extended creative-destructive dialectic, is productive of meaning.

Writing has its history, and so does reading. We have advanced beyond traditional readers, for the canonical form is not the only one *we* have. We have recovered other forms; now we must learn how to read them.

---

[31] This is not always the case; the Deuteronomist often speaks in his own voice.

APPENDIX A:

LXX-AT EQUIVALENTS

The following passages generally (but sometimes loosely) correspond (* = loose correspondence; - = omitted).

LXX	AT	LXX	AT
A 1-2	i 1	5:11	-
A 3-17	i 2-18	5:12-15	vi 21b-24
1:1-14	ii 1-14	6:1-3	vii 1-4
1:15	-	-	vii 5-6a
1:16-17	ii 16	6:4-10	vii 6b-12
1:18	-	-	vii 13
1:19, 20, 21	ii 18, 20, 21	6:11	vii 14
1:22	-	-	vii 15-17
2:1-9	iii 1-9a	6:12-14	vii 18-23a
2:10-15	-	7:1-5	vii 23b-viii 5
2:16-18	iii 9b-18	-	viii 6-7
2:19-23	-	7:6-10	viii 8-13b
3:1-6	iv 1-6	8:1-2	viii 15*
3:7-13	iv 8, 9, 11, 10, 7, 13	8:3-12	-
		-	viii 16-21
B 1-7	iv 14-18	E 1-24	viii 22-32
3:14-15	iv 19*	8:13-14	-
4:1-4	v 1-4a	-	viii 33-38
4:5	-	8:15-16	viii 39-40
[MT 4:6 om.]	same	8:17a	-
4:7-11	v 4b-8*	8:17b	viii 41a
4:12	-	9:1	-
4:13-17	v 9-12a	9:2-15	viii 41b-46
C 1-10	v 12b-17	9:16-19	-
C 11	-	9:20-21	viii 47-48*
C 12-30	v 18-29	9:22-25	-
D 1-16	vi 1-12	9:26a	viii 49
5:3-8	vi 13-18	9:26b-31	-
-	vi 19	10:1-3	viii 50-52
5-9	-	F 1-11	viii 53-59
5:10	vi 21a		

155

APPENDIX B:

THE AT

Sigla for AT Manuscripts

Göttingen	Cambridge			
19	=	b′	Vatican, Chigi R. VI.38	12th c.
93	=	e₂	British Museum, Royal 1 D.II.	13th c.
108	=	b	Vatican, Vat. Gr. 330	13th c.
319	=	y	Athos, Vatopethi 513	1021 CE
392		not used	Grottaferrata, A.γ.I	10th c.

Readings which differ in Hanhart's edition (apart from orthographic variations) are inserted at the bottom of the page and marked by "H."

ΕΣΘΗΡ Α

¹ᵃἜτους δευτέρου βασιλεύοντος Ἀσσυήρου τοῦ μεγάλου, μιᾷ τοῦ μηνὸς Αδαρ Νισαν (ὅς 1 (A) 1
ἐστι Δύστρος Ξανθικός), ἐνύπνιον εἶδε Μαρδοχαῖος ὁ τοῦ Ἰαείρου τοῦ Σεμείου τοῦ Κισαίου
τῆς φυλῆς Βενιαμιν, ⁽²⁾ ἄνθρωπος μέγας ² ⁽³⁾ τῆς αἰχμαλωσίας ἧς ᾐχμαλώτευσε Ναβουχοδονοσορ 2 (2)(3)
ὁ βασιλεὺς Βαβυλῶνος μετὰ Ἰεχονίου τοῦ βασιλέως τῆς Ἰουδαίας. ³⁽⁴⁾ καὶ τοῦτο ἦν αὐτοῦ 3 (4)
τὸ ἐνύπνιον. καὶ ἰδοὺ φωνὴ καὶ κραυγὴ θορύβου, βρονταὶ καὶ σεισμὸς καὶ τάραχος ἐπὶ τῆς
γῆς. ⁴⁽⁵⁾ καὶ ἰδοὺ δύο δράκοντες, καὶ προσῆλθον ἀμφότεροι παλαίειν. ⁵ καὶ ἐγένετο αὐτῶν ⁴₅ (5)
φωνή, ⁽⁶⁾ καὶ ἐταράσσετο πάντα ἀπὸ τῆς φωνῆς τῆς κραυγῆς ταύτης. ⁶ μαρτυρομένη πᾶσι 6 (6)
τοῖς λαοῖς ⁽⁷⁾ ἡμέρα σκότους καὶ γνόφου ⁽⁸⁾ καὶ ταραχὴ πολέμου, καὶ ἡτοιμάσατο πᾶν ἔθνος (7)(8)
πολεμῆσαι, ⁽⁹⁾ καὶ ἀνεβοήσαμεν πρὸς κύριον ἀπὸ φωνῆς τῆς κραυγῆς αὐτῶν. ⁷ καὶ ἐγένετο ἐκ 7 (9)
πηγῆς μικρᾶς ὕδωρ πολύ, ποταμὸς μέγας· ⁸⁽¹⁰⁾ φῶς, ἥλιος ἀνέτειλε, καὶ οἱ ποταμοὶ ὑψώθησαν 8 (10)
καὶ κατέπιον τοὺς ἐνδόξους. ⁹⁽¹¹⁾ καὶ ἀναστὰς Μαρδοχαῖος ἐκ τοῦ ὕπνου αὐτοῦ, ἐμερίμνα τί 9 (11)
τὸ ἐνύπνιον καὶ τί ὁ δυνατὸς ἑτοιμάζει ποιῆσαι. ¹⁰ καὶ τὸ ἐνύπνιον αὐτοῦ κεκρυμμένον ἦν ἐν 10
τῇ καρδίᾳ αὐτοῦ, καὶ ἐν παντὶ καιρῷ ἦν ἀναζητῶν αὐτό· ¹¹ ἐπίκρισις διασαφηθήσεται αὐτῷ 11
ἕως τῆς ἡμέρας ⁽¹²⁾ ἧς ὕπνωσε Μαρδοχαῖος ἐν τῇ αὐλῇ τοῦ βασιλέως μετὰ Ασταου καὶ Θεδεύτου (12)
τῶν δύο εὐνούχων τοῦ βασιλέως. ¹²⁽¹³⁾ καὶ ἤκουσε τοὺς λόγους αὐτῶν καὶ τὰς διαβολὰς αὐτῶν, 12 (13)
ὡς ἐξηγοῦντο τοῦ ἐπιθέσθαι Ἀσσυήρῳ τῷ βασιλεῖ τοῦ ἀνελεῖν αὐτόν. ¹³ εὖ δὲ φρονήσας ὁ 13
Μαρδοχαῖος ἀπήγγειλε περὶ αὐτῶν. ¹⁴ καὶ ἤτασεν ὁ βασιλεὺς τοὺς δύο εὐνούχους, καὶ εὗρε 14
τοὺς λόγους Μαρδοχαίου. καὶ ὁμολογήσαντες οἱ εὐνοῦχοι ἀπήχθησαν. ¹⁵ καὶ ἔγραψεν 15
Ἀσσυῆρος ὁ βασιλεὺς περὶ τῶν λόγων τούτων. καὶ ἐγράφη Μαρδοχαῖος ἐν τῷ βιβλίῳ τοῦ
βασιλέως περὶ τοῦ μνημονεύειν τῶν λόγων τούτων. ¹⁶ καὶ ἐνετείλατο ὁ βασιλεὺς περὶ τοῦ 16
Μαρδοχαίου, θεραπεύειν αὐτὸν ἐν τῇ αὐλῇ τοῦ βασιλέως καὶ πᾶσαν θύραν ἐπιφανῶς τηρεῖν,
¹⁷ καὶ ἔδωκεν αὐτῷ περὶ τούτων ⁽¹⁷⁾ Αμαν Ἀμαδάθου Μακεδόνα κατὰ πρόσωπον τοῦ 17 (17)
βασιλέως. ¹⁸ καὶ ἐζήτει ὁ Αμαν κακοποιῆσαι τὸν Μαρδοχαῖον καὶ πάντα τὸν λαὸν αὐτοῦ 18
ὑπὲρ τοῦ λελαληκέναι αὐτὸν τῷ βασιλεῖ περὶ τῶν εὐνούχων, δι' ὅτι ἀνῃρέθησαν.

¹ καὶ ἐγένετο μετὰ τοὺς λόγους τούτους ἐν ἡμέραις Ἀσσυήρου τοῦ βασιλέως τοῦ μεγάλου, 1 (I) II
ὑπετάγησαν αὐτῷ ἀπὸ τῆς Ἰνδικῆς ἕως τῆς Αἰθιοπίας ἑκατὸν εἴκοσι ἑπτὰ χῶραι. ² ἐν τῷ 2
καθῆσθαι Ἀσσυῆρον ἐπὶ τοῦ θρόνου τῆς βασιλείας αὐτοῦ, ³ καὶ ἐποίησεν ὁ βασιλεὺς πότον τοῖς 3
ἄρχουσι τῆς αὐλῆς Περσῶν καὶ Μήδων, καὶ οἱ ἄρχοντες τῶν χωρῶν κατὰ πρόσωπον αὐτοῦ, ⁴ εἰς 4
τὸ ἐπιδειχθῆναι τὸν πλοῦτον τῆς δόξης τοῦ βασιλέως καὶ τὴν τιμὴν τῆς καυχήσεως αὐτοῦ ἐπὶ
ὀγδοήκοντα καὶ ἑκατὸν ἡμέρας, ⁵ ἕως ἀνεπληρώθησαν αἱ ἡμέραι ἃς ἐποίησεν ὁ βασιλεὺς πᾶσι τοῖς 5
εὑρεθεῖσιν ἐν Σούσοις τῇ πόλει ἀπὸ μεγάλου ἕως μικροῦ, πότον ἐν ἡμέραις ἑπτὰ ἔνδον ἐν τῇ αὐλῇ

i 11 (after ἐπικρισις). H: + αυτου

ΕΣΘΗΡ Α   III 14

6 τοῦ βασιλέως, ἄγων τὰ σωτήρια αὐτοῦ. ⁶ἦν δὲ ἐξεστρωμένα βύσσινα καὶ καρπάσινα καὶ ὑακίνθινα καὶ κόκκινα ἐμπεπλεγμένα ἐν ἄνθεσιν, καὶ σκηνὴ τεταμένη ἐν σχοινίοις βυσσίνοις καὶ πορφυροῖς ἐπὶ κύβοις ἀργυροῖς καὶ στύλοις παρίνοις καὶ περιχρύσοις, καὶ κλῖναι χρυσαῖ ἐπὶ λιθόστρωτον 7 σμαράγδου, καὶ κύκλῳ ῥόδα, ⁷καὶ ποτήρια χρυσᾶ ἔξαλλα καὶ οἶνος βασιλικὸς ὃν ὁ βασιλεὺς πίνει, 8 ⁸καὶ πότος κατὰ τὸν νόμον. οὕτως γὰρ ἐπέταξεν ὁ βασιλεὺς ποιῆσαι τὸ θέλημα τῶν ἀνθρώπων.

9 ⁹καὶ Ουαστιν ἡ βασίλισσα ἐποίησε δοχὴν μεγάλην πάσαις ταῖς γυναιξὶν ἐν τῇ αὐλῇ τοῦ 10 βασιλέως. ¹⁰ἐγένετο δὲ τῇ ἡμέρᾳ τῇ ἑβδόμῃ ἐν τῷ εὐφρανθῆναι τὸν βασιλέα ἐν τῷ οἴνῳ εἶπεν ὁ 11 βασιλεὺς τοῖς παισὶν αὐτοῦ ¹¹ἀγαγεῖν Ουαστιν τὴν βασίλισσαν εἰς τὸ συνεστηκὸς συμπόσιον ἐν 12 τῷ διαδήματι τῆς βασιλείας αὐτῆς κατὰ πρόσωπον τῆς στρατιᾶς αὐτοῦ. ¹²καὶ οὐκ ἠθέλησεν Ουαστιν ποιῆσαι τὸ θέλημα τοῦ βασιλέως διὰ χειρὸς τῶν εὐνούχων. ὡς δὲ ἤκουσεν ὁ βασιλεὺς 13 ὅτι ἠκύρωσεν Ουαστιν τὴν βουλὴν αὐτοῦ, ἐλυπήθη σφόδρα, καὶ ὀργὴ ἐξεκαύθη ἐν αὐτῷ. ¹³καὶ εἶπεν ὁ βασιλεὺς πᾶσι τοῖς σοφοῖς τοῖς εἰδόσι νόμον καὶ κρίσιν τί ποιῆσαι τῇ βασιλίσσῃ περὶ τοῦ 14 μὴ τεθεληκέναι αὐτὴν ποιῆσαι τὸ θέλημα τοῦ βασιλέως. ¹⁴καὶ προσῆλθον πρὸς αὐτὸν οἱ ἄρχοντες Περσῶν καὶ Μήδων καὶ οἱ ὁρῶντες τὸ πρόσωπον τοῦ βασιλέως καὶ οἱ καθήμενοι ἐν τοῖς βασιλείοις. 16 ¹⁶καὶ παρεκάλεσεν αὐτὸν Βουγαῖος λέγων Οὐ τὸν βασιλέα μόνον ἠδίκηκεν Ουαστιν ἡ βασίλισσα, ἀλλὰ καὶ τοὺς ἄρχοντας Περσῶν καὶ Μήδων· καὶ εἰς πάντας τοὺς λαοὺς ἡ ἀδικία αὐτῆς ἐξῆλθεν, ₍₁₉₎¹⁸ὅτι ἠκύρωσε τὸ πρόσταγμα τοῦ βασιλέως. ¹⁸ ⁽¹⁹⁾εἰ δοκεῖ οὖν τῷ κυρίῳ ἡμῶν, καὶ ἀρεστὸν τῷ φρονήματι αὐτοῦ, γραφήτω εἰς πάσας τὰς χώρας καὶ πρὸς πάντα τὰ ἔθνη, καὶ γνωσθήτω ἠθετηκυῖα τὸν λόγον τοῦ βασιλέως Ουαστιν, ἡ δὲ βασιλεία δοθήτω ἄλλῃ, κρείττονι οὔσῃ αὐτῆς. 20 ²⁰καὶ φαινέσθω ὑπακούουσα τῆς φωνῆς τοῦ βασιλέως, καὶ ποιήσει ἀγαθὸν πάσαις ταῖς βασιλείαις, καὶ πᾶσαι αἱ γυναῖκες δώσουσι τιμὴν καὶ δόξαν τοῖς ἀνδράσιν αὐτῶν ἀπὸ πτωχῶν ἕως πλουσίων. 21 ²¹καὶ ἀγαθὸς ὁ λόγος ἐν καρδίᾳ τοῦ βασιλέως, καὶ ἐποίησεν ἑτοίμως κατὰ τὸν λόγον τοῦτον.

III (II) 1 ¹καὶ οὕτως ἔστη τοῦ μνημονεύειν τῆς Ουαστιν καὶ ὧν ἐποίησεν Ἀσσυήρῳ τῷ βασιλεῖ. ₍₃₎ ²καὶ εἶπον οἱ λειτουργοὶ τοῦ βασιλέως Ζητήσωμεν παρθένους καλὰς τῷ εἴδει, ⁽³⁾καὶ δοθήτωσαν προστατεῖσθαι ὑπὸ χεῖρα Γωγαίου τοῦ εὐνούχου τοῦ φύλακος τῶν γυναικῶν. ⁴καὶ ἡ παῖς ἣ ἐὰν 5 ἀρέσῃ τῷ βασιλεῖ, κατασταθήσεται ἀντὶ Ουαστιν. καὶ ἐποίησαν ἑτοίμως κατὰ ταῦτα. ⁵καὶ ἀνὴρ Ἰουδαῖος ἐν Σούσοις τῇ πόλει ᾧ ὄνομα Μαρδοχαῖος υἱὸς Ἰαείρου τοῦ Σεμείου τοῦ Κεισαίου 7 τῆς φυλῆς Βενιαμιν. ⁷καὶ ἦν ἐκτρέφων πιστῶς τὴν Εσθηρ θυγατέρα ἀδελφοῦ τοῦ πατρὸς αὐτοῦ. 8 καὶ ἦν ἡ παῖς καλὴ τῷ εἴδει σφόδρα καὶ ὡραία τῇ ὄψει. ⁸καὶ ἐλήμφθη τὸ κοράσιον εἰς τὸν οἶκον ₍₉₎τοῦ βασιλέως· καὶ εἶδε Βουγαῖος ὁ εὐνοῦχος ὁ φυλάσσων τὸ κοράσιον, ⁽⁹⁾καὶ ἤρεσεν αὐτῷ ὑπὲρ 9 πάσας τὰς γυναῖκας. ⁹καὶ εὗρεν Εσθηρ χάριν καὶ ἔλεον κατὰ πρόσωπον αὐτοῦ, καὶ ἔσπευσε προστατῆσαι αὐτῆς, καὶ ἐπέδωκεν ὑπὲρ τὰ ἑπτὰ κοράσια, τὰς ἅβρας αὐτῆς. ὡς δὲ εἰσήχθη 14 Εσθηρ πρὸς τὸν βασιλέα, ἤρεσεν αὐτῷ σφόδρα. ¹⁴καὶ ὅταν ἐγένετο ἑσπέρα, εἰσήγετο, καὶ τὸ

iii 5 (after και). H: + ην

πρωὶ ἀπελύετο. ¹⁷ὡς δὲ κατεμάνθανεν ὁ βασιλεὺς πάσας τὰς παρθένους, ἐφάνη ἐπιφανεστάτη ¹⁷ Εσθηρ. καὶ εὗρε χάριν καὶ ἔλεον κατὰ πρόσωπον αὐτοῦ, καὶ ἐπέθηκε τὸ διάδημα τῆς βασιλείας ἐπὶ τὴν κεφαλὴν αὐτῆς. ¹⁸καὶ ἤγαγεν ὁ βασιλεὺς τὸν γάμον τῆς Εσθηρ ἐπιφανῶς, καὶ ἐποίησεν ¹⁸ ἀφέσεις πάσαις ταῖς χώραις.

¹καὶ ἐγένετο μετὰ τοὺς λόγους τούτους, ἐμεγάλυνεν ὁ βασιλεὺς Ἀσσυῆρος Αμαν Αμαδάθου ι (III) IV Βουγαῖον, καὶ ἐπῆρεν αὐτόν, καὶ ἔθηκε τὸν θρόνον αὐτοῦ ὑπὲρ ἄνω τῶν φίλων αὐτοῦ, ὥστε κάμπτεσθαι καὶ προσκυνεῖν αὐτῷ ἐπὶ τὴν γῆν πάντας. ²πάντων οὖν προσκυνούντων αὐτῷ κατὰ ² τὸ πρόσταγμα τοῦ βασιλέως, Μαρδοχαῖος οὐ προσεκύνει αὐτῷ. ³καὶ εἶδον οἱ παῖδες τοῦ βασιλέως 3 ὅτι ὁ Μαρδοχαῖος οὐ προσκυνεῖ τὸν Αμαν, καὶ εἶπον οἱ παῖδες τοῦ βασιλέως πρὸς τὸν Μαρδοχαῖον Τί σὺ παρακούεις τοῦ βασιλέως καὶ οὐ προσκυνεῖς τὸν Αμαν; ⁴καὶ ἀπήγγειλεν αὐτοῖς ὅτι ₄ Ἰουδαῖός ἐστιν. καὶ ἀπήγγειλαν περὶ αὐτοῦ τῷ Αμαν. ⁵ὡς δὲ ἤκουσεν Αμαν, ἐθυμώθη τῷ Μαρ- 5 δοχαίῳ, καὶ ὀργὴ ἐξεκαύθη ἐν αὐτῷ, καὶ ἐζήτει ἀνελεῖν τὸν Μαρδοχαῖον καὶ πάντα τὸν λαὸν αὐτοῦ ἐν ἡμέρᾳ μιᾷ. ⁶καὶ παραζηλώσας αὐτὸν ἐξ ὀφθαλμῶν αὐτοῦ, καὶ καρδίᾳ φαύλη ἐλάλει τῷ βασιλεῖ κακὰ περὶ Ισραηλ ⁸λέγων Ἔστι λαὸς διεσπαρμένος ἐν πάσαις ταῖς βασιλείαις, λαὸς πολέμιος καὶ ἀπειθής, ἔξαλλα 8 νόμιμα ἔχων, τοῖς δὲ νομίμοις σου, βασιλεῦ, οὐ προσέχουσι, γνωριζόμενοι ἐν πᾶσι τοῖς ἔθνεσι πονηροὶ ὄντες, καὶ τὰ προστάγματά σου ἀθετοῦσι πρὸς καθαίρεσιν τῆς δόξης σου. ⁹εἰ δοκεῖ οὖν 9 τῷ βασιλεῖ, καὶ ἀγαθὴ ἡ κρίσις ἐν καρδίᾳ αὐτοῦ, δοθήτω μοι τὸ ἔθνος εἰς ἀπώλειαν, καὶ διαγράψω εἰς τὸ γαζοφυλάκιον ἀργυρίου τάλαντα μύρια. ¹¹καὶ εἶπεν αὐτῷ ὁ βασιλεὺς Τὸ μὲν ἀργύριον ἔχε, 11 τῷ δὲ ἔθνει χρῶ ὡς ἄν σοι ἀρεστὸν ᾖ. ¹⁰καὶ περιείλετο ὁ βασιλεὺς τὸ δακτύλιον ἀπὸ τῆς χειρὸς 10 αὐτοῦ καὶ ἔδωκε τῷ Αμαν λέγων Γράφε εἰς πάσας τὰς χώρας, καὶ σφραγίζου τῷ δακτυλίῳ τοῦ βασιλέως· οὐ γὰρ ἔστιν ὃς ἀποστρέψει τὴν σφραγῖδα. ⁷καὶ ἐπορεύθη Αμαν πρὸς τοὺς θεοὺς 7 αὐτοῦ τοῦ ἐπιγνῶναι ἡμέραν θανάτου αὐτῶν. καὶ βάλλει κλήρους ἕως τρισκαιδεκάτην τοῦ μηνὸς Αδαρ Νισαν φονεύειν πάντας τοὺς Ἰουδαίους ἀπὸ ἀρσενικοῦ ἕως θηλυκοῦ καὶ διαρπάζειν τὰ νήπια. ¹³καὶ ἔσπευσε καὶ ἔδωκεν εἰς χεῖρας τρεχόντων ἱππέων. ¹⁴ B⁽¹⁾καὶ ὑπέγραψε τὴν ¹³ B(ı) ὑποτεταγμένην ἐπιστολήν· Βασιλεὺς μέγας Ἀσσυῆρος τοῖς ἀπὸ τῆς Ἰνδικῆς ἕως τῆς Αἰθιοπίας ἑκατὸν καὶ εἴκοσι καὶ ἑπτὰ χωρῶν ἄρχουσι καὶ σατράπαις τάδε γράφει· ¹⁵⁽²⁾πολ- 15 (2) λῶν ἄρξας ἐθνῶν καὶ πάσης ἐπικρατήσας τῆς οἰκουμένης ἐβουλήθην—μὴ τῷ θράσει τῆς ἐξουσίας ἐπαιρόμενος, ἐπιεικέστερον δὲ καὶ μετὰ ἠπιότητος ἀεὶ διεξάγων—τοὺς τῶν ὑποτεταγμένων ἀταράχους διὰ παντὸς καταστῆσαι βίους, τὴν δὲ βασιλείαν ἥμερον καὶ πορευτὴν ἄχρι περάτων παρεχόμενος, ἀνανεώσασθαι τὴν πᾶσιν ἀνθρώποις ποθουμένην εἰρήνην. ¹⁶⁽³⁾πυνθανομένου δέ μου τῶν συμβούλων πῶς ἄν ἀχθείη τοῦτο ἐπὶ πέρας, ὁ σωφροσύνῃ παρ' 16 (3)

ΕΣΘΗΡ Α v ii

(4) ἡμῖν διενηνοχώς, εὐνοίᾳ ἀπαραλλάκτῳ καὶ βεβαίᾳ πίστει τὸ δεύτερον τῶν βασιλειῶν γέρας ἀπενεγκάμενος Αμαν [4] ὑπέδειξεν ἡμῖν πάροικον ἐν πάσαις ταῖς κατὰ τὴν οἰκουμένην φυλαῖς ἀναμεμῖχθαι δυσμενῆ τινὰ λαόν, τοῖς μὲν νόμοις ἀντιδικοῦντα πρὸς πᾶν ἔθνος, τὰ δὲ τῶν βασιλέων παραπέμποντα διηνεκῶς προστάγματα πρὸς τὸ μηδέποτε τὴν βασιλείαν εὐσταθείας

(5) 17 τυγχάνειν. 17 [5] διειληφότες οὖν μονώτατον τὸ ἔθνος ἐν ἀντιπαραγωγῇ παντὸς κείμενον τῶν ἀνθρώπων διὰ τῶν νόμων ξενίζουσαν παραγωγήν, καὶ δυσνοοῦν τοῖς ἡμετέροις προστάγμασιν ἀεὶ τὰ χείριστα συντελεῖν κακὰ πρὸς τὸ μηδέποτε κατατίθεσθαι τῇ ὑφ' ἡμῶν κατευθυνομένῃ

(6) 18 μοναρχίᾳ, 18 [6] προστετάχαμεν οὖν ὑμῖν τοὺς σημαινομένους ὑμῖν ἐν τοῖς γεγραμμένοις ὑπὸ Αμαν τοῦ τεταγμένου ἐπὶ τῶν πραγμάτων καὶ δευτέρου πατρὸς ἡμῶν ὁλορρίζους ἀπολέσαι σὺν γυναιξὶ καὶ τέκνοις ταῖς τῶν ἐχθρῶν μαχαίραις ἄνευ παντὸς οἴκτου καὶ φειδοῦς τῇ τεσσαρεσκαιδεκάτῃ τοῦ μηνὸς τοῦ δωδεκάτου (οὗτος ὁ μὴν Αδαρ, ὅς ἐστι Δύστρος), φονεύειν πάντας

(7) τοὺς Ἰουδαίους καὶ ἁρπάζειν τὰ νήπια, [7] ἵνα οἱ πάλαι δυσμενεῖς καὶ νῦν ἐν ἡμέρᾳ μιᾷ συνελθόντες εἰς τὸν ᾅδην εἰς τὰ μετ' ἔπειτα εὐσταθήσωσιν, καὶ μὴ διὰ τέλους παρέχωσιν 19 ἡμῖν πράγματα. 19 [III 15] καὶ ἐν Σούσοις ἐξετέθη τὸ πρόσταγμα τοῦτο.

v (IV) 1 1 ὁ δὲ Μαρδοχαῖος ἐπέγνω πάντα τὰ γεγονότα, καὶ ἡ πόλις Σοῦσα ἐταράσσετο ἐπὶ τοῖς 2 γεγενημένοις, καὶ πᾶσι τοῖς Ἰουδαίοις ἦν πένθος μέγα καὶ πικρὸν ἐν πάσῃ πόλει. 2 ὁ δὲ Μαρδοχαῖος ἐλθὼν εἰς τὸν οἶκον αὐτοῦ περιείλετο τὰ ἱμάτια αὐτοῦ καὶ περιεβάλετο σάκκον, καὶ σποδωθεὶς ἐξῆλθεν ὡς ἐπὶ τὴν αὐλὴν τὴν ἔξω καὶ ἔστη· οὐ γὰρ ἠδύνατο εἰσελθεῖν εἰς τὰ

(4) 3 βασίλεια ἐν σάκκῳ. 3 [4] καὶ ἐκάλεσεν εὐνοῦχον ἕνα καὶ ἀπέστειλε πρὸς Εσθηρ. καὶ εἶπεν ἡ

(8) 4 βασίλισσα Περίελεσθε τὸν σάκκον καὶ εἰσαγάγετε αὐτόν. 4 ὃς δὲ οὐκ ἤθελεν, [8] ἀλλ' εἶπεν Οὕτως ἐρεῖτε αὐτῇ Μὴ ἀποστρέψῃς τοῦ εἰσελθεῖν πρὸς τὸν βασιλέα καὶ κολακεῦσαι τὸ πρόσωπον αὐτοῦ ὑπὲρ ἐμοῦ καὶ τοῦ λαοῦ, μνησθεῖσα ἡμερῶν ταπεινώσεώς σου ὧν ἐτράφης ἐν τῇ χειρί μου, ὅτι Αμαν ὁ δευτερεύων λελάληκε τῷ βασιλεῖ καθ' ἡμῶν εἰς θάνατον. 5 5 ἐπικαλεσαμένη οὖν τὸν θεὸν λάλησον περὶ ἡμῶν τῷ βασιλεῖ, καὶ ῥῦσαι ἡμᾶς ἐκ θανάτου.

(9) (10) 6 6 [9] καὶ ἀπήγγειλεν αὐτῇ τὴν ὀδύνην τοῦ Ισραηλ. 7 [10] καὶ ἀπέστειλεν αὐτῷ κατὰ τάδε λέγουσα

(11) 7 [11] Σὺ γινώσκεις παρὰ πάντας ὅτι ὃς ἂν εἰσέλθῃ πρὸς τὸν βασιλέα ἄκλητος ᾧ οὐκ ἐκτενεῖ 8 τὴν ῥάβδον αὐτοῦ τὴν χρυσῆν, θανάτου ἔνοχος ἔσται. 8 καὶ ἐγὼ οὐ κέκλημαι πρὸς αὐτόν,

(13) 9 ἡμέραι εἰσὶ τριάκοντα· καὶ πῶς εἰσελεύσομαι νῦν, ἄκλητος οὖσα; 9 [13] καὶ ἀπέστειλε πρὸς

(14) αὐτὴν Μαρδοχαῖος καὶ εἶπεν αὐτῇ [14] Ἐὰν ὑπερίδῃς τοῦ ἔθνους σου τοῦ μὴ βοηθῆσαι αὐτοῖς, ἀλλ' ὁ θεὸς ἔσται αὐτοῖς βοηθὸς καὶ σωτηρία, σὺ δὲ καὶ ὁ οἶκος τοῦ πατρός σου ἀπολεῖσθε.

(15) 10 10 καὶ τίς οἶδεν εἰ εἰς τὸν καιρὸν τοῦτον ἐβασίλευσας; 11 [15] καὶ ἀπέστειλεν ἡ βασίλισσα

(16) 11 λέγουσα [16] Παραγγείλατε θεραπείαν καὶ δεήθητε τοῦ θεοῦ ἐκτενῶς, κἀγὼ δὲ καὶ τὰ κοράσιά μου ποιήσομεν οὕτως· καὶ εἰσελεύσομαι πρὸς τὸν βασιλέα ἄκλητος, εἰ δέοι καὶ ἀποθανεῖν με.

iv 17 (for εν αντιπαραγωγη). Η: εναντια παραγωγη
v 9 (for του εθνους). Η: το εθνος

v 12 ΕΣΘΗΡ Α

¹²⁽¹⁷⁾καὶ ἐποίησεν οὕτως Μαρδοχαῖος, (C₁) καὶ ἐδεήθη τοῦ κυρίου, μνημονεύων αὐτοῦ τὰ ἔργα, 12 (17)
⁽²⁾καὶ εἶπεν ¹³Δέσποτα παντοκράτορ οὗ ἐν τῇ ἐξουσίᾳ ἐστὶ τὰ πάντα, καὶ οὐκ ἔστιν ὃς 13 (2)
ἀντιτάξεταί σοι ἐν τῷ θέλειν σε σῶσαι τὸν οἶκον Ισραηλ, ⁽³⁾ὅτι σὺ ἐποίησας τὸν οὐρανὸν καὶ (3)
τὴν γῆν καὶ πᾶν τὸ θαυμαζόμενον ἐν τῇ ὑπ᾽ οὐρανόν, ⁽⁴⁾καὶ σὺ κυριεύεις πάντων. ¹⁴⁽⁵⁾σὺ γὰρ 14 (⁴)(⁵)
πάντα γινώσκεις, καὶ τὸ γένος Ισραηλ σὺ οἶδας. ¹⁵καὶ οὐχ ὅτι ἐν ὕβρει οὐδὲ ἐν φιλοδοξίᾳ 15
ἐποίησα τοῦ μὴ προσκυνεῖν τὸν ἀπερίτμητον Αμαν, ⁽⁶⁾ἐπεὶ εὐδόκουν φιλῆσαι τὰ πέλματα (6)
τῶν ποδῶν αὐτοῦ ἕνεκεν τοῦ Ισραηλ, ⁽⁷⁾ἀλλ᾽ ἐποίησα ἵνα μηδένα προτάξω τῆς δόξης σου, (7)
δέσποτα, καὶ μηδένα προσκυνήσω πλὴν σοῦ τοῦ ἀληθινοῦ, καὶ οὐ ποιήσω αὐτὸ ἐν πειρασμῷ.
¹⁶⁽⁸⁾καὶ νῦν, κύριε, ὁ διαθέμενος πρὸς Αβρααμ φεῖσαι τοῦ λαοῦ σου ὅτι ἐπιτέθεινται ἡμῖν εἰς 16 (8)
καταφθοράν, καὶ ἐπιθυμοῦσιν ἀφανίσαι καὶ ἐξᾶραι τὴν ἐξ ἀρχῆς κληρονομίαν σου, ⁽⁹⁾μὴ (9)
ὑπερίδῃς τὴν μερίδα σου ἣν ἐλυτρώσω ἐκ γῆς Αἰγύπτου· ¹⁷⁽¹⁰⁾ἐπάκουσον τῆς δεήσεως ἡμῶν 17 (10)
καὶ ἱλάσθητι τῆς κληρονομίας σου, καὶ στρέψον τὸ πένθος ἡμῶν εἰς εὐφροσύνην, ἵνα ζῶντες
ὑμνήσωμέν σε. καὶ μὴ ἀφανίσῃς στόμα ὑμνούντων σε. ¹⁸⁽¹²⁾καὶ Εσθηρ ἡ βασίλισσα κατέ- 18 (12)
φυγεν ἐπὶ τὸν κύριον ἐν ἀγῶνι θανάτου κατειλημμένη. ⁽¹³⁾καὶ ἀφείλατο τὰ ἱμάτια τῆς δόξης (13)
ἀφ᾽ ἑαυτῆς καὶ πᾶν σημεῖον ἐπιφανείας αὐτῆς, καὶ ἐνεδύσατο στενοχωρίαν καὶ πένθος, καὶ
ἀντὶ ὑπερηφάνων ἡδυσμάτων σποδοῦ καὶ κόπρου ἔπλησε τὴν κεφαλὴν αὐτῆς, καὶ τὸ σῶμα
αὐτῆς ἐταπείνωσε σφόδρα, καὶ πᾶν σημεῖον κόσμου αὐτῆς καὶ ἀγαλλιάματος τερπνῶν τριχῶν
ἔπλησε ταπεινώσεως. ¹⁹⁽¹⁴⁾καὶ ἐδεήθη τοῦ κυρίου καὶ εἶπεν Κύριε βασιλεῦ, σὺ εἶ μόνος βοηθός· 19 (14)
βοήθησόν μοι τῇ ταπεινῇ καὶ οὐκ ἐχούσῃ βοηθὸν πλὴν σοῦ, ⁽¹⁵⁾ὅτι κίνδυνός μου ἐν τῇ χειρί (15)
μου. ²⁰⁽¹⁶⁾ἐγὼ δὲ ἤκουσα πατρικῆς μου βίβλου ὅτι ἐλυτρώσω τὸν Ισραηλ ἐκ πάντων τῶν 20 (16)
ἐθνῶν, καὶ τοὺς πατέρας αὐτῶν ἐκ τῶν προγόνων αὐτῶν, ἐπιθέμενος αὐτοῖς Ισραηλ
κληρονομίαν αἰώνιον. καὶ ἐποίησας αὐτοῖς ἃ ἐλάλησας αὐτοῖς, καὶ παρέσχου ὅσα ᾔτησαν.
²¹⁽¹⁷⁾ἡμάρτομεν ἐναντίον σου, καὶ παρέδωκας ἡμᾶς εἰς χεῖρας τῶν ἐχθρῶν ἡμῶν, ⁽¹⁸⁾εἰ 21 (17)(18)
ἐδοξάσαμεν τοὺς θεοὺς αὐτῶν. ²²δίκαιος εἶ, κύριε· ⁽¹⁹⁾καὶ νῦν οὐχ ἱκανώθησαν ἐν πικρασμῷ 22 (19)
δουλείας ἡμῶν, ἀλλ᾽ ἐπέθηκαν τὰς χεῖρας αὐτῶν ἐπὶ τὰς χεῖρας τῶν εἰδώλων αὐτῶν, ⁽²⁰⁾ἐξᾶραι (20)
ὁρισμὸν στόματος αὐτῶν, ἀφανίσαι κληρονομίαν σου, καὶ ἐμφράξαι στόμα αἰνούντων σε, καὶ
σβέσαι δόξαν οἴκου σου καὶ θυσιαστηρίου σου, ⁽²¹⁾καὶ ἀνοῖξαι στόματα ἐχθρῶν εἰς ἀρετὰς (21)
ματαίων, καὶ θαυμασθῆναι βασιλέα σάρκινον εἰς τὸν αἰῶνα. ²³⁽²²⁾μὴ δὴ παραδῷς, κύριε, τὸ 23 (22)
σκῆπτρόν σου τοῖς μισοῦσί σε ἐχθροῖς, καὶ μὴ χαρείησαν ἐπὶ τῇ πτώσει ἡμῶν. στρέψον
τὰς βουλὰς αὐτῶν ἐπ᾽ αὐτούς, τὸν δὲ ἀρξάμενον ἐφ᾽ ἡμᾶς εἰς κακὰ παραδειγμάτισον. ²⁴⁽²³⁾ἐπι- 24 (23)
φάνηθι ἡμῖν, κύριε, καὶ γνώσθητι ἐν καιρῷ θλίψεως ἡμῶν, καὶ μὴ θραύσῃς ἡμᾶς. ²⁵⁽²⁴⁾δὸς 25 (24)
λόγον εὔρυθμον εἰς τὸ στόμα μου, καὶ χαρίτωσον τὰ ῥήματά μου ἐνώπιον τοῦ βασιλέως, καὶ
μετάστρεψον τὴν καρδίαν αὐτοῦ εἰς μῖσος τοῦ πολεμοῦντος ἡμᾶς, εἰς συντέλειαν αὐτοῦ καὶ
τῶν ὁμονοούντων αὐτῷ· ⁽²⁵⁾ἡμᾶς δὲ ῥῦσαι ἐν τῇ χειρί σου τῇ κραταιᾷ, καὶ βοήθησόν μοι, ὅτι (25)
σὺ πάντων γνῶσιν ἔχεις, ⁽²⁶⁾καὶ οἶδας ὅτι βδελύσσομαι κοίτην ἀπεριτμήτου, καὶ ἐμίσησα (26)
δόξαν ἀνόμου καὶ παντὸς ἀλλογενοῦς. ²⁶⁽²⁷⁾σύ, κύριε, οἶδας τὴν ἀνάγκην μου, ὅτι βδελύσσομαι 26 (27)

v 22 (for στοματος αυτων). H: στοματος σου
v 24 (after γνωσθητι). H: + ημιν

ΕΣΘΗΡ Α   (D) VI 19

τὸ σημεῖον τῆς ὑπερηφανίας ὅ ἐστιν ἐπὶ τῆς κεφαλῆς μου, καὶ οὐ φορῶ αὐτὸ εἰ μὴ ἐν ἡμέρᾳ
(28) 27 ὀπτασίας μου, καὶ βδελύσσομαι αὐτὸ ὡς ῥάκος ἀποκαθημένης. 27 (28) καὶ οὐκ ἔφαγεν ἡ δούλη
28 σου ἐπὶ τῶν τραπεζῶν αὐτῶν ἅμα. 28 καὶ οὐκ ἐδόξασα βασιλέως συμπόσια, καὶ οὐκ ἔπιον
(29) σπονδῆς οἶνον, (29) καὶ οὐκ εὐφράνθη ἡ δούλη σου ἐφ' ἡμέραις μεταβολῆς μου εἰ μὴ ἐπὶ σοί,
(30) 29 δέσποτα. 29 (30) καὶ νῦν, δυνατὸς ὢν ἐπὶ πάντας, εἰσάκουσον φωνῆς ἀπηλπισμένων, καὶ ῥῦσαι
ἡμᾶς ἐκ χειρὸς τῶν πονηρευομένων ἐφ' ἡμᾶς, καὶ ἐξελοῦ με, κύριε, ἐκ χειρὸς τοῦ φόβου μου.
VI   1   1 καὶ ἐγενήθη ἐν τῇ ἡμέρᾳ τῇ τρίτῃ ὡς ἐπαύσατο Εσθηρ προσευχομένη, ἐξεδύσατο τὰ (D)
2 ἱμάτια τῆς θεραπείας, καὶ περιεβάλετο τὰ ἱμάτια τῆς δόξης. 2 καὶ γενομένη ἐπιφανὴς καὶ
(3) ἐπικαλεσαμένη τὸν πάντων γνώστην καὶ σωτῆρα θεὸν παρέλαβε μεθ' ἑαυτῆς δύο ἄβρας, (3) καὶ
(4) τῇ μὲν μιᾷ ἐπηρείδετο ὡς τρυφερευομένη, (4) ἡ δὲ ἑτέρα ἐπηκολούθει ἐπικουφίζουσα τὸ ἔνδυμα
(5) 3 αὐτῆς. 3 (5) καὶ αὐτὴ ἐρυθριῶσα ἐν ἀκμῇ κάλλους αὐτῆς, καὶ τὸ πρόσωπον αὐτῆς ὡς προσφιλές,
(6) 4 ἡ δὲ καρδία αὐτῆς ἀπεστενωμένη. 4 (6) καὶ εἰσελθοῦσα τὰς θύρας ἔστη ἐνώπιον τοῦ βασιλέως.
καὶ ὁ βασιλεὺς ἐκάθητο ἐπὶ τοῦ θρόνου τῆς βασιλείας αὐτοῦ, καὶ πᾶσαν στολὴν ἐπιφανείας
(7) 5 ἐνδεδύκει, ὅλος διάχρυσος, καὶ λίθοι πολυτελεῖς ἐπ' αὐτῷ, καὶ φοβερὸς σφόδρα. 5 (7) καὶ ἄρας
τὸ πρόσωπον αὐτοῦ πεπυρωμένον ἐν δόξῃ ἐνέβλεψεν αὐτῇ ὡς ταῦρος ἐν ἀκμῇ θυμοῦ αὐτοῦ.
6 6 καὶ ἐφοβήθη ἡ βασίλισσα, καὶ μετέβαλε τὸ πρόσωπον αὐτῆς ἐν ἐκλύσει, καὶ ἐπέκυψεν ἐπὶ
(8) 7 τὴν κεφαλὴν τῆς ἄβρας τῆς προπορευομένης. 7 (8) καὶ μετέβαλεν ὁ θεὸς τὸ πνεῦμα τοῦ
8 βασιλέως καὶ μετέθηκε τὸν θυμὸν αὐτοῦ εἰς πραότητα, 8 καὶ ἀγωνιάσας ὁ βασιλεὺς κατε-
πήδησεν ἀπὸ τοῦ θρόνου αὐτοῦ, καὶ ἀνέλαβεν αὐτὴν ἐπὶ τὰς ἀγκάλας αὐτοῦ καὶ παρεκάλεσεν
(9) 9 αὐτὴν (9) καὶ εἶπεν Τί ἐστιν, Εσθηρ· ἐγώ εἰμι ἀδελφός σου. 9 θάρσει, (10) οὐ μὴ ἀποθάνῃς,
(10)
(11) ὅτι κοινόν ἐστι τὸ πρᾶγμα ἡμῶν, (11) καὶ οὐ πρὸς σὲ ἡ ἀπειλή. ἰδοὺ τὸ σκῆπτρον ἐν τῇ χειρί
(12) 10 σου. 10 (12) καὶ ἄρας τὸ σκῆπτρον ἐπέθηκεν ἐπὶ τὸν τράχηλον αὐτῆς, καὶ ἠσπάσατο αὐτήν,
(13) 11 καὶ εἶπεν Λάλησόν μοι. 11 (13) καὶ εἶπεν αὐτῷ Εἶδόν σε ὡς ἄγγελον θεοῦ, καὶ ἐτάκη ἡ καρδία
(14) 12 μου ἀπὸ τῆς δόξης τοῦ θυμοῦ σου, κύριε. 12 (14) καὶ ἐπὶ τὸ πρόσωπον αὐτῆς μέτρον ἱδρώτος.
(16) 13 (16) καὶ ἐταράσσετο ὁ βασιλεὺς καὶ πᾶσα ἡ θεραπεία αὐτοῦ, καὶ παρεκάλουν αὐτήν. 13 V (3) καὶ
(V, 3)
εἶπεν ὁ βασιλεὺς Τί ἐστιν, Εσθηρ; ἀνάγγειλόν μοι, καὶ ποιήσω σοι· ἕως ἡμίσους τῆς βασι-
(4) 14 λείας μου. 14 (4) καὶ εἶπεν Εσθηρ Ἡμέρα ἐπίσημός μοι αὔριον· εἰ δοκεῖ οὖν τῷ βασιλεῖ,
(5) 15 εἰσελθε σὺ καὶ Αμαν ὁ φίλος σου εἰς τὸν πότον ὃν ποιήσω αὔριον. 15 (5) καὶ εἶπεν ὁ βασιλεὺς
16 Κατασπεύσατε τὸν Αμαν, ὅπως ποιήσωμεν τὸν λόγον Εσθηρ. 16 καὶ παραγίνονται ἀμφότεροι
(6) 17 εἰς τὴν δοχὴν ἣν ἐποίησεν Εσθηρ, δεῖπνον πολυτελές. 17 (6) καὶ εἶπεν ὁ βασιλεὺς πρὸς Εσθηρ
Ἡ βασίλισσα, τί τὸ θέλημά σου; αἴτησαι ἕως ἡμίσους τῆς βασιλείας μου, καὶ ἔσται σοι ὅσα
(7) 18 ἀξιοῖς. 18 (7) καὶ εἶπεν Εσθηρ Τὸ αἴτημά μου καὶ τὸ ἀξίωμά μου, (8) εἰ εὗρον χάριν ἐναντίον
σου, βασιλεῦ, καὶ εἰ ἐπὶ τὸν βασιλέα ἀγαθὸν δοῦναι τὸ αἴτημά μου καὶ ποιῆσαι τὸ ἀξίωμά
μου, ἐλθέτω ὁ βασιλεὺς καὶ Αμαν εἰς τὴν δοχὴν ἣν ποιήσω αὐτοῖς καὶ τῇ αὔριον· καὶ αὔριον
19 γὰρ ποιήσω κατὰ τὰ αὐτά. 19 καὶ εἶπεν ὁ βασιλεὺς Ποίησον κατὰ τὸ θέλημά σου.

(D) VI 20   ΕΣΘΗΡ Α

²⁰⁽⁹⁾ καὶ ἀπηγγέλη τῷ Αμαν κατὰ τὰ αὐτά, καὶ ἐθαύμασεν, καὶ ὁ βασιλεὺς ἀναλύσας ἡσύχασεν. 20 (9)
²¹⁽¹⁰⁾ ὁ δὲ Αμαν εἰσῆλθεν εἰς τὸν οἶκον αὐτοῦ, καὶ συνήγαγε τοὺς φίλους αὐτοῦ καὶ τοὺς υἱοὺς 21 (10)
αὐτοῦ καὶ Ζωσάραν τὴν γυναῖκα αὐτοῦ, ⁽¹²⁾ καὶ ἐκαυχᾶτο λέγων ὡς οὐδένα κέκληκεν ἡ βασί- (12)
λισσα ἐν ἐπισήμῳ ἡμέρᾳ αὐτῆς εἰ μὴ τὸν βασιλέα καὶ ἐμὲ μόνον· καὶ αὔριον κέκλημαι. ²² ⁽¹³⁾ τοῦτο 22 (13)
δὲ λυπεῖ με μόνον ὅταν ἴδω τὸν Μαρδοχαῖον τὸν Ἰουδαῖον ἐν τῇ αὐλῇ τοῦ βασιλέως, καὶ μὴ
προσκυνεῖ με. ²³ ⁽¹⁴⁾ καὶ εἶπεν αὐτῷ Ζωσάρα ἡ γυνὴ αὐτοῦ Ἐκ γένους Ἰουδαίων ἐστίν· ἐπεὶ 23 (14)
συγκεχώρηκέ σε ὁ βασιλεὺς ἀφανίσαι τοὺς Ἰουδαίους, καὶ ἔδωκάν σοι οἱ θεοὶ εἰς ἐκδίκησιν
αὐτῶν ἡμέραν ὀλέθριον, κοπήτω σοι ξύλον πηχῶν πεντήκοντα, καὶ κείσθω, καὶ κρέμασον
αὐτὸν ἐπὶ τοῦ ξύλου, ὀρθρίσας δὲ πρὸς τὸν βασιλέα λαλήσεις αὐτῷ· καὶ νῦν εἰσελθὼν
εὐφραίνου πρὸς τὸν βασιλέα. ²⁴ καὶ ἤρεσε τῷ Αμαν, καὶ ἐποίησεν οὕτως. 24
¹ ὁ δὲ δυνατὸς ἀπέστησε τὸν ὕπνον τοῦ βασιλέως τὴν νύκτα ἐκείνην, καὶ ἦν ἀγρυπνῶν. 1   (VI) VII
² καὶ ἐκλήθησαν οἱ ἀναγνῶσται, καὶ τὸ βιβλίον τῶν μνημοσυνῶν ἀνεγινώσκετο αὐτῷ. 3 ⁽²⁾ καὶ 3 (2)
ἦν ὑπόθεσις τῶν εὐνούχων καὶ ὃ ἐποίησε Μαρδοχαῖος εὐεργέτημα τῷ βασιλεῖ. ⁴ καὶ ἐπέστη- 4
σεν ὁ βασιλεὺς τὸν νοῦν σφόδρα, λέγων Πιστὸς ἀνὴρ Μαρδοχαῖος εἰς παραφυλακὴν τῆς
ψυχῆς μου, δι' ὅτι αὐτὸς ἐποίησέ με ζῆν ἄχρι τοῦ νῦν, καὶ κάθημαι σήμερον ἐπὶ τοῦ θρόνου
μου, καὶ οὐκ ἐποίησα αὐτῷ οὐθέν· οὐκ ὀρθῶς ἐποίησα. ⁵ ⁽³⁾ καὶ εἶπεν ὁ βασιλεὺς τοῖς παισὶν 5 (3)
αὐτοῦ Τί ποιήσομεν τῷ Μαρδοχαίῳ τῷ σωτῆρι τῶν κακῶν; καὶ νοήσαντες οἱ νεανίσκοι διε-
φθόνουν αὐτῷ· ἐνέκειτο γὰρ φόβος Αμαν ἐν τοῖς σπλάγχνοις αὐτῶν. ⁶ καὶ ἐνενόησεν ὁ 6
βασιλεύς. καὶ ἐγένετο ὄρθρος. ⁽⁴⁾ καὶ ἠρώτησεν ὁ βασιλεὺς Τίς ἐστιν ἔξω; καὶ ἦν Αμαν. (4)
⁷ Αμαν δὲ ὠρθρίκει λαλῆσαι τῷ βασιλεῖ ἵνα κρεμάσῃ τὸν Μαρδοχαῖον. ⁸ ⁽⁵⁾ καὶ εἶπεν ὁ βασι- 7 (5)
λεὺς εἰσαγαγεῖν αὐτόν. ⁹ ⁽⁶⁾ ὡς δὲ εἰσῆλθεν, εἶπεν αὐτῷ ὁ βασιλεὺς Τί ποιήσομεν τῷ ἀνδρὶ 9 (6)
τῷ τὸν βασιλέα τιμῶντι, ὃν ὁ βασιλεὺς βούλεται δοξάσαι; ¹⁰ καὶ ἐλογίσατο ὁ Αμαν λέγων 10
ὅτι Τίνα βούλεται ὁ βασιλεὺς δοξάσαι εἰ μὴ ἐμέ; ¹¹ ⁽⁷⁾ καὶ εἶπεν ὁ Αμαν Ἄνθρωπος ὃν ὁ 11 (7)
βασιλεὺς βούλεται δοξάσαι, ⁽⁸⁾ ληφθήτω στολὴ βασιλικὴ καὶ ἵππος βασιλικὸς ἐφ' ᾧ ὁ (8)
βασιλεὺς ἐπιβαίνει, ⁽⁹⁾ καὶ εἷς τῶν ἐνδόξων, τῶν φίλων τοῦ βασιλέως, λαβέτω ταῦτα, καὶ (9)
ἐνδυσάτω αὐτόν, καὶ ἀναβιβασάτω αὐτὸν ἐπὶ τὸν ἵππον, καὶ περιελθέτω τὴν πόλιν ἔμπροσ-
θεν αὐτοῦ κηρύσσων Κατὰ τάδε ποιηθήσεται τῷ τὸν βασιλέα τιμῶντι, ὃν ὁ βασιλεὺς βούλεται
δοξάσαι. ¹² ⁽¹⁰⁾ καὶ εἶπεν ὁ βασιλεὺς τῷ Αμαν Ταχὺ δράμε καὶ λαβὲ τὸν ἵππον καὶ στολὴν 12 (10)
ὡς εἴρηκας, καὶ ποίησον Μαρδοχαίῳ τῷ Ἰουδαίῳ τῷ καθημένῳ ἐν τῷ πυλῶνι· καὶ μὴ παρα-
πεσάτω ὁ λόγος σου. ¹³ ὡς δὲ ἔγνω Αμαν ὅτι οὐκ ἦν αὐτὸς ὁ δοξαζόμενος, ἀλλ' ὅτι 13
Μαρδοχαῖος, συνετρίβη ἡ καρδία αὐτοῦ σφόδρα, καὶ μετέβαλε τὸ πνεῦμα αὐτοῦ ἐν ἐκλύσει.
¹⁴ ⁽¹¹⁾ καὶ ἔλαβεν Αμαν τὴν στολὴν καὶ τὸν ἵππον, ἐντρεπόμενος τὸν Μαρδοχαῖον καθ' ὅτι 14 (11)
ἐκείνῃ τῇ ἡμέρᾳ ἐκεκρίκει ἀνασκολοπίσαι αὐτόν. ¹⁵ καὶ εἶπε τῷ Μαρδοχαίῳ Περιελοῦ τὸν 15
σάκκον. ¹⁶ καὶ ἐταράχθη Μαρδοχαῖος ὡς ἀποθνήσκων, καὶ ἀπεδύσατο μετ' ὀδύνης τὸν σάκκον 16

vii 5 (for ποιησομεν). Η: ποιησωμεν
vii 5 (after λογων). Η: τουτων
vii 6 (for ενενοησεν). Η: ενοησεν
vii 11 (for ω). Η: ον

ΕΣΘΗΡ Α   VIII 16

17 καὶ ἐνεδύσατο τὰ ἱμάτια δόξης. ¹⁷καὶ ἐδόκει Μαρδοχαῖος τέρας θεωρεῖν, καὶ ἡ καρδία αὐτοῦ
18 πρὸς τὸν κύριον. καὶ ἐξίστατο ἐν ἀφασίᾳ. ¹⁸καὶ ἔσπευσεν Αμαν ἀναλαβεῖν αὐτὸν ἔφιππον.
19 ¹⁹καὶ ἐξήγαγεν Αμαν τὸν ἵππον ἔξω, καὶ προσήγαγεν αὐτὸν ἔξω κηρύσσων Κατὰ τάδε
(12) 20 ποιηθήσεται τῷ ἀνδρὶ τῷ τὸν βασιλέα τιμῶντι, ὃν ὁ βασιλεὺς βούλεται δοξάσαι. ²⁰⁽¹²⁾καὶ ὁ
     μὲν Αμαν ἀπῆλθε πρὸς ἑαυτὸν ἐσκυθρωπωμένος, ὁ δὲ Μαρδοχαῖος ἀπῆλθεν εἰς τὸν οἶκον
(13) ²¹⁄₂₂ αὐτοῦ. ²¹⁽¹³⁾καὶ διηγήσατο Αμαν τῇ γυναικὶ αὐτοῦ πάντα τὰ γενόμενα αὐτῷ. ²²καὶ εἶπεν ἡ
     γυνὴ αὐτοῦ καὶ οἱ σοφοὶ αὐτοῦ Ἀφ' ὅτε λαλεῖς περὶ αὐτοῦ κακά, προσπορεύεταί σοι τὰ κακά·
(14) 23 ἡσύχαζε, ὅτι ὁ θεὸς ἐν αὐτοῖς. ²³⁽¹⁴⁾καὶ αὐτῶν λαλούντων παρῆν τις ἐπὶ τὸν πότον σπουδάζων
(VII 1) αὐτόν, καὶ οὕτως ἱλαρώθη, ⁽ᵛᴵᴵ¹⁾καὶ πορευθεὶς ἀνέπεσε μετ' αὐτῶν ἐν ὥρᾳ.
VIII (2) 1   ¹⁽²⁾ὡς δὲ προῆγεν ἡ πρόποσις, εἶπεν ὁ βασιλεὺς τῇ Εσθηρ Τί ἐστιν ὁ κίνδυνος; καὶ τί τὸ
      2 αἴτημά σου; ἕως τοῦ ἡμίσους τῆς βασιλείας μου. ²καὶ ἠγωνίασεν Εσθηρ ἐν τῷ ἀπαγγέλλειν,
      ὅτι ὁ ἀντίδικος ἐν ὀφθαλμοῖς αὐτῆς, καὶ ὁ θεὸς ἔδωκεν αὐτῇ θάρσος ἐν τῷ αὐτὴν ἐπικαλεῖσθαι
      3 αὐτόν. ³καὶ εἶπεν Εσθηρ Εἰ δοκεῖ τῷ βασιλεῖ, καὶ ἀγαθὴ ἡ κρίσις ἐν καρδίᾳ αὐτοῦ, δοθήτω
      4 ὁ λαός μου τῷ αἰτήματί μου καὶ τὸ ἔθνος τῆς ψυχῆς μου. ⁴ἐπράθημεν γὰρ ἐγὼ καὶ ὁ λαός
      μου εἰς δούλωσιν, καὶ τὰ νήπια αὐτῶν εἰς διαρπαγήν, καὶ οὐκ ἤθελον ἀπαγγεῖλαι, ἵνα μὴ
      λυπήσω τὸν κύριόν μου· ἐγένετο γὰρ μεταπεσεῖν τὸν ἄνθρωπον τὸν κακοποιήσαντα ἡμᾶς.
      5 ⁵καὶ ἐθυμώθη ὁ βασιλεὺς καὶ εἶπεν Τίς ἐστιν οὗτος ὃς ἐτόλμησε ταπεινῶσαι τὸ σημεῖον τῆς
      6 βασιλείας μου ὥστε παρελθεῖν τὸν φόβον σου; ⁶ὡς δὲ εἶδεν ἡ βασίλισσα ὅτι δεινὸν ἐφάνη
      τῷ βασιλεῖ, καὶ μισοπονηρεῖ, εἶπεν Μὴ ὀργίζου, κύριε· ἱκανὸν γὰρ ὅτι ἔτυχον τοῦ ἱλασμοῦ
      7 σου· εὐωχοῦ, βασιλεῦ· αὔριον δὲ ποιήσω κατὰ τὸ ῥῆμά σου. ⁷καὶ ὤμοσεν ὁ βασιλεὺς τοῦ
      ἀπαγγεῖλαι αὐτὴν αὐτῷ· τὸν ὑπερηφανευσάμενον τοῦ ποιῆσαι τοῦτο, καὶ μετὰ ὅρκου ὑπέσχετο
(6) 8 ποιῆσαι αὐτῇ ὃ ἂν βούληται. ⁸⁽⁶⁾καὶ θαρσήσασα ἡ Εσθηρ εἶπεν Αμαν ὁ φίλος σου ὁ
(7) 9 ψευδὴς οὑτοσί, ὁ πονηρὸς ἄνθρωπος οὗτος. ⁹⁽⁷⁾ἔκθυμος δὲ γενόμενος ὁ βασιλεὺς καὶ πλησθεὶς
     10 ὀργῆς ἀνεπήδησε, καὶ ἦν περιπατῶν. ¹⁰καὶ ὁ Αμαν ἐταράχθη, καὶ προσέπεσεν ἐπὶ τοὺς πόδας
(8) 11 Εσθηρ τῆς βασιλίσσης ἐπὶ τὴν κοίτην ἔτι ἀνακειμένης. ¹¹⁽⁸⁾καὶ ὁ βασιλεὺς ἐπέστρεψεν ἐπὶ
      τὸ συμπόσιον. καὶ ἰδὼν εἶπεν Οὐχ ἱκανόν σοι ἡ ἁμαρτία τῆς βασιλείας, ἀλλὰ καὶ τὴν
      12 γυναῖκά μου ἐκβιάζει ἐνώπιόν μου; ἀπαχθήτω Αμαν, καὶ μὴ ζήτω. ¹²καὶ οὕτως ἀπήγετο.
(9) .   ⁽⁹⁾καὶ εἶπεν Αγαθας εἷς τῶν παίδων αὐτοῦ Ἰδοὺ ξύλον ἐν τῇ αὐλῇ αὐτοῦ πηχῶν πεντήκοντα,
      ὃ ἔκοψεν Αμαν ἵνα κρεμάσῃ τὸν Μαρδοχαῖον τὸν λαλήσαντα ἀγαθὰ περὶ τοῦ βασιλέως· κέλευσον
      13 οὖν, κύριε, ἐπ' αὐτῷ αὐτὸν κρεμασθῆναι. ¹³καὶ εἶπεν ὁ βασιλεὺς Κρεμασθήτω ἐπ' αὐτῷ. καὶ
      ἀφεῖλεν ὁ βασιλεὺς τὸ δακτύλιον ἀπὸ τῆς χειρὸς αὐτοῦ, καὶ ἐσφραγίσθη ἐν αὐτῷ ὁ βίος αὐτοῦ.
      14 ¹⁴καὶ εἶπεν ὁ βασιλεὺς τῇ Εσθηρ Καὶ Μαρδοχαῖον ἐβουλεύσατο κρεμάσαι τὸν σώσαντά με ἐκ
      15 χειρὸς τῶν εὐνούχων; οὐκ ᾔδει ὅτι πατρῷον αὐτοῦ γένος ἐστὶν ἡ Εσθηρ; ¹⁵καὶ ἐκάλεσεν ὁ
      16 βασιλεὺς τὸν Μαρδοχαῖον, καὶ ἐχαρίσατο αὐτῷ πάντα τὰ τοῦ Αμαν. ¹⁶καὶ εἶπεν αὐτῷ Τί θέλεις;

vii 16 (τα). H: om
vii 19 (εξω 2°). H: om
viii 11 (for εκβιαζει). H: εκβιαζη

VIII 16   ΕΣΘΗΡ Α

καὶ ποιήσω σοι. καὶ εἶπε Μαρδοχαῖος "Οπως ἀνέλῃς τὴν ἐπιστολὴν τοῦ Αμαν. ¹⁷καὶ ἐνεχείρισεν 17
αὐτῷ ὁ βασιλεὺς τὰ κατὰ τὴν βασιλείαν. ¹⁸καὶ εἶπεν Εσθηρ τῷ βασιλεῖ τῇ ἑξῆς Δός μοι κολάσαι 18
τοὺς ἐχθρούς μου φόνῳ. ¹⁹ἐνέτυχε δὲ ἡ βασίλισσα Εσθηρ καὶ κατὰ τέκνων Αμαν τῷ βασιλεῖ, 19
ὅπως ἀποθάνωσι καὶ αὐτοὶ μετὰ τοῦ πατρὸς αὐτῶν. καὶ εἶπεν ὁ βασιλεὺς Γινέσθω. ²⁰καὶ 20
ἐπάταξε τοὺς ἐχθροὺς εἰς πλῆθος. ²¹ἐν δὲ Σούσοις ἀνθωμολογήσατο ὁ βασιλεὺς τῇ βασιλίσσῃ 21
ἀποκτανθῆναι ἄνδρας, καὶ εἶπεν Ἰδοὺ δίδωμί σοι τοῦ κρεμάσαι. καὶ ἐγένετο οὕτως.

²²⁽ᴱ ¹⁾καὶ ἔγραψε τὴν ὑποτεταγμένην ἐπιστολήν· Βασιλεὺς μέγας Ἀσσυῆρος τοῖς ἀπὸ τῆς 22 (E 1)
Ἰνδικῆς ἕως τῆς Αἰθιοπίας ἑκατὸν καὶ εἴκοσι καὶ ἑπτὰ χωρῶν ἄρχουσι καὶ σατράπαις τοῖς
τὰ ἡμέτερα φρονοῦσι χαίρειν. ²³⁽²⁾πολλοὶ τῇ πλείστῃ τῶν εὐεργετούντων χρηστότητι πυκ- 23 (2)
νότερον τιμώμενοι, μεῖζον φρονήσαντες, ⁽³⁾οὐ μόνον τοὺς ὑποτεταγμένους ἡμῖν ζητοῦσι κακο- (3)
ποιεῖν, τὸν δὲ κόρον οὐ δυνάμενοι φέρειν καὶ τοῖς ἑαυτῶν εὐεργέταις ἐπιχειροῦσι μηχανᾶσθαι
κακά, ⁽⁴⁾καὶ τὴν εὐχαριστίαν οὐ μόνον ἐκ τῶν ἀνθρώπων ἀναιροῦντες, ἀλλὰ καὶ τοῖς τῶν· (4)
ἀπειραγάθων κόμποις παρελθόντες, τὸ τοῦ πάντα δυναστεύοντος δικαιοκρίτου μισοπόνηρον
ἐκφυγεῖν διειληφότες, τὴν δίκην ⁽⁵⁾πολλάκις ἐπ' ἐξουσιῶν τεταγμένοι τὰ τῶν ἐμπιστευομένων (5)
φίλων πράγματα χειρίζειν αἰτίους ἀθώων αἱμάτων καταστήσαντες περιέβαλον συμφοραῖς
ἀνηκέστοις, ⁽⁶⁾τῷ τῆς κακοποιίας ψεύδει παραλογισάμενοι τὴν τῶν ἐπικρατούντων ἀκέραιον (6)
εὐγνωμοσύνην. ²⁴⁽⁷⁾σκοπεῖν δὲ ἔστιν ἐκ τῶν παραδεδομένων ἡμῖν ἱστοριῶν καὶ ὅσον τὸ παρὰ 24 (7)
πόδας θεωρουντες ἀξίως τῇ τῶν δυναστευόντων ὠμότητι ⁽⁸⁾προσέχειν εἰς τὰ μετ' ἔπειτα, καὶ (8)
τὴν βασιλείαν ἀτάραχον παρέχειν πᾶσι τοῖς ἔθνεσι μετ' εἰρήνης, ⁽⁹⁾οὐ χρώμενοι ταῖς διαβολαῖς, (9)
τὰ δὲ ὑπὸ τὴν ὄψιν ἐρχόμενα μετ' ἐπιεικείας διεξάγοντες.

²⁵⁽¹⁰⁾ἐπιξενωθεὶς γὰρ ἡμῖν Αμαν Ἀμαδάθου ὁ Βουγαῖος ταῖς ἀληθείαις ἀλλότριος τοῦ 25 (10)
τῶν Περσῶν φρονήματος καὶ πολὺ διεστὼς τῆς ἡμετέρας χρηστότητος ⁽¹¹⁾ἔτυχε τῆς ἐξ ἡμῶν (11)
πρὸς πᾶν ἔθνος φιλανθρωπίας ἐπὶ τοσοῦτον, ὥστε ἀναγορευθῆναι πατέρα ἡμῶν καὶ προσ-
κυνεῖσθαι ὑπὸ πάντων τὸ δεύτερον τῶν βασιλικῶν θρόνων διατελεῖν. ²⁶⁽¹²⁾οὐκ ἐνεγκὼν δὲ τὴν 26 (12)
ὑπερηφανίαν, ἐπετήδευσεν ἡμᾶς τῆς ἀρχῆς καὶ τοῦ πνεύματος μεταστῆναι, ⁽¹³⁾τὸν δὲ ἡμέτερον (13)
σωτῆρα διὰ παντὸς Μαρδοχαῖον καὶ τὴν ἄμεμπτον τούτου κοινωνὸν Εσθηρ σὺν τῷ παντὶ
τούτων ἔθνει πολυπλόκοις μεθοδείαις διαρτησάμενος εἰς ἀπώλειαν· ⁽¹⁴⁾διὰ γὰρ τούτων τῶν (14)
τρόπων ᾠήθη λαβὼν ἡμᾶς ἐρήμους ἐξαλλοτριῶσιν τῆς τῶν Περσῶν ἐπικρατείας ἕως εἰς τοὺς
Μακεδόνας ἀγαγεῖν. ²⁷⁽¹⁵⁾τοὺς οὖν ὑπὸ τοῦ τρισαλιτηρίου παραδεδομένους ὑμῖν Ἰουδαίους 27 (15)
εὑρίσκομεν μὴ ὄντας κακούργους, δικαιοτάτοις δὲ πολιτευομένους νόμοις, ⁽¹⁶⁾ὄντας δὲ καὶ υἱοὺς (16)
τοῦ μόνου θεοῦ καὶ ἀληθινοῦ, τοῦ κατευθύναντος ἡμῖν τὴν βασιλείαν μέχρι τοῦ νῦν ἐν τῇ
καλλίστῃ διαθέσει. ²⁸⁽¹⁷⁾καλῶς οὖν ποιήσατε μὴ προσέχοντες τοῖς προαπεσταλμένοις ὑμῖν 28 (17)
ὑπὸ Αμαν γράμμασιν, διὰ τὸ καὶ αὐτὸν τὸν τὰ τοιαῦτα ἐργασάμενον πρὸς ταῖς Σούσων (18)
πύλαις ἐσταυρῶσθαι, ἀποδεδωκότος αὐτῷ τὴν κατ' ἀξίαν δίκην τοῦ τὰ πάντα κατοπτεύοντος

viii 19 (after κατα). H: + των
viii 26 (for μεθοδειαις). H: μεθοδοις

ΕΣΘΗΡ Α   VIII 48

(19) 29 ἀεὶ κριτοῦ. ²⁹⁽¹⁹⁾ἐκτεθήτω δὲ τὸ ἀντίγραφον τῆς ἐπιστολῆς ἐν παντὶ τόπῳ, χρῆσθαί τε τοὺς
(20)   Ἰουδαίους τοῖς ἑαυτῶν νόμοις ⁽²⁰⁾καὶ ἐπισχύειν αὐτοῖς, ὅπως τοὺς ἐν καιρῷ θλίψεως ἐπιθεμέ-
30   νους ἀμύνωνται. ³⁰ἐκρίθη δὲ ὑπὸ τῶν κατὰ τὴν βασιλείαν Ἰουδαίων ἄγειν τὴν τεσσαρεσκαι-
(21)   δεκάτην τοῦ μηνός, ὅς ἐστιν Αδαρ, καὶ τῇ πεντεκαιδεκάτῃ ἑορτάσαι, ⁽²¹⁾ὅτι ἐν αὐταῖς ὁ
(23) 31 παντοκράτωρ ἐποίησεν αὐτοῖς σωτηρίαν καὶ εὐφροσύνην. ³¹⁽²³⁾καὶ νῦν μετὰ ταῦτα σωτηρίαν
(24) 32 μὲν εὖ ποιοῦσι τοῖς Πέρσαις, τῶν δὲ ἐπιβουλευσάντων μνημόσυνον τῆς ἀπωλείας. ³²⁽²⁴⁾ἡ δὲ
   πόλις καὶ ἡ χώρα ἥτις κατὰ ταῦτα μὴ ποιῆσαι, δόρατι καὶ πυρὶ καταναλωθήσεται μετ᾽ ὀργῆς,
33   καὶ οὐ μόνον ἀνθρώποις ἄβατος, ἀλλὰ καὶ θηρίοις καὶ πετεινοῖς ἐκταθήσεται. ³³⁽ᵛⁱⁱⁱ ¹⁴⁾ἐξετέθη
   δὲ καὶ ἐν Σούσοις ἔκθεμα περιέχον τάδε, καὶ ὁ βασιλεὺς ἐνεχείρισε τῷ Μαρδοχαίῳ γράφειν
34 ὅσα βούλεται. ³⁴ἐπέστειλε δὲ Μαρδοχαῖος διὰ γραμμάτων, καὶ ἐσφραγίσατο τῷ τοῦ βασιλέως
35 δακτυλίῳ, μένειν τὸ ἔθνος αὐτοῦ κατὰ χώρας ἕκαστον αὐτῶν καὶ ἑορτάζειν τῷ θεῷ. ³⁵ἡ δὲ
36 ἐπιστολὴ ἣν ἀπέστειλεν ὁ Μαρδοχαῖος ἣν ἔχουσα ταῦτα· ³⁶Αμαν ἀπέστειλεν ὑμῖν γράμματα
   ἔχοντα οὕτως· Ἔθνος Ἰουδαίων ἀπειθὲς σπουδάσατε ταχέως ἀναπέμψαι μοι εἰς ἀπώλειαν.
37 .³⁷ἐγὼ δὲ ὁ Μαρδοχαῖος μηνύω ὑμῖν τὸν ταῦτα ἐργασάμενον πρὸς ταῖς Σούσων πύλαις κεκρε-
38 μάσθαι καὶ τὸν οἶκον αὐτοῦ διακεχειρίσθαι· ³⁸οὗτος γὰρ ἐβούλετο ἀποκτεῖναι ἡμᾶς τῇ τρίτῃ
   καὶ δεκάτῃ τοῦ μηνὸς ὅς ἐστιν Αδαρ.
(15)   39 ³⁹⁽ᵛⁱⁱⁱ ¹⁵⁾καὶ ὁ Μαρδοχαῖος ἐξῆλθεν ἐστολισμένος τὴν βασιλικὴν ἐσθῆτα καὶ διάδημα
(16) 40 βύσσινον περιπόρφυρον. ⁴⁰ἰδόντες δὲ οἱ ἐν Σούσοις ἐχάρησαν. ⁽¹⁶⁾καὶ τοῖς Ἰουδαίοις ἐγένετο
(17) 41 φῶς, πότος, κώθων. ⁴¹⁽¹⁷⁾καὶ πολλοὶ τῶν Ἰουδαίων περιετέμνοντο, καὶ οὐδεὶς ἐπανέστη αὐτοῖς·
   42 ἐφοβοῦντο γὰρ αὐτούς. ⁴²⁽ⁱˣ ³⁾οἱ δὲ ἄρχοντες καὶ οἱ τύραννοι καὶ οἱ σατράπαι καὶ οἱ βασι-
   λικοὶ γραμματεῖς ἐτίμων τοὺς Ἰουδαίους· ὁ γὰρ φόβος Μαρδοχαίου ἐπέπεσεν ἐπ᾽ αὐτούς.
(4) 43 ⁴³⁽⁴⁾καὶ προσέπεσεν ἐν Σούσοις ὀνομασθῆναι Αμαν καὶ τοὺς ἀντικειμένους ἐν πάσῃ βασιλείᾳ.
(6)
(7) 44 ⁴⁴⁽⁶⁾καὶ ἀπέκτεινον ἐν Σούσοις οἱ Ἰουδαῖοι ἄνδρας ἑπτακοσίους ⁽⁷⁾καὶ τὸν Φαρσαν καὶ τὸν
(8)   ἀδελφὸν αὐτοῦ καὶ τὸν Φαρνα ⁽⁸⁾καὶ τὸν Γαγαφαρδαθα ⁽⁹⁾καὶ τὸν Μαρμασαιμα καὶ τὸν
(9)
(10)   Ιζαθουθ ⁽¹⁰⁾καὶ τοὺς δέκα υἱοὺς Αμαν Αμαδάθου τοῦ Βουγαίου τοῦ ἐχθροῦ τῶν Ἰουδαίων,
(11) 45 καὶ διήρπασαν πάντα τὰ αὐτῶν. ⁴⁵⁽¹²⁾καὶ εἶπεν ὁ βασιλεὺς τῇ Εσθηρ Πῶς σοι οἱ ἐνταῦθα
(13) 46 καὶ οἱ ἐν τῇ περιχώρῳ κέχρηνται; ⁴⁶⁽¹³⁾καὶ εἶπεν Εσθηρ Δοθήτω τοῖς Ἰουδαίοις οὓς ἐὰν
(16)   θέλωσιν ἀνελεῖν καὶ διαρπάζειν. καὶ συνεχώρησεν. ⁽¹⁶⁾καὶ ἀπώλεσαν μυριάδας ἑπτὰ καὶ
(20) 47 ἑκατὸν ἄνδρας. ⁴⁷⁽²⁰⁾ἔγραψε δὲ Μαρδοχαῖος τοὺς λόγους τούτους εἰς βιβλίον, καὶ ἐξαπέστειλε
(21)   τοῖς Ἰουδαίοις οἳ ἦσαν ἐν τῇ Ἀρταξέρξου βασιλείᾳ, τοῖς μακρὰν καὶ τοῖς ἐγγύς, ⁽²¹⁾στῆσαι
   τὰς ἡμέρας ταύτας εἰς ὕμνους καὶ εὐφροσύνας ἀντὶ ὀδυνῶν καὶ πένθους, τὴν τεσσαρεσκαι-
(22)
(27) 48 δεκάτην καὶ τὴν πεντεκαιδεκάτην. ⁴⁸⁽²²⁾καὶ ἀπέστειλε μερίδας τοῖς πένησιν, ⁽²⁷⁾καὶ προσεδέ-

viii 34 (for επεστειλε). H: απεστειλε
viii 47 (for Αρταξερξου). H: Ασσυηρου

VIII 48   ΕΣΘΗΡ Α

ξαντο. ⁴⁹⁽²⁶⁾διὰ τοῦτο ἐκλήθησαν αἱ ἡμέραι αὗται φουρδαια διὰ τοὺς κλήρους τοὺς πεσόντας 49 (26)
εἰς τὰς ἡμέρας ταύτας εἰς μνημόσυνον. ⁵⁰⁽ˣ¹⁾καὶ ἔγραψεν ὁ βασιλεὺς τὰ τέλη τῆς γῆς καὶ 50
θαλάσσης ⁽²⁾καὶ τὴν ἰσχὺν αὐτοῦ, πλοῦτόν τε καὶ δόξαν τῆς βασιλείας αὐτοῦ. ⁵¹καὶ ἐδόξασε 51 (2)
Μαρδοχαῖος καὶ ἔγραψεν ἐν τοῖς βιβλίοις Περσῶν καὶ Μήδων εἰς μνημόσυνον. ⁵²⁽³⁾ὁ δὲ 52 (3)
Μαρδοχαῖος διεδέχετο τὸν βασιλέα Ξέρξην, καὶ μέγας ἦν ἐν τῇ βασιλείᾳ καὶ φιλούμενος
ὑπὸ πάντων τῶν Ἰουδαίων, καὶ ἡγεῖτο αὐτῶν, καὶ δόξαν παντὶ τῷ ἔθνει αὐτοῦ περιετίθει.
⁵³⁽F¹⁾καὶ εἶπε Μαρδοχαῖος Παρὰ τοῦ θεοῦ ἐγένετο ταῦτα. ⁵⁴ἐμνήσθη γὰρ τοῦ ἐνυπνίου οὗ 53
εἶδεν. καὶ ἀπετελέσθη καὶ εἶπεν ⁽³⁾Ἡ μικρὰ πηγὴ Εσθηρ ἐστίν, ⁽⁴⁾καὶ οἱ δύο δράκοντες ἐγώ   (3)
                                                                                                        (4)
εἰμι καὶ Αμαν· ⁽⁵⁾ποταμὸς τὰ ἔθνη τὰ συναχθέντα ἀπολέσαι τοὺς Ἰουδαίους· ἥλιος καὶ φῶς 57   (5)
οἳ ἐγένοντο τοῖς Ἰουδαίοις ἐπιφανεία τοῦ θεοῦ, τοῦτο τὸ κρίμα. ⁵⁵⁽⁶⁾καὶ ἐποίησεν ὁ θεὸς τὰ 55 (6)
σημεῖα καὶ τὰ τέρατα ταῦτα ἃ οὐ γέγονεν ἐν τοῖς ἔθνεσιν. ⁽⁷⁾καὶ ἐποίησε κλήρους δύο, ἕνα τῷ (7)
λαῷ τοῦ θεοῦ καὶ ἕνα τοῖς ἔθνεσιν. ⁵⁶⁽⁸⁾καὶ προσῆλθον οἱ δύο κλῆροι οὗτοι εἰς ὥρας κατὰ 56 (8)
καιρὸν καὶ ἡμέρας κυριεύσεως τοῦ αἰωνίου ἐν πᾶσι τοῖς ἔθνεσιν. ⁵⁷⁽⁹⁾καὶ ἐμνήσθη ὁ θεὸς τοῦ 57 (9)
λαοῦ αὐτοῦ, καὶ ἐδικαίωσε τὴν κληρονομίαν αὐτοῦ. ⁵⁸καὶ πᾶς ὁ λαὸς ἀνεβόησε φωνῇ μεγάλῃ 58
καὶ εἶπεν Εὐλογητὸς εἶ, κύριε, ὁ μνησθεὶς τῶν διαθηκῶν τῶν πρὸς τοὺς πατέρας ἡμῶν· ἀμήν.
⁵⁹⁽¹⁰⁾καὶ ἔσονται αὐτοῖς αἱ ἡμέραι αὗται ἐν μηνὶ Αδαρ, ἐν τῇ τεσσαρεσκαιδεκάτῃ καὶ τῇ 59 (10)
πεντεκαιδεκάτῃ τοῦ αὐτοῦ μηνός, μετὰ συναγωγῆς καὶ χαρᾶς καὶ εὐφροσύνης ἐνώπιον τοῦ
θεοῦ κατὰ γενεὰς εἰς τὸν αἰῶνα ἐν τῷ λαῷ αὐτοῦ Ισραηλ.

viii 49 (for φουρδαια). H: Φουραια
viii 52 (for Ξερξην). H: Ασσυηρον
viii 54 (for δι' εγενοντο). H: η εγενετο

BIBLIOGRAPHY

References are by author and date. Commentaries are referenced by author's name and *ad loc.*

Ackerman, James S.
1967   *On Teaching the Bible as Literature.* Bloomington, IN.
Ackroyd, Peter
1984   *T. S. Eliot.* London.
Alter, Robert
1981   *The Art of Biblical Narrative.* New York.
Alter, Robert and Kermode, Frank
1987   *The Literary Guide to the Bible.* Cambridge, MA.
Avi-Yonah, Michael
1984   *The Jews Under Roman and Byzantine Rule.* Jerusalem. (1st English edn. 1972)
Bardtke, Hans
1963   *Das Buch Esther.* KAT XVII 5. Gütersloh.
Barthélemy, D.; Gooding, D. W.; Lust, J.; and Tov, E.
1986   *The Story of David and Goliath: Textual and Literary Criticism.* Göttingen.
Barton, John
1984   *Reading the Old Testament.* Philadelphia.
Battersby, James L.
1988   "The Inevitability of Professing Literature." In *Criticism, History and Intertextuality*, ed. Richard Fleming and Michael Payne, pp. 61-76. Lewisburg, PA.
Berg, Sandra
1979   *The Book of Esther.* SBLDS 44. Missoula, MT.
Berlin, Adele
1983   *Poetics and Interpretation of Biblical Narrative.* Sheffield.
Bickermann, Elias J.
1944   "The Colophon of the Greek Book of Esther." *JBL* 63:339-62.
1951   "Notes on the Greek book of Esther." *PAAJR* 20:101-33.
1967   *Four Strange Books of the Bible.* New York.

Bloom, Harold
  1973   *The Anxiety of Influence*. New York.
  1975   *A Map of Misreading*. New York.
Boorer, Suzanne
  1989   "The Importance of a Diachronic Approach: the Case of Genesis-Kings." *CBQ* 51:195-208.
Booth, Wayne C.
  1988   *The Company We Keep*. Berkeley, CA.
Brooke, Alan E.; McLean, Norman; and Thackery, H. St. John, eds.
  1940   *Esther, Judith, Tobit*. The Old Testament in Greek: Vol. III, Part I. Cambridge.
Carpenter, J.E. and Harford, G. B.
  1900   *The Hexateuch*.
Cazelles, Henri
  1961   "Note sur la composition du rouleau d'Esther." In *Lex tua veritas*: Festschrift für Hubert Junker, ed. by H. Gross and F. Mussner, pp. 17-29. Trier.
Clines, David J. A.
  1984   *The Esther Scroll*. JSOTSup 30. Sheffield.
Cook, Herbert J.
  1969   "The A Text of the Greek Versions of the Book of Esther." *ZAW* 81:369-76.
Cooper, Alan
  1987   "Reading the Bible Critically and Otherwise." In *The Future of Biblical Studies*, ed. R. E. Friedman and H. G. M. Williamson, pp. 61-79. Atlanta.
Culler, Jonathan
  1981   *The Pursuit of Signs*. Ithaca, NY.
Damrosch, David
  1987   *The Narrative Covenant*. San Francisco.
Daube, David
  1946-47 "The Last Chapter of Esther." *JQR* 37:139-47.
Dhorme, Edouard
  1984   *A Commentary on the Book of Job*. Nashville. [French original Paris 1926].
Dommershausen, Werner
  1968   *Die Estherrolle*. SBM 6. Stuttgart.
Driver, Samuel R.
  1967   *An Introduction to the Literature of the Old Testament*. [1891]. Cleveland and New York.
Ehrlich, Arnold B.
  1914   *Randglossen zur hebräischen Bibel*. Leipzig (repr. Hildesheim 1968).

Eissfeldt, Otto
1966   *The Old Testament: an Introduction.* Oxford.
Field, Leslie A.
1987   *Thomas Wolfe and his Editors.* Norman OK.
Fishbane, Michael
1985   *Biblical Interpretation in Ancient Israel.* Oxford.
Fox, Michael V.
1983   "The Structure of the Book of Esther." In the Isaac L.
            Seeligmann Memorial Volume, ed. A. Rofé and Y. Zakovitch,
            pp. 291-304. Jerusalem.
1988   [Review of] D. J. Clines' *The Esther Scroll. Hebrew Studies*
            29:103-10.
Fritzsche, Otto F.
1848   ΕΣΘΗΡ. *Duplicem libri textum ad optimos codices emenda-
            vit et cum selecta lectionis varietate edidit.* Zurich.
1851   *Zusätze zu den Buche Esther* (Kurzgefasstes exegetisches
            Handbuch zu dem Apokryphen des ATs, I). Leipzig.
Gan, Moshe
1961-62   *Megillat Esther Be'aspeqlariyat Qorot Yoseph Bemitzrayim.
            Tarbiz* 31:144-49.
Gerleman, Gillis
1982   *Esther.* BKAT XXI. Neukirchen.
Gros Louis, Kenneth R. R.
1982   *Literary Interpretations of Biblical Narratives.* Vol. II.
            Nashville.
Grossfeld, Bernard
1990   *The Two Esther Targums.* New York.
Gunkel, Hermann
1925   "Fundamental Problems of Hebrew Literary History" [orig.
            1906]. In *What Remains of the Old Testament* (tr. A. K.
            Dallas) (1958), pp. 57-67. New York.
Haelewyck, J.-C.
1985   "Le Texte dit 'Lucianique' du livre d'Esther, son étendue et
            sa cohérence." *Le Muséon* 98:5-44.
Halpern, Baruch
1988   *The First Historians.* San Francisco.
Hanhart, Robert, ed.
1983   *Esther.* Göttingen Septuagint, VIII, 3. Göttingen.
Herodotus
1968   *Herodotus: the Histories.* Translated by Aubrey de Sélin-
            court. Baltimore.
Hertzberg, Hans Wilhelm
1964   I & II Samuel. OTL. Philadelphia.

Hoschander, Jacob
    1923   *The Book of Esther in the Light of History.* Philadelphia.

Jacob, B.
    1890   "Das Buch Esther bei den LXX." *ZAW* 10:241-98.

Jones, Bruce
    1977   "Two Misconceptions about the Book of Esther." *CBQ* 39:171-81.

Kaufman, Stephen A.
    1982   "The Temple Scroll and Higher Criticism." *HUCA* 53:29-43.

Knierim, Rolf
    1985   "Criticism of Literary Features: Form, Tradition, and Redaction." In *The Hebrew Bible and its Modern Interpreters*, ed. Douglas A. Knight and Gene M. Tucker, pp. 123-65. Philadelphia.

Koch, Klaus
    1969   *The Growth of the Biblical Tradition.* New York.

Kristeva, Julia
    1969   Σημειωτική: *Recherches pour une sémanalyse.* Paris.

Kugel, James
    1981   "On the Bible and Literary Criticism." *Prooftexts* 1:217-36.
    1982   "James Kugel responds [to A. Berlin]." *Prooftexts* 2:328-32.

Lagarde, Paul de
    1883   *Librorum Veteris Testamenti Canonicorum Pars Prior Graece.* Göttingen.

Langen, Joseph
    1860   "Die beiden griechischen Texte des Buches Esther." *Tübinger Theologische Quartalschrift* 42:244-72.

Lebram, J. C. H.
    1972   "Purimfest und Estherbuch." *VT* 22:208-22.

Leitch, Vincent B.
    1983   *Deconstructive Criticism.* New York.

Lewy, Julius
    1939a   "The Feast of the 14th Day of Adar." *HUCA* 14:127-51.
    1939b   "Old Assyrian *puru'um* and *pūrum.*" *Revue Hittite et Asianique* 5:117-24.

Lichtheim, Miriam
    1973   *Ancient Egyptian Literature.* Vol. I. Berkeley, CA.

Liddell, Henry George and Scott, Robert
    1968   *A Greek-English Lexicon.* Revised by H. S. Jones. Oxford.

Loewenstamm, Samuel E.
    1971   "Esther 9:29-32: the Genesis of a Late Addition." *HUCA* 42:117-24.

Martin, Raymond A.
　1974　　*Syntactical Evidence of Semitic Sources in Greek Documents*
　　　　　(SBLSCS 3). Cambridge, MA.
　1975　　"Syntax Criticism of the LXX Additions to the Book of
　　　　　Esther." *JBL* 94:65-72.
McCarter, P. Kyle, Jr.
　1986　　*II Samuel* (AB 9). Garden City, NY.
McEvenue, Sean E.
　1971　　*The Narrative Style of the Priestly Writer* (AnBib 50). Rome.
Meinhold, Arndt
　1975　　"Die Gattung der Josephgeschichte und des Estherbuches:
　　　　　Diasporanovelle." Part I: ZAW 87:306-24.
　1976　　"Die Gattung der Josephgeschichte und des Estherbuches:
　　　　　Diasporanovelle." Part II: ZAW 88:72-93.
　1983a　*Das Buch Esther.* Zürcher Bibelkommentare. Zurich.
　1983b　"Zu Aufbau und Mitte des Estherbuches." *VT* 33:435-45.
Michaelis, Johann David
　1783　　*Deutsche Uebersetzung des Alten Testaments, mit Anmer-*
　　　　　kungen für Ungelehrte. Vol. XIII. Göttingen.
Miles, John A., Jr.
　1981　　"Radical editing: *Redaktionsgeschichte* and the Aesthetic of
　　　　　Willed Confusion." In *Traditions in Transformation*, ed.
　　　　　Baruch Halpern and John Levenson, pp. 9-31. Winona Lake,
　　　　　IN.
Moore, Carey A.
　1965　　*The Greek Text of Esther.* PhD diss., Johns Hopkins. Univer-
　　　　　sity Microfilms, Ann Arbor, MI.
　1967　　"A Greek Witness to a Different Hebrew Text of Esther."
　　　　　ZAW 79:351-58.
　1971　　*Esther.* AB 7B. Garden City, NY.
　1977　　*Daniel, Esther, and Jeremiah: the Additions.* AB 44. Garden
　　　　　City, NY.
Motzo, Bacchisio R.
　1927　　"La storia del testo di Ester." *Ricerche Religiose* 3:205-08.
Moulton, Richard G.
　1896　　*The Literary Study of the Bible.* Boston.
Noth, Martin
　1981　　*The Deuteronomistic History.* JSOTSup 15. Sheffield.
　　　　　[= *Ueberlieferungsgeschichtliche Studien*, 1957).
Orlinsky, Harry M.
　1957　　"Studies in the Septuagint of the Book of Job. Part I." *HUCA*
　　　　　28:1957:53-73.
Paton, Lewis B.
　1908　　*The Book of Esther.* ICC. Edinburgh.

Richter, Wolfgang
    1971   *Exegese als Literaturwissenschaft.* Göttingen.

Robertson, David
    1977   *The Old Testament and the Literary Critic.* Philadelphia.

Rosenthal, Ludwig A.
    1895   *Die Josephgeschichte mit den Büchern Ester und Daniel verglichen.* ZAW 15:278-84 (see also 17 [1897]125-38).

Rosenzweig, Franz
    1964   *Die Schrift.* Ed. Karl Thieme. Frankfurt am Main.

Ryssel, V.
    1900   *Zusätze zum Buch Esther.* In *Die Apokryphen und Pseudepigraphen des ATs,* vol. I.

Samuel, Alan
    1972   *Greek and Roman Chronology.* Munich.

Sandmel, Samuel
    1961   "The Haggada within Scripture." *JBL* 80:105-22.

Schneider, B.
    1962-63   "Esther Revised According to the Maccabees." *Liber Annus* 13:190-218.

Scholz, Anton
    1892   *Commentar über das Buch 'Esther.'* Würzburg-Wien.

Schütz, Dionys
    1933   "Das hebräische Buch Esther." *BZ* 21:255-76.

Schürer, Emil; revised by G. Vermes and F. Millar
    1973   *The History of the Jewish People in the Age of Jesus Christ.* Edinburgh.

Schwarz, Adolf
    1923   "Taanith Esther." Festschrift David Simonsens. Copenhagen.

Sternberg, Meir
    1985   *The Poetics of Biblical Narrative.* Bloomington, IN.

Talmon, Shemaryahu
    1975   "The textual study of the Bible--a new outlook." In *Qumran and the History of the Biblical Text,* ed. S. Talmon and F. M. Cross. Cambridge, MA.

Tigay, Jeffrey H., ed.
    1982   *The Evolution of the Gilgamesh Epic.* Philadelphia.
    1985   *Empirical Models for Biblical Criticism.* Philadelphia.

Torrey, Charles C.
    1944   "The Older Book of Esther." *HTR* 37:1-40.

Tov, Emanuel
    1982   "The 'Lucianic' text of the Canonical and Apocryphal Sections of Esther: a Rewritten Biblical Book." *Textus* 10:1-25.

1985a   "The Composition of 1 Samuel 16-18 in the Light of the Sep-
             tuagint Version." In Tigay 1985:97-130.
1985b   "The Literary History of the Book of Jeremiah in the Light
             of its Textual History." In Tigay 1985:211-37.

Ulrich, Eugene
1988   "Double Literary Editions of Biblical Narratives." In
             *Perspectives on the Hebrew Bible: Essays in Honor of Walter
             J. Harrelson*, ed. J. L. Crenshaw, ed., pp. 101-16. Macon, GA.

Usher, James
1665   *De Graeca Septuaginta interpretum versione syntagma*, etc.
             London.

Volz, Paul and Rudolph, R.
1933   *Der Elohist als Erzähler: ein Irrweg der Pentateuchkritik?*.
             Giessen.

Warshaw, Thayer S.
1978   *On Teaching the Bible in Literature Classes*. Nashville, TN.

Weiss, Meir
1984   *The Bible from Within*. Jerusalem.

Wellhausen, Julius
1902   [Review of] G. Jahn, *Das Buch Esther*. *Göttingische gelehrte
             Anzeigen* 164:127-47.

Willis, John
1979   "Redaction Criticism and Historical Reconstruction." In
             Encounter with the Text, ed. M. J. Buss, pp. 83-89.
             Philadelphia.

Zimmermann, Frank
1958   *The Book of Tobit* (Dropsie College Edition). New York.

INDEXES

I. TOPICS

175

II. AUTHORS

III. AT REFERENCES

IV. MT-LXX REFERENCES
(in MT canonical order)

V. MT REFERENCES

VI. SEPTUAGINT REFERENCES
(in MT canonical order)

VII. GREEK WORDS AND PHRASES
(alphabetized by main item in phrase, according to specific form used)

VIII. HEBREW WORDS
(alphabetized by Hebrew root)

DATE DUE

MAY 1			

HIGHSMITH # 45220